THE

EVERYTHING

PARENT'S GUIDE TO

ADHD IN CHILDREN

Dear Reader,

Childhood attention-deficit/hyperactivity disorder (ADHD)
affects the lives of millions of children. Whether your child
has ADHD, you know other children who have the disorder, or
you are curious to learn more about the disorder, we hope
you will find this book a helpful and informative resource.

Although no one knows exactly what causes childhood
ADHD, and there is no cure, rapid advances in technology are
leading to more effective diagnostic and treatment modalities.

Today, most children with ADHD who receive appropriate treatment go on to lead happy, productive lives. In fact,
throughout history, many children with ADHD have become
adults with ADHD who have achieved great fame and fortune,
and made lasting contributions to society. Just a few ADHD
"greats" your child is familiar with include Cher, Tom Cruise,
Walt Disney, Benjamin Franklin, Bill Gates, Whoopi Goldberg,
Magic Johnson, Babe Ruth, Will Smith, and Steven Spielberg.

Hopefully, this guide will inform and inspire the parents
of children with ADHD about a wide range of issues regarding
the disorder, and affect them and their children's lives in a
positive way.

Carole Jacobs and Isadore Wendel, PhD, MSCP

WELCOME TO THE

EVERYTHING
PARENT'S GUIDES

Everything® Parent's Guides are a part of the bestselling
Everything® series and cover common parenting issues
like childhood illnesses and tantrums, as well as medical
conditions like asthma and juvenile diabetes. These family-
friendly books are designed to be a one-stop guide for
parents. If you want authoritative information on specific
topics not fully covered in other books, *Everything*®
Parent's Guides are your perfect solution.

 Alerts

Urgent warnings

 Facts

Important snippets of information

 **Essentials**

Quick handy tips

 Questions

Answers to common questions

When you're done reading, you can finally say you know **EVERYTHING**®!

PUBLISHER Karen Cooper

DIRECTOR OF ACQUISITIONS AND INNOVATION Paula Munier

MANAGING EDITOR, EVERYTHING® SERIES Lisa Laing

COPY CHIEF Casey Ebert

ACQUISITIONS EDITOR Brett Palana-Shanahan

SENIOR DEVELOPMENT EDITOR Brett Palana-Shanahan

EDITORIAL ASSISTANT Ross Weisman

EVERYTHING® SERIES COVER DESIGNER Erin Alexander

LAYOUT DESIGNERS Colleen Cunningham, Michelle Roy Kelly,
Elisabeth Lariviere, Ashley Vierra, Denise Wallace

Visit the entire Everything® series at *www.everything.com*

THE

EVERYTHING

PARENT'S GUIDE TO

ADHD IN CHILDREN

A reassuring guide to getting the right diagnosis, understanding treatments, and helping your child focus

Carole Jacobs and Isadore Wendel, PhD, MSCP

Avon, Massachusetts

This book is dedicated to all children, parents,
and families who are living with childhood ADHD.

Thanks to Brett Shanahan at Adams Media, and
Robert G. DiForio of D4EO Literary Agency.

An Everything® Series Book.
Everything® and everything.com® are registered trademarks of F+W Media, Inc.

Published by Adams Media, a division of F+W Media, Inc.
57 Littlefield Street, Avon, MA 02322 U.S.A.
www.adamsmedia.com

ISBN 10: 1-60550-678-8
ISBN 13: 978-1-60550-678-4
eISBN 10: 1-60550-679-6
eISBN 13: 978-1-60550-679-1

Printed in the United States of America.

10 9 8 7 6 5 4 3 2 1

Library of Congress Cataloging-in-Publication Data
is available from the publisher.

This publication is designed to provide accurate and authoritative information with regard to the subject matter covered. It is sold with the understanding that the publisher is not engaged in rendering legal, accounting, or other professional advice. If legal advice or other expert assistance is required, the services of a competent professional person should be sought.
—From a *Declaration of Principles* jointly adopted by a Committee of the American Bar Association and a Committee of Publishers and Associations

Many of the designations used by manufacturers and sellers to distinguish their products are claimed as trademarks. Where those designations appear in this book and Adams Media was aware of a trademark claim, the designations have been printed with initial capital letters.

This book is available at quantity discounts for bulk purchases.
For information, please call 1-800-289-0963.

All the examples and dialogues used in this book are fictional, and have been created by the author to illustrate different situations.

Contents

Introduction

Parenting a child with attention-deficit/hyperactivity disorder (ADHD) can be an exhausting, frustrating, bewildering, and overwhelming experience. But as a parent, there is a lot you can do to help your child manage and control his or her symptoms, and to quiet the chaos that the disorder often imposes on families and marriages. It all begins with a complete understanding of childhood ADHD.

The Everything® Parent's Guide to ADHD in Children is a comprehensive resource for parents of children of all ages and provides detailed information on recognizing and managing your child's disorder from preschool through high school. This health guide offers practical advice on the telltale signs and symptoms of childhood ADHD and information on getting a reliable diagnosis, evaluation, and treatment for your child.

By reading this book, you'll glean the basic medical knowledge necessary to talk intelligently about your child's condition to his or her doctor. You'll also learn about the condition's classic symptoms, new diagnostic and evaluation techniques, and an increasingly sophisticated arsenal of high-tech treatment and medication modalities used to treat childhood ADHD.

While practically all children have days when they don't complete their homework, blurt out the wrong things in class, or forget where they put their backpack, those days are the norm, rather than the exception for children with ADHD. As you'll learn by reading *The Everything® Parent's Guide to ADHD in Children*, not every child has the same ADHD symptoms, and a child's symptoms may change over time. While some children with ADHD are hyperactive, others are quiet dreamers who stare into space, miles away from their teacher and homework at hand. Still others are so impulsive that they butt into every conversation, are overly blunt and tactless, or invade everyone's space.

The Everything® Parent's Guide to ADHD in Children will also help remove any blame, shame, or guilt you may be harboring about having caused or contributed to your child's disorder. You'll learn that your child's ADHD was not caused by bad parenting, by eating a poor diet, or by watching too much television, but that it is a neurobiological disorder caused by biochemical imbalances in the brain. Scientists now believe that childhood ADHD is not one single disorder, but a cluster of disorders that affect different parts of the brain. Researchers also know that childhood ADHD is a genetic disorder. That means if you or your spouse have ADHD, all of your children are at a higher risk of developing it, too.

While there's no cure to date for childhood ADHD, perhaps the best news about this disorder is that most of your child's symptoms can be successfully managed and controlled through a combination of medication and behavior therapy.

It's not easy for parents or children to live with childhood ADHD. While early intervention won't cure your child's disorder, it can dramatically improve his chances of managing his ADHD symptoms and doing well academically and emotionally. In fact, studies show that most children with ADHD can be successfully diagnosed and treated and go on to lead more productive lives.

But the key to your child getting and staying well is parental knowledge. By picking up this book, you've made a commitment to learn as much as you can about childhood ADHD and taken the first step in you and your child's journey to improved health and happiness.

CHAPTER 1

Understanding the Symptoms

In the past, children were diagnosed with attention deficit disorder (ADD) because they didn't pay attention, had poor organizational skills, and did poorly on tasks requiring sustained mental activity, such as schoolwork. Children were diagnosed with hyperactivity if they were constantly on the go and behaved impulsively. Now the two diagnoses have been combined into attention-deficit/hyperactivity disorder (ADHD), and the definitions have been expanded. Today almost any child can be diagnosed with ADHD. That includes youngsters with a low energy level and a tendency to daydream.

Dealing with Parent Denial

Perhaps one of the most important things that you as a parent should understand about childhood ADHD is that it is not a lifestyle condition caused by an improper diet, environmental agents, a poor upbringing, watching too much TV, or other factors. Childhood ADHD is a neurobiological disorder of the brain caused by an imbalance of chemicals in the brain. While experts now believe the condition may be genetic, it's important not to blame yourself for your child's condition.

Diet Is Not a Universal Cure

While dietary changes may help relieve isolated symptoms of childhood ADHD, there is no scientific proof that certain foods cause or exacerbate ADHD. Neither is there any proof that exposure to lead, mercury, or other heavy metals cause the condition.

According to the American Academy of Pediatrics (AAP), "childhood ADHD is a condition of the brain that makes it hard for children to control their behavior, and is also one of the most common chronic conditions of childhood." While all children have behavior problems at times, children with ADHD have frequent, severe problems that interfere with their ability to live normal lives.

 Essential

An exceptionally high activity level, inattentiveness, and impulsiveness are all part of being a toddler. Little people are very reactive to stress, which can make them hyperactive. Inattentiveness is often due to their poor language abilities. Research indicates that parents think children understand far more than they actually do.

Parent Training

Another important part of treatment for a child with ADHD is parent training. Children with ADHD may not respond to the usual parenting practices, so experts recommend parent education. This approach has been successful in educating parents on how to help their children develop better organizational skills, problem-solving skills, and how to cope with their ADHD symptoms.

Parent training can be conducted in groups or with individual families and is offered by therapists or in special classes. The national organization CHADD (Children and Adults with Attention-Deficit/Hyperactivity Disorder) offers a unique education program to help parents and individuals navigate the challenges of ADHD across the lifespan. Find more information about CHADD's "Parent to Parent" program by visiting CHADD's website at *www.chadd.org.*

The Three Types of Childhood ADHD

To cover their bases, psychiatrists decided in 1980 to reclassify ADHD as two separate subsets. One was attention deficit disorder with hyperactivity, or ADD–H. The other was attention deficit disorder without hyperactivity, or ADD with no "H." On further study, researchers realized hyperactivity/impulsivity was actually a larger problem than inattention, and decided to change the name of the disorder to reflect their findings.

 Essential

The symptom of inattention in childhood ADHD actually refers to a whole galaxy of attention problems, not just a lack of attention. Your child could also be so focused on one thing that she can't pay attention to anything else. Or she may not be able to decide what to focus on, how to maintain her attention, or how to shift her focus when necessary.

In 1987, the disorder was renamed attention-deficit/hyperactivity disorder, or ADHD, and reclassified as a disorder with not two, but three distinct subsets: inattentive, hyperactive/impulsive, and combination (children who display both inattentive and hyperactive/impulsive symptoms). For the purpose of this book, the disorder will be called childhood ADHD to comply with current psychiatric terminology.

The "predominantly inattentive type" is for children with attention deficits but no problems with hyperactivity. The "predominantly hyperactive/impulsive type" diagnosis is used for hyperactive children, who may also be impulsive. The "combined type" is for children with both inattentive and hyperactive/impulsive behaviors.

Outgrowing the Disorder?

Adolescents and adults may outgrow or overcome their symptoms. If so, they are diagnosed as being "in partial remission." This reflects the new view that people do not outgrow the disorder, but may learn to compensate so that the symptoms are not disabling. There is also a catch-all diagnosis for children who don't meet the standard criteria. If they don't have enough symptoms or their symptoms aren't severe enough, they can be diagnosed with an atypical form of ADHD called attention-deficit/hyperactivity disorder not otherwise specified or ADHD-NOS.

Predominantly Inattentive

Many people used to refer to the "predominantly inattentive type" of attention-deficit/hyperactivity disorder simply as "ADD." Symptoms include:

- Difficulty listening, even when being directly addressed
- Trouble continuing to pay attention to activities involving either work or play
- Difficulty paying attention to details and avoiding careless mistakes
- Problems completing tasks, chores, and assignments
- Difficulty organizing activities and tasks
- Trouble doing tasks that require sustained mental effort, like that required for schoolwork
- Difficulty keeping track of possessions and materials, such as toys, clothes, homework papers, and school supplies
- Being easily distracted
- Difficulty remembering things

In order for his symptoms to be considered bona fide, it should be clear that a child cannot sustain attention and cannot concentrate on mental tasks for extended periods. Problems stemming from boredom, disinterest, lack of motivation, and defiance are not supposed to be counted as ADHD symptoms—though they often are.

It is easy to see why attention deficits create problems in school. Students with short attention spans cannot concentrate on schoolwork for the long periods required to do their work. Being easily distracted poses a major problem in crowded classrooms, which are filled with continuous rustles and murmurs. If students' attention wanders at unpredictable moments, they miss portions of lectures and don't hear explanations about assignments and tests.

Lapses of attention when a parent gives directions and instructions can result in considerable frustration and upset at home. A parent might send a child to clean up his room and later discover him playing with baseball cards instead of doing his chore. If the child's attention strayed while the parent was giving instructions, the youngster might have understood that he was to go to his room but missed what he was expected to do when he arrived. Or, after going to his room to clean it, he might see his box of baseball cards and spend an hour going through them without giving another thought to what he was supposed to do.

Poor Organizational Skills

Poor organizational skills can cause a host of problems in school and at home. Many children get confused during projects and tasks to the point that they don't know how to proceed.

Some youngsters become upset and cry over seemingly simple homework assignments and chores, claiming they don't know how to do them. If parents and teachers are convinced that a youngster is bright enough and possesses the skills needed to do the work, they may conclude that the child is overly emotional.

Other youngsters don tough-guy masks and display an "I couldn't care less" attitude, so it is hard for adults to recognize that poor organization is at the heart of many of their problems. The solution may be to break long assignments and projects into a number of small steps and have students complete them one at a time.

Predominantly Hyperactive

The second type of attention-deficit/hyperactivity disorder, which includes hyperactivity and impulsiveness, is technically known as the "predominantly hyperactive type." Most people refer to it simply as ADHD.

For this type, children's difficulties must stem from hyperactivity or from a combination of hyperactive and impulsive behaviors. *The Diagnostic and Statistical Manual of Mental Disorders, Fourth Edition, Text Revision (DSM-IV-TR)*, lists six symptoms of hyperactive behavior and three symptoms of impulsive behavior. A child must have six out of the nine symptoms to be diagnosed with the predominantly hyperactive type.

 Fact

The Diagnostic and Statistical Manual of Mental Disorders, Fourth Edition, Text Revision (DSM-IV-TR), which was published by the American Psychiatric Association in 2000, is a list of mental and behavior disorders recognized by U.S. doctors.

Symptoms of Hyperactivity

Hyperactive children have an energy level that their parents and teachers consider excessive. They may appear to be driven by a motor, so that they continue to wiggle even when at rest. Symptoms include:

- Squirming and fidgeting even when seated
- Getting up when expected to remain seated
- Running excessively and climbing in inappropriate situations
- Difficulty playing quietly
- Being always on the go
- Talking excessively

Some youngsters squirm and fidget while sitting at their school desks, while watching television at home, and while listening to bedtime stories. Hyperactive adolescents may swing their legs, tap their feet, drum their fingers on their desk, pop their chewing gum, or chew their fingernails. They are more likely to report that they feel restless much of the time. Some say that when they must remain seated for more than a few minutes, they feel as though they're about to jump out of their skin.

 Essential

> According to a new study conducted by the University of Central Florida, children with ADHD are overly active and move around a lot because its helps them better focus on challenging tasks like learning letters and numbers.

Professionals believe that ADHD sufferers share a common problem: They require much more stimulation to remain attentive than the average youngster. As anyone who has sat through a long sermon or attempted to read a book they find boring knows, the mind must have enough stimulation to remain attentive.

Hyperfocus

Despite their short attention spans and inability to pay attention in school, children with ADHD can concentrate on a video game or television program so well that they don't even notice when someone is standing two feet away, yelling for their attention. Most parents find this extremely irritating. They think their child is defiant, pointing out that he concentrates and sits still well enough "when he wants to."

When children diagnosed with ADHD are fully engaged in a highly stimulating activity such as a television program or interactive game, they become so attentive that they cannot readily shift their attention away from it. Do the minds of children diagnosed with ADHD move at the same speed as a fast-action video game and rock video? This seems to be a possibility.

Impulsivity

Many children with ADHD also have impulsivity. Impulsive children have difficulty inhibiting the urge to act or speak and often seem unable to contain themselves. There are three main signs doctors look for:

- Blurting answers before the teacher or parent has finished asking the question
- Not waiting his turn
- Interrupting conversations or intruding into other's activities

Impulsive children reach for fragile objects despite repeated reminders not to touch. They grab other children's toys without asking permission. At school, they get up to sharpen their pencils the moment they determine their tip is dull or broken without waiting to ask permission.

 Alert

Peers dislike having other students disrupt the classroom, interrupt their conversations, and intrude in their games, so impulsive children often have social difficulties. Some impulsive children alienate others because they have hair-trigger tempers and are quick to take affront.

Parents and teachers spend a good deal of time and effort admonishing impulsive youngsters to slow down and think before they do or say something, but they seem incapable of remembering. Many parents come to doubt the intelligence of children who don't anticipate the consequences of their actions. But for those diagnosed with ADHD, the problem is not lack of intelligence or willful misbehavior. Their minds simply work differently.

The knee-jerk reactions of impulsive children may occur because they are actually wired differently. Scientists hypothesize that the part of the brain controlling automatic reactions propels them to react before the part that handles conscious thought can process and evaluate information (see Chapter 2).

Common Diagnostic Challenges of Childhood ADHD

Although virtually every child could qualify for a diagnosis of atypical ADHD, the requirements for a standard ADHD diagnosis are quite stringent. Besides having enough symptoms of attention deficits, hyperactivity, and/or impulsiveness, signs of these problems must have been present early in childhood—at least before age seven. While a child might not have been evaluated by a professional until after that age, the developmental history must indicate that the behavior was present early in life.

In addition, the current troublesome behavior must have been present for at least six months. Behavior problems that have been going on for shorter periods are more likely to be reactions to a specific trauma or life change, such as the birth of a sibling or a family move.

Symptoms Present in Several Settings

To be considered symptoms of ADHD, the behavior in question must be more frequent as well as more severe than is typical for youngsters at the same level of development. Children must have serious behavior problems in two or more important settings (e.g. at home, at school, with peers) for a standard ADHD diagnosis.

Behavior problems that are limited to home are more likely to stem from family stress, poor parenting, or difficult family dynamics. If students have problems at school but get along well in other environments, this usually suggests they are struggling with teaching or learning difficulties. If the problem is limited to not getting along with peers, it's usually because of poor social skills.

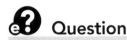 **Question**

My child keeps getting in trouble at school. Could she have ADHD?
If she is doing well in other settings, the first step is to find out if there is a problem at school that needs attention. Everything from being bullied to having an especially strict or permissive teacher can cause children to act up. Sit in the classroom to observe.

Problems that are confined to the playground and unsupervised playtime in the neighborhood suggest problems coping with unstructured situations, or having a personality trait known as risk-taking or thrill-seeking. People with this trait require more stimulation to avoid boredom, and they are drawn to activities that most youngsters would view as overly dangerous or frightening.

Diagnostic Considerations

In addition to having serious difficulty managing in several environments, the standard ADHD diagnosis requires "clear evidence" of "significant impairment in social, academic, or occupational functioning," according to the *DSM-IV-TR*. Impaired social functioning might mean that the child cannot make or keep friends because of her off-putting behavior.

For the standard (as opposed to "atypical") ADHD diagnosis, a child must have many specific symptoms reflecting difficulty with attention, hyperactivity, and impulsivity. In addition, the problems must have started before age seven, and they must be pervasive and severe. However, a child can be diagnosed with attention-deficit/hyperactivity disorder not otherwise specified (ADHD-NOS) with just a few symptoms that only create problems in one setting and that started later in life. The *DSM-IV-TR* indicates that this diagnosis is even appropriate for children with "a behavior pattern marked by sluggishness, daydreaming, and hypoactivity" or low energy level. Many combinations of problematic behaviors can now be diagnosed as ADHD.

Primary and Secondary Symptoms

While childhood ADHD is characterized by the three primary symptoms of hyperactivity, inattention, and impulsivity, there are also many secondary symptoms your child may exhibit. For many children, secondary symptoms are more problematic than the core symptoms of ADHD.

Common Secondary Symptoms

Here are just a few of the typical secondary symptoms suffered by children with ADHD:

- **Anticipating failure.** Because many children have a habit of repeated failures, whether it's losing things, forgetting their homework, being late, or losing track of their thoughts, they suffer a great deal of anxiety over expecting to fail.
- **Excessive worrying.** Often accompanied by anxiety and restlessness, children with ADHD worry about anything and everything. The worry often makes them appear detached or disinterested.
- **Boredom.** Children with ADHD are easily bored and often need continual stimulation, change, and even conflict. Getting bored also makes them prone to high-risk behavior, such as smoking, drug abuse, and promiscuity.
- **Frustration.** Children with ADHD are easily frustrated and impatient with themselves and others, often over the smallest things. They also tend to have short, explosive tempers.
- **Low self-esteem.** Children with ADHD are frequently criticized and blamed for their shortcomings, whether it is at home, at

school, or in social situations. Years of feeling as if they haven't measured up erodes their self-esteem and confidence.

- **Insomnia or sleep disturbances.** Many children with ADHD have trouble falling asleep and/or staying asleep. Causes range from hyperactivity and restlessness to side effects from stimulant medications.
- **Alcohol and substance abuse.** Some adolescents and teens with ADHD use drugs and alcohol to numb their feelings of frustration and low self-esteem. Others use alcohol and drugs because they are drawn to daring or risky behavior.

Conditions and Diseases that Mimic and Overlap Childhood ADHD

Many psychiatric conditions—including anxiety, depression, substance abuse, and personality disorders—mimic or mask the symptoms of ADHD. Sometimes it's hard for a medical expert to know which disease or condition is causing which symptoms and how to best treat it.

A high percentage of children with ADHD also suffer from the comorbid disorders that commonly occur alongside ADHD, and which may exacerbate a physician's attempt to isolate and treat symptoms.

The most common overlapping diseases and conditions include clinical depression and anxiety, bipolar disorder, substance abuse, alcoholism, learning disorders, dyslexia, brain injuries, dementia, psychosis, hypothyroidism, hyperthyroidism, conduct disorder, speech and communication problems, sensory integration disorders, oppositional defiant disorder, and sleep disorders.

Depression

Research shows that children with ADHD have three times the risk as the general population of suffering from major depression, and more than seven times the risk of suffering from dysthymia, or chronic low-level depression—the "never really happy" depression sometimes portrayed by comedian Woody Allen.

Researchers believe depression is more common among children with ADHD because the same neurobiological systems in the brain that control mood also control attention.

Another prominent theory holds that the relationship between ADHD and depression may result from the social and interpersonal difficulties experienced by many children with the disorder.

 Fact

While no one is sure why children with ADHD tend to be moody, grumpy, depressed, and pessimistic, scientists today believe the ADHD "downer personality" may be the result of neurological dysfunctions in the brain combined with a patient's emotional response to repeated failure, frustration, and disappointment in his life.

It takes a real pro—and often, many diagnostic tests—to differentiate between depression and ADHD. Both disorders are marked by moodiness, forgetfulness, an inability to pay attention, a lack of motivation, and feelings of helplessness and hopelessness. Complicating things is the fact that many medications used to treat childhood ADHD may also increase symptoms of depression.

Medications that May Mask Childhood ADHD Symptoms

Although you may normally think of medication as something that heals or cures a condition, some medications produce symptoms that actually mimic childhood ADHD. For instance, that flu medicine your child took this morning may have left her feeling nervous, jittery, and irritable, while antihistamines for allergies and rashes may cause your child to become sleepy and confused.

Whether it's a seemingly benign over-the-counter pill for a head-ache, a prescription drug your doctor ordered, or an illegal drug your teen with ADHD took because she thought it might help her relax, nearly every drug has side effects that can affect your child.

 Alert

Studies show that children with ADHD are twice as likely to smoke as people who don't have the disorder, and that teens with ADHD are also more inclined to be heavy coffee drinkers. In addition, adolescents and teenagers with the condition are also at a much higher risk for abusing illegal drugs, prescription drugs, and alcohol.

If you think your child has ADHD, your doctor will probably ask her to stop taking all medications until he can figure out which symptoms are caused by the medication and which symptoms are caused by the disorder. If your child is already addicted to one or more illegal drugs, your doctor may recommend that she undergo detoxification or enter a rehab program before starting treatment for ADHD.

Over-the-Counter Drugs

Allergy medications like Claritin and Zyrtec can cause restlessness, nervousness, sleeplessness, excitability, and poor coordination. Diet pills may contain excessive amounts of stimulants like caffeine or green tea that result in nervousness, anxiety, restlessness, an inability to focus, and insomnia. Sleeping pills can cause confusion, lethargy, and apathy. Cold and flu tablets and syrups that contain antihistamine-decongestant combinations like pseudoenephedrine and/or phenyl-ephrine can cause excitability, nervousness, anxiety, and sleeplessness.

Over-the-counter drugs are easy to abuse. To ensure your doctor doesn't confuse the side effects of over-the-counter medications with symptoms of childhood ADHD, write down a list of everything your child takes, including dosage.

Prescription Drugs

Many prescription drugs also have side effects that can mimic symptoms of ADHD. Here is a list of some prescription drugs whose side effects may be mistaken for ADHD symptoms:

- **Beta blockers.** Common side effects include confusion, depression, and memory loss.
- **Anticonvulsants, like Klonopin.** Common side effects include poor muscle control and behavior changes.
- **Benzodiazepam tranquilizers like Valium and Ativan.** Side effects include confusion, depression, lethargy, nervousness, hysteria, and tremors.
- **Selective serotonin reuptake inhibitors (SSRIs) prescribed for depression.** Common side effects include anxiety, nervousness, sleeplessness, and changes in sex drive.
- **Thyroid replacement drugs.** Common side effects include nervousness, anxiety, sleeplessness, and heart palpitations.

As with over-the-counter drugs, make a list and give it to your medical doctor so he doesn't confuse side effects for symptoms that may indicate childhood ADHD.

Substance Abuse

Unfortunately, many children and teens with undiagnosed ADHD use illegal drugs to mask symptoms of their disorder. In fact, studies show childhood ADHD is associated with an earlier onset of substance abuse, a longer period of active abuse, and a lower rate of recovery. Teens and adolescents with ADHD may use a variety of illegal drugs to mask social phobias, nervousness, anxiety, insomnia, an inability to concentrate and focus, and other telltale signs of childhood ADHD. These include cocaine, marijuana, street amphetamines, street tranquilizers, and the illegal use of stimulant prescription drugs like Ritalin, Adderall, and Concerta.

CHAPTER 2

Searching for Causes

S cientists still don't know exactly what causes childhood ADHD or what conditions are responsible for the disorder. Most agree that the condition is a neurobiological disorder that affects several areas of the brain, including those responsible for behavior, working memory, and executive functions. Researchers also know that childhood ADHD is a highly genetic disease. Because the symptoms of the disease manifest differently in different children, it can be difficult to recognize and diagnose.

Current Theories

One of the first questions you may ask after your child has been diagnosed with ADHD is "Did I do something wrong to cause it?" Over the years, medical science has come up with many theories regarding what might cause childhood ADHD. Today, most researchers agree that the disorder is not only highly genetic, but that it also has a neurobiological cause.

Here are five current theories as to what may cause childhood ADHD:

1. **ADHD is caused by structural abnormalities in the brain.** Research using magnetic resonance imagers (MRIs) has shown that four brain regions in children with ADHD are smaller than those in children without ADHD.

2. **ADHD is caused by an insufficient supply of the neurotransmitter dopamine in the brain.** This theory would explain why stimulant medications that increase dopamine in the brain are effective in controlling ADHD symptoms. Researchers speculate that the lack of dopamine may affect how it interacts with two other neurotransmitters, norepinephrine and serotonin.

3. **ADHD is really a sleep disorder in disguise.** Some researchers believe the disorder may be caused by a sleep-deprived brain, and the hyperactivity children with ADHD exhibit may be an effort to compensate for drowsiness. Many kids with ADHD have sleep disorders, while others sleep so soundly it's hard to wake them up.

4. **ADHD is a hereditary condition.** While researchers don't fully understand why and how ADHD is passed from one generation to the next, they agree there is a strong genetic component. Children with ADHD are extremely likely to have at least one close relative with the disorder.

5. **Environmental agents such as cigarette and alcohol use during pregnancy may increase the risk of ADHD in children.** High levels of lead may also cause ADHD.

Ten ADHD Myths

Here are ten popular misconceptions that continue to exist about childhood ADHD, and the truth behind them. Beware that even some unenlightened physicians and ADHD "experts" still continue to give these theories credence, despite scientific evidence.

Myth 1: Food additives and sugar cause ADHD in children. Fact: A study conducted in 1982 by the National Institutes for Health (NIH) found that restricting sugar in the diets of children with ADHD was beneficial in just 5 percent of cases, mostly in children who already had food allergies. There is no research indicating that excess sugar consumption causes ADHD, although it may cause hyperactivity in some people.

Myth 2: The dramatic rise of ADHD is caused by increased toxins in the environment. Fact: While it's true that the incidence of ADHD in children has increased, there are no studies indicating a link between the two. In fact, experts largely attribute the increase in ADHD to advances in diagnostic tools.

Myth 3: Exposure to lead leads to childhood ADHD. Fact: The accumulation of lead in the brain was once believed to cause ADHD. While research has shown that some people with ADHD may not tolerate lead as well as people who don't have the disorder, research linking lead to childhood ADHD is tentative at best.

Myth 4: ADHD is caused by brain damage. Fact: This early theory originated around the time of the 1918 flu epidemic, when affected children came down with symptoms that resembled ADHD, including hyperactivity, inattentiveness, and impulsivity. This theory was later refuted.

Myth 5: ADHD is caused by traumatic brain injury resulting from a lack of oxygen during birth or from a head injury in early childhood. Fact: That brain injuries have many symptoms that overlap or mimic the symptoms of ADHD led researchers to suspect a correlation between the two. No studies have confirmed this theory.

Myth 6: Allergies and food sensitivities trigger ADHD. Fact: While these conditions have symptoms that may mimic or overlap with the symptoms of ADHD, there is no research showing a connection between the two. Most people see a dramatic reduction or elimination of their supposed food allergy symptoms when they begin medication for the condition.

Myth 7: A poor diet causes ADHD. Fact: While malnutrition has not been linked with childhood ADHD, some studies show that a lack of omega-3 fatty acids in the diet may exacerbate ADHD symptoms. These fats are important for brain development and function, and having insufficient amounts may contribute to, if not actually cause, developmental disorders in children. Fish oil supplements appear to decrease the symptoms of ADHD in some children and may even help them improve their performance at school and at work.

Myth 8: ADHD is the result of "moral defectiveness." Fact: This early theory claimed that children with ADHD were morally defective by nature. While many children with ADHD suffer from behavior issues that lead to criminal problems or arrest, there is no evidence the disorder is caused by an inherent moral defectiveness.

Myth 9: ADHD is a willful behavior caused by defiance. Fact: This theory puts the blame on parents, claiming that children who fail to pay attention could be "cured" if parents taught them not to misbehave or daydream. It assumes that children with ADHD were being inattentive, impulsive, and defiant by choice.

Myth 10: ADHD is caused by a poor upbringing. Fact: This early theory remains one of the leading misconceptions about ADHD today. While improper parenting can exacerbate the symptoms of ADHD, research shows that being overly strict with children and teenagers who suffer from the disorder nearly always backfires. Studies show that while ADHD symptoms can't be scolded or disciplined away, a variety of treatment modalities, including medication, psychotherapy, and bio-feedback, can help decrease or even eliminate them.

Research Overview

ADHD has had many different names since the early 1900s, many of which reflected the current thinking of the time. Before the disorder was officially recognized by the American Psychiatric Association (APA) as a mental disorder in the mid-1980s, ADHD was called minimal brain damage and minimal brain dysfunction.

Since then, the disorder has been renamed many times in the APA's *Diagnostic and Statistic Manual of Mental Disorders (DSM)*. The first edition of the *DSM* called it "hyperactivity of childhood." The second edition, published in 1968, changed the name to "hyperkinetic reaction of children." In 1980, the third edition of the *DSM* renamed it "attention deficit disorder with or without hyperactivity.

So What's Taking So Long?

Given the dramatic advances in technology, you may be wondering how and why scientists could figure out how to send a man to the moon, but still not understand what causes a biological disorder that affects millions of children.

The easiest answer is that the human brain is a complicated labyrinth. Scientists now know that the primary symptom of childhood ADHD is an inability to self-regulate, or to control attention, temper, moods, and impulses.

 Fact

The NIH conducted a landmark study in 1990 that showed there was reduced glucose uptake in the brains of children with ADHD compared with "normal" people. This study established a biological basis for ADHD by providing a measurable difference between the ADHD and non-ADHD brain. But scientists still don't understand where the difference comes from or exactly what it means.

With advances in technology, scientists are now able to explore the brain for abnormalities that could result in childhood ADHD. While past research focused almost exclusively on external factors like parental upbringing, environmental causes, and toxic culprits like sugar and lead, research today targets genetic, anatomical, functional, and chemical brain dysfunctions as potential causes of the disorder.

Search for Genetic Causes

There's much disagreement when it comes to the causes of childhood ADHD, but many scientists agree that ADHD has a strong genetic basis in the majority of cases. In fact, the first thing your physician may ask if he suspects your child has ADHD is if anyone else in your family has it.

Searching for ADHD Genes

Genetic researchers now believe childhood ADHD is actually an umbrella term for several slightly different disorders. Because ADHD is one of the most heritable of psychiatric disorders, researchers have been searching for genes that underlie the disorder in the hopes that gene discovery will lead to better treatments.

Studies also suggest that genes are involved in ADHD and that each of these have small effects, although larger studies are needed to confirm the initial findings and fully understand the genetic mechanisms underlying ADHD.

 Fact

The largest genetic study of ADHD was recently conducted at the International ADHD Multicenter Genetics (IMAGE) project at the State University of New York (SUNY) Upstate Medical Center. The studies examined more than 600,000 genetic markers in more than 900 families and found one genetic marker that may be associated with ADHD symptoms.

Research from all over the world is being collected and published by the ADHD Molecular Genetics Network. While scientists have been able to identify some genes that may be associated with ADHD, it still isn't clear what causes those genes to become defective.

Environment versus Genetics

Research has also followed the impact of hereditary versus environmental factors on adopted children with ADHD raised by nonbiological parents. One study concluded that genes had more influence on childhood ADHD than upbringing or environment.

Another study showed that adopted children had a more than 30 percent chance of having ADHD. While this contradicts claims that genetics overrides environment when it comes to ADHD, it fits in well with psychodynamic theories claiming the trauma of early separation from biological parents can result in hyperactivity and behavior problems.

A Rare Thyroid Disorder Provides Clues

The NIH discovered a startling association between ADHD and a rare genetic thyroid disorder. The condition, called generalized resistance to thyroid hormone, occurs in just 1 in 100,000 people, or about fifty families in the United States. People with the disorder are resistant to the action of the thyroid hormone, which regulates a host of important functions in the body, including metabolism, bone growth, and brain development.

Advances in Nuclear Medicine and ADHD

With the advent of brain imaging technology such as the MRI, and positron emission tomography (PET) and single proton emission computed tomography (SPECT) scans, scientists no longer have to guess what's going on in your child's brain. While they can't see your child's actual thought process, they are able to measure the size, shape, and symmetry of his brain and compare it against the brains of children who don't have ADHD.

 Essential

Researchers still don't know what causes "bad connections" in the brains of children with ADHD. Is it caused by a smaller-sized brain or one that's not quite symmetrical? Do connections somehow misfire and get lost? Or is it a problem with the neurotransmitters, the brain's miniscule messengers?

Despite the dramatic increase in research, many answers continue to elude scientists, although they have made one major discovery. Using MRIs to scan the brains of people with ADHD, researchers have discovered that four regions in their brains are smaller than in "normal" brains. Those four regions of the brain include the frontal lobes, the corpus callosum, the basal ganglia, and the cerebellum.

- **The frontal lobes are critical for executive functions like planning and organizing.** Researchers already know that damage to the frontal lobes resulting from injury can result in mood swings, impulsivity, lack of inhibition, and hyperactivity.
- **The corpus callosum is the rope of nerves that connects the two hemispheres of your brain.** Studies have shown that this area of the brain, besides being smaller in children with ADHD, also operates differently than in those who don't have the disorder.
- **The basal ganglia are a set of nuclei deep within your child's brain that connects the left and right frontal lobes and lets them talk to each other.** Research has shown that basal ganglia that are asymmetrical or smaller in size may indicate a higher incidence of ADHD.
- **The cerebellum is the part of the brain responsible for balance and motor coordination.** Having a smaller cerebellum than normal could explain why some people with undiagnosed ADHD have problems with hand-eye coordination.

The Role of Brain Function in Childhood ADHD

Brains of children with ADHD not only look different from brains without it, they also function differently. Scientists can now compare the functioning of ADHD brains and "normal" brains.

One study used brain scans on children with and without ADHD to measure the level of brain activity in their frontal lobes when they were concentrating, and again when they were at rest. The differences were startling.

When children with ADHD concentrated, the activity level in the frontal lobe decreased from its level at rest. In people without ADHD, just the opposite was true. This was a giant stepping stone in establishing ADHD as a biological disease.

Are Brain Chemical Deficiencies the Culprit?

The brain and central nervous system work like a command center to coordinate every system in the human body. Comprising millions of nerve cells, the command center receives and transmits signals from one part of the body to another.

Impulses are carried along the length of nerve cells and "jump" from one cell to another. The gap between nerve cells is called a synapse. The chemical messengers that carry the impulse across the gap are called neurotransmitters.

Epinephrine and norepinephrine are two neurotransmitters that mobilize the body's reaction to danger and trigger the "fight or flight" response your child has probably experienced as a racing heart and heightened senses. Dopamine is a neurotransmitter that helps regulate your child's general activity level, whether she's active or passive, alert or disinterested, awake or asleep.

Many studies have shown a link between ADHD and an imbalance of neurotransmitters in the brain. Stimulant drugs used to treat ADHD relieve symptoms by increasing dopamine levels in the brain. Using indirect drug response research, researchers have discovered that insufficient levels of dopamine may be associated with ADHD.

Other studies associated ADHD with an imbalance of norepinephrine and dopamine in the brain. Having too much norepinephrine could make your child feel agitated and in a constant state of fight or flight, a common symptom in children with ADHD.

Could Your Child's Diet Be the Culprit?

Although it has become increasingly popular to blame certain foods and diets for causing or aggravating childhood ADHD, and there are many fad diets today that allege to cure childhood ADHD or alleviate symptoms, there is no scientific evidence proving that certain foods or diets ease ADHD symptoms.

Just a few diets around today that claim to ease ADHD symptoms include the Feingold Diet, the casein-free/gluten free diet, and diets that are low in sugar, high in protein, and high in omega-3 fatty acids. None of these dietary approaches have been proven to alleviate ADHD symptoms, although eliminating or limiting certain foods may ease symptoms in some children. For more information on the connection between ADHD and diet, see Chapter 17.

The Controversy over ADHD and Environmental Toxins

Unfortunately, there is a great deal of hysteria concerning the alleged connection between environmental toxins and ADHD. Controlled scientific studies have not shown a direct correlation between environmental toxins and ADHD, although early studies have shown that exposure to lead may cause ADHD-like symptoms.

There's a big difference between claiming lead causes ADHD and claiming lead causes ADHD-like symptoms. Unfortunately, many reports and press releases have blurred or ignored that important distinction. Also, many symptoms of ADHD, such as anxiety, depression, hyperactivity, and inattention, are very common disorders that are found in countless other diseases. For more information on the connection between ADHD and environmental toxins, see Chapter 19.

CHAPTER 3

Getting a Diagnosis

Many parents don't know where to begin when they suspect their child has ADHD. Unlike diseases and conditions that can be easily diagnosed by getting a blood test or an x-ray, there is no one simple test that confirms the presence of the condition. For most parents, getting the right diagnosis for their child usually entails going through a series of assessments from one or more medical professionals. Most experts believe that the best diagnostic and treatment plan is a multidisciplinary approach that involves a team of medical and ADHD experts.

Where Should You Start?

The choice of where to start your search can be bewildering, especially since different medical specialists have different strengths and are qualified to do different things. For instance, while both psychiatrists and psychologists treat mental disorders, most psychologists cannot prescribe medication or medical tests and must refer patients to someone else for those.

Further complicating matters is the fact that methods of evaluating children for ADHD are not as scientific as most people assume. In fact, they are not scientific at all. There are no tests for this condition. Because children's behavior typically improves in unfamiliar environments such as waiting rooms and examining offices, doctors do not expect to personally witness the behavior problems that are of concern. Many rely exclusively on information provided by a parent or teacher.

How to Find a Specialist

The best way to locate a specialist to do an ADHD evaluation is to contact your child's pediatrician or a child guidance clinic for a referral. Ask if there are any clinics specializing in ADHD in your area. The tests your child needs cut across a number of specialties, and a clinic is likely to house most of the professionals under one roof.

However, clinics specifically designed to evaluate and treat ADHD are few and far between, so most families use their child's physician, a psychologist, or a psychiatrist to coordinate the referrals to various specialists, compile all of the test results, pull together the recommendations, and conduct checkups after treatment has begun.

 Essential

Support groups can serve as an informal clearinghouse of information on recommended physicians, specialists, and treatments in your area, and may also offer you and your child the moral support you both need. To find one near you, talk to ADHD specialists, local universities, or the national organization of Children and Adults with ADD at *www.chadd.org*.

Types of Specialists That Treat ADHD

For a comprehensive evaluation, many professionals need to be involved, they include:

- MD (medical doctor) or DO (doctor of osteopathic medicine)
- Child psychologist
- Child psychiatrist

- Neurologist
- Audiologist
- Educational diagnostician
- Allergist
- Clinical nutritionist (licensed by the Clinical Nutrition Certification Board)

Any state-licensed physician or psychologist can legally diagnose and treat ADHD. Psychiatrists are physicians and can prescribe medication. Psychologists specialize in psychological testing. (Both may also provide counseling and psychotherapy.) They do not prescribe medication in most states, although this is changing. Licensed educational diagnosticians can diagnose disorders and make treatment recommendations if they have a doctorate, but they do not usually provide treatment.

 Fact

If you are in need of a new physician, a doctor of osteopathic medicine (DO) may be a good choice. Like other physicians, DOs attend medical school, but their curriculum places more emphasis on preventative, family, and community medicine. DOs prescribe medication and perform surgeries but tend to be broader in their approach and more concerned with holistic healing. Be sure to ask if the doctor works with children before scheduling an appointment.

Other Specialists that Treat Childhood ADHD

There are many other types of specialists who diagnose and help treat childhood ADHD and who may be able to offer additional assistance with assessment, coping skills, behavior modification, and problem solving.

- **Neuropsychologists** are trained in the biological and neurological basis of thought and learning. They may use a battery of tests to measure cognitive and behavior functioning. Neuropsychologists are usually less expensive than psychiatrists, but more expensive than psychologists.
- **Neurologists** are medical doctors who specialize in diagnosing and treating diseases and disorders of the brain and nervous system. Neurologists may be able to differentiate between symptoms of childhood ADHD and overlapping conditions like seizure disorder or brain injury. They can also prescribe medications and medical tests. They tend to be very expensive.
- **Psychiatric nurse practitioners and nurse practitioners,** or ARNPs, are generally well trained and knowledgeable about the diagnosis and treatment of ADHD. They are usually less expensive and more available than medical professionals, and may be helpful with life management skills.
- **Registered nurses, or RNs,** may also be able to make an initial diagnosis and offer assistance with life skills. As with psychiatric nurses, they can't prescribe medical testing and medication and must refer patients to other medical professionals. But they are usually less expensive and easier to schedule than psychologists or psychiatrists.
- **Master and doctoral level counselors** have advanced degrees in psychology or counseling, but they are not medical doctors. They can do an initial assessment and help your child deal with a wide variety of everyday life skills and problems. However, they must refer your child to a doctor or another professional for medication and medical testing. They may also provide services like neurofeedback and biofeedback.
- **Individual, group, family, and marriage counselors and therapists** can provide you, your spouse, your family, and your child with help in dealing with specific issues like getting along in social settings, functioning at work, parenting,

organizational issues at home, and dealing with childhood ADHD-related problems in relationships and marriage.

- **Social workers** are usually employed by public or private health care agencies to offer counseling to people served by the agency. Treatment is generally affordable. While social workers may be able to offer an initial diagnosis, they may lack the training necessary to distinguish between the symptoms of childhood ADHD and overlapping conditions like clinical depression, anxiety or bipolar disorder. Social workers also can't prescribe medications or medical tests.

- **ADHD coaches** specialize in helping children and teenagers manage everyday problems and situations, such as organization, time management, memory, follow-through, and motivation. Unlike psychiatrists and psychologists, they don't give advice or counsel. Instead, they address the present, using an approach that asks children and teenagers to focus on where they are now, where they want to be, and how they can get there. While generally less expensive than psychologists, coaches aren't cheap. Many coaches request that your child commits to four to six hourly sessions over several weeks or months. Fees range anywhere from $75 an hour on up, and are not covered by health insurance.

 Alert

Unlike doctors, coaches are not licensed by regulatory boards, nor are they required to undergo special training or licensing to practice. For this reason, some medical and psychological professionals question the validity of coaching as supplemental therapy. For more information on accredited coaches in your area, visit the International Coaching Federation website at *www.coachfederation.org.*

Importance of Medical Examination

If your family physician has known your child since he was born, it may be easier for her to arrive at a diagnosis than a physician who has never met your child before. Either way, any diagnosis for childhood ADHD should begin with a complete medical examination to rule out other diseases and disorders that may be masquerading as childhood ADHD. See Chapter 2 for more information on the many disorders that look like childhood ADHD.

As an MD, your family physician can also order the necessary medical tests and procedures your child may require, as well as prescribe prescription drugs. It may be easier to get in to see your family physician than to get an appointment with a specialist who doesn't know you or your child. Your family physician is also likely to charge less than some specialists.

Why You May Need More than a Family Physician

While family physicians are becoming increasingly aware of childhood ADHD, your family physician may not have the expertise or experience in diagnosing and treating the condition. In addition, she may not be comfortable diagnosing a condition in which a common treatment is the long-term use of a stimulant medication. But getting a medical checkup with your family doctor is a very good place to start if you suspect your child has ADHD.

Help Your Doctor Develop a History of Behavior

No matter what type of specialist your child sees first, an important first step in the evaluation process is for you, your child, and your child's doctor to work together to collect background information and take a detailed developmental history. The goal of a personal history is to ascertain the exact nature of the behavior problems, determine that they have been present for at least six months, establish that they occur in multiple settings, identify any special stresses your child has been under, find out what has been done at school and at home to try to help, and ensure that another diagnosis does not better explain the difficulties.

 Essential

To prepare for your first interview with a physician, collect your youngster's medical and school records and take them with you to the appointment unless your doctor requests them in advance. If you have recorded information in a baby book about the age at which your child first sat up alone, walked, talked, etc., be sure to have it with you as well.

Your physician will also want to interview you about your family medical history, and find out if anyone else in the family has ADHD, which is believed to be a hereditary condition.

Teacher Evaluations

Your child's doctor may ask her teachers to fill out an evaluation of your child. Often the evaluations are mailed to the school before the first appointment so the doctor can review the information in advance.

Classroom teachers are usually the first to urge parents to seek an ADHD evaluation. Because they work with so many students, teachers have a better basis than parents for judging whether behavior is typical. Because teachers are less emotionally involved, they also tend to be more objective than parents.

Parents also complete a checklist of problem behavior. Although parents and teachers tend to report different problems on the behavior checklists, they usually agree that the youngster's behavior is difficult, trying, and frustrating. Many doctors consider teacher reports of behavior problems relayed by an upset parent sufficient for an ADHD diagnosis and a prescription for amphetamines.

Tests Your Doctor May Use

Children with ADHD symptoms are typically prescribed a battery of medical tests. A neurological evaluation is important, since petit mal seizures can cause "spaciness" and lapses of attention. Thyroid problems can cause children's activity level to be abnormally high or low, and can cause inattentiveness. Some practitioners may also test for lead poisoning, allergies, and nutritional deficiencies, although there is no scientific evidence linking these factors to ADHD.

Hearing Tests

Children should have their hearing checked. Middle ear infections can be so minor that there is no fever, but the combination of muffled sounds and feeling under the weather can make children distracted, inattentive, and irritable. An audiologist should investigate the possibility of language processing problems. If all of those tests are passed, it is time for a psychological evaluation and educational testing.

Mental Health Screening

Children should be screened for other emotional and mental disorders before a diagnosis is made. Depression, anxiety, and stress reactions ("post-traumatic stress disorder") cause difficulties with sustaining attention and produce agitation that can look so much like hyperactivity, even seasoned professionals cannot tell them apart. Moreover, almost two-thirds of children diagnosed with ADHD also have another psychological, behavior, or learning disorder.

Psychological Evaluation

If mental health screening suggests that a child has another psychological problem in addition to or instead of ADHD, further evaluation by a psychologist, psychiatrist, or another credentialed mental health provider is in order.

A psychological evaluation involves taking a psychosocial history by interviewing parents in order to identify current and past individual, family, and social problems. Trauma from parental divorce, abandonment, alcoholism, abuse, domestic violence, and stress from chronic family tension can cause ADHD symptoms and other psychological, behavior, and learning problems.

Older children are then interviewed at length and younger children are observed in a playroom. Children ages six to twelve typically undergo a combination of interviews and playroom observations. If the interviews and observations suggest a need for further evaluation, the next step is likely to be psychological testing.

A complete psychological evaluation includes personality, intelligence, neuropsychological, and educational testing. A school psychologist or educational diagnostician employed by the school district may be legally obligated to administer some or even all of the tests, which relieves the family of this financial burden.

Educational Testing

Students diagnosed with ADHD should undergo educational and intelligence testing. The required tests can be administered by the psychologist during the psychological evaluation or by a qualified educational diagnostician, either through the school or privately. Learning disabilities are rampant among children with ADHD, so there is a good chance that special education services will be helpful.

Moreover, students with severe learning problems often misbehave in school or simply stop paying attention because they are frustrated and overwhelmed by the work. They act up at home because they are so upset about their inability to succeed academically. Their ADHD symptoms disappear once they receive instruction targeted to their particular learning style and needs.

The same applies to students who are especially academically advanced, except that their inattention, frustration, and classroom behavior problems are more likely to stem from boredom. They settle down and their concentration improves when they are given more challenging work. Educational testing can often pinpoint issues that are causing children to misbehave.

Quiz: Is This Specialist Right for Your Child?

Finding the right medical team for childhood ADHD is probably going to require more time and effort on your part than trying to find a doctor to set a broken leg. This is especially true if you feel you've already wasted a lot of time and money on specialists and treatments that didn't help.

While your child may be smarter and more intuitive than the average patient, on the minus side, your child may have less patience and tolerance, and have a much lower frustration level, as well as an innate distrust or disrespect of the medical profession.

Here are ten things to consider.

1. Has the specialist in question been recommended by friends or family members with childhood ADHD, members of your support group, medical experts, or other people or professionals you already admire, respect, and trust?
2. Does the specialist have the requisite academic and professional credentials and experience as well as a proven track record in treating children with ADHD? This includes being a member in good standing of national boards and professional organizations devoted to psychiatry, psychology, etc.
3. Is he informed about the latest medications, treatments, therapies, diagnostic tools, and tests for childhood ADHD?
4. Is he open to exploring new medications and approaches that you've always wanted to explore, or is he inflexible and stuck in his ways?
5. Do you and your child like the specialist enough to sense your child can hang in there for the duration, and/or when the going gets tough?

6. During your first meeting, did your specialist do as much listening as talking, or did you and your child have trouble getting a word in edgewise?

7. Does the specialist seem to "get" your child and regard him as a unique human being, or do you get the feeling he's already pegged your child as Type 1, 2, or 3 on the basis of a short test or conversation?

8. Can you afford to see the specialist regularly without going into foreclosure or emptying your bank account?

9. Is your specialist someone you think your child can easily fool? For example, can he see through little white lies, sins of omission, exaggerations, misleading statements, or false bravado your child might be tempted to use?

10. Will your specialist be there for your child when things get difficult? Or would he be more likely to write your child off, and send you a bill?

Scoring: If you and your child answered "yes" to questions 1–7, and "no" to questions 8–10, you are probably on the right track. If you scored any differently, you may want to keep looking.

Getting a Second Opinion

Maybe your child doesn't feel comfortable talking with your doctor, you're not confident the approach she's taking with your child will work, or perhaps the doctor wants your child to undergo an expensive test or treatment that isn't covered by your insurance.

Whatever you and your child's concerns may be, sometimes it pays to get a second opinion, especially when faced with a disorder that has many different treatment options, but no magic bullet. To find the names of ADHD specialists in your area, call your local branch of CHADD. You may also want to ask someone at your child's school for a recommendation, talk to other parents of children with ADHD for names of good specialists, or seek out good doctors from members of your ADHD support group.

CHAPTER 4

The Controversy Surrounding Preschool Children and ADHD

W hile infants and preschoolers may display some telltale signs of ADHD, they are generally not diagnosed or treated with ADHD until they reach age six. Because preschoolers are by nature hyperactive, impulsive, and inattentive at times, it can be difficult to distinguish normal hyperactivity from that associated with ADHD. And while there are hundreds of scientific studies on how to diagnose ADHD in grade school children, there are very few studies on how to detect the disorder in infants, toddlers, and preschool children.

Can You Really Diagnose ADHD in Toddlers?

Most ADHD experts caution that it is very difficult to diagnose an infant or preschooler with ADHD. That's because many exhibit some ADHD symptoms in various situations that are actually developmentally appropriate for their age.

This is not to suggest that infant and preschoolers are never diagnosed with the condition. Some physicians believe it's prudent to diagnose the disorder in preschoolers and infants when impulsivity, hyperactivity, and inattention are extreme. For instance, a preschooler who can't focus on anything at all for any length of time and requires constant monitoring may be suspected of having ADHD by some diagnosticians.

Remember that your child's suspect behaviors must occur in and adversely affect at least two areas of her life, such as home, school, day-care, or in her relationships with friends, and also must have been present consistently for at least six months.

 Alert

If your child is overly aggressive, exhibits behavior that is more extreme or very different than her peers, and has problems making friends, you may want to take her to a pediatrician or child psychologist for evaluation, especially if you or your spouse suffers from ADHD.

ADHD experts must look at the root of a child's behavior before making a definitive diagnosis, as many other things are often mistaken for ADHD, such as separation anxiety, poor motor skills or sensory problems, developmental disorders, oppositional disorder, and bipolar disorder.

Behavior that Predicts ADHD Later in Life

Although most physicians will not diagnose an infant, toddler, or preschooler with ADHD, some believe there are certain behaviors in early childhood that can predict the onset of ADHD in later life. They include:

- Expulsion from preschool because of aggressive behavior
- Refusal to take part in school activities
- Unwillingness to respect other children's property and boundaries
- Being rejected, avoided, or shunned by peers

Again, these behaviors may not be enough to diagnose the condition in infants and toddlers, because they are naturally hyperactive.

Does My Toddler Have ADHD?

Although all toddlers have a short attention span and are only able to entertain themselves for a few minutes at a time, toddlers who may develop ADHD are often unable to sustain their attention for more than a few minutes on their favorite toys or games, and are often distracted by the slightest sound or motion. They may also exhibit poor eye contact during conversation, and require far more one-on-one contact than other children to stay occupied and out of trouble.

Hyper Hyperactive

Although toddlers are also known for their high energy and activity levels and are naturally hyperactive, toddlers prone to ADHD are often in motion at all times and difficult to hold or cuddle and too hyperactive to eat or use the toilet. They are usually messy and careless and are constantly breaking or losing their toys. When these infants become excited, it can take hours to calm them down. With too much stimulation, they can exhibit wild behavior, such as hitting others and screaming at the top of their lungs.

Overly Impulsive

Normal impulsiveness is also exaggerated in toddlers who go on to develop ADHD. They are likely to experience more falls and injuries, throw and break their toys more often, and experience trouble falling and staying asleep. A toddler who may develop ADHD is likely to wake up in the middle of the night with energy to burn and demanding to play or run around. A lack of sleep is likely to make him more irritable and inattentive than other children.

Does My Preschooler Have ADHD?

Although children in this age group are usually still pretty inattentive, most children without ADHD are able to sit and do some activity on their own, such as listening to a story, coloring, or playing with toys.

By way of contrast, preschoolers who will develop ADHD are usually unable to sit still and listen, play with toys on their own without problems, or concentrate on coloring for any length of time. While a child without ADHD can do the same activity for ten to fifteen minutes, a preschooler who may develop ADHD may need to change activities every few minutes.

Hyperactivity in Preschool Children

Preschoolers who go on to develop ADHD may pick fights with their classmates, run out into the street without looking, fall out of trees, or get bitten by dogs they have pestered. They are usually in such a hurry that they can't sit still for a meal. Many preschoolers prone to the disorder will also become very talkative. If they have friends, they are likely to be very active children. Others may be expelled from school for hitting fellow classmates, destroying classroom materials, or displaying wild, uncontrollable behavior.

 Fact

Research shows that many preschool children who go on to develop ADHD are very aggressive and have poor social skills. Studies show they are twice as disobedient as other children, are responsible for three times the stress in families, and misbehave five times as often as children without the disorder.

The Dangers of Early Diagnosis

One real danger of attempting to diagnose an infant, toddler, or preschooler with ADHD is that normal behavior is easy for teachers, parents, and even some ADHD experts to mistake for ADHD symptoms.

The *DSM-IV* criteria used to diagnose ADHD points to red flags like "out of seat during school," "does not follow through on instructions," "avoids tasks with sustained mental effort," and "fidgety and restless while sitting"—behavior that is demonstrated by nearly every toddler and preschooler.

Wasted Time and Expense

Another reason many experts are reluctant to diagnose ADHD in infants, toddlers, and preschoolers is that their bodies and brain are growing and changing so quickly that isolating symptoms of ADHD can be difficult or impossible, especially since a diagnosis of ADHD rests on symptoms being present for at least six months in two different scenarios, such as at home, at school, and in social settings.

How Do You Treat an Infant?

There's also the problem of how to treat an infant if she's been diagnosed with ADHD. Some experts claim that many parents can see signs of ADHD in children before they can even walk. They claim that infants who go on to develop ADHD often are squirmier, less able to cuddle, and have a difficult temperament. They may also be easily frustrated, impatient, and require more care and attention than other babies, and suffer from more colic.

 Essential

One study suggests that infant sleep patterns can predict ADHD in later years. The study examined infants with severe or chronic sleep problems and then looked at them again when they were five and a half years old. One in four of the infants had developed ADHD compared to one in twenty children in the general population who had developed ADHD.

But many physicians question how they can monitor infants and toddlers who are being treated for ADHD. Very few physicians would agree to give ADHD stimulant drugs to an infant who has been diagnosed with ADHD because they would have no way of knowing if the medication was working.

Pros and Cons of a "Wait and See" Approach

Studies show that young children diagnosed with the condition between the ages of two and four have a 50 percent chance of outgrowing it, while children diagnosed after age five have only a 25 percent chance. Considering the odds, some experts believe that when it comes to diagnosing ADHD, the younger the better.

On the other hand, diagnosing an infant or preschooler with a disorder that isn't normally diagnosed until age six opens a Pandora's box. You and your child could go through a lot of expense and heartache for nothing. There's also the chance that diagnosing an infant or toddler with what appears to be ADHD will distract you or your physician from recognizing telltale signs of disorders that mimic ADHD, or have similar symptoms, and which are far more common in infants and toddlers.

The Preschool ADHD Treatment Study (PATS)

Another problem in diagnosing infants, toddlers, and preschoolers with ADHD is how to effectively treat symptoms. PATS, a study conducted by the National Institute of Mental Health (NIMH) in 2006, was the first long-term study designed to look at the effectiveness of treating preschoolers with ADHD with behavior therapy and/or methylphenidate. The study looked at 300 preschoolers with severe ADHD, including a history of preschool expulsion and rejection by peers.

Parent Training

In the first stage of the study, the preschoolers and their parents took part in a ten-week behavior therapy course. Parents were trained in behavior modification techniques, including using consistent praise, ignoring negative behavior, and using timeouts. More than a third of the children responded so favorably to behavior modification that they did not go on to the medication phase of the study.

Medicating Preschoolers

Children with extreme ADHD symptoms who did not improve with behavior therapy participated in a double-blind study comparing low doses of methylphenidate (Ritalin) with a placebo. Methylphenidate treatment resulted in a significant reduction in ADHD symptoms, as measured by standard rating forms and observations at home and at school.

However, the study reported that the children's ability to tolerate the drugs was less than expected. Eleven percent of the children ultimately stopped treatment, despite improvements in ADHD symptoms, because of moderate to severe side effects. These included a reduction in appetite, an increase in insomnia and anxiety, emotional outbursts, repetitive behaviors and thoughts, and irritability. Preschoolers appeared to be more susceptible to side effects than children in elementary school.

 Alert

One adverse effect of stimulant medication is that it appears to slow the growth rate of preschoolers. Children who participated in the PATS study and took stimulant drugs grew a half inch less and weighed three pounds less than normal growth rates.

The Medication Controversy

Experts remain divided on whether preschool children should take drugs to control ADHD symptoms. Some feel that the methodology for diagnosing infants and toddlers is unreliable, as is the effect of drugs on a developing brain, and that more research is needed before infants, toddlers, and preschoolers are given medication for ADHD. Others argue that because the PATS study showed that some young children with ADHD benefited from ADHD medication, those with severe ADHD should be treated to control out-of-control behavior.

Is It ADHD or Bipolar Disorder?

Studies show that up to 15 percent of young children diagnosed with ADHD actually have bipolar disorder, a debilitating disorder that until recently was rarely diagnosed in children.

Research suggests that bipolar disorder that begins in childhood may be a different and possibly more severe form of the disorder than that suffered by those with adolescent and adult-onset forms of the disorder. Studies show children who are bipolar are likely to suffer the following symptoms:

- Night terrors and nightmares filled with blood and gore
- Hypersexuality
- Feelings of elation and grandiosity
- Racing thoughts and ideas
- Less need for sleep

If your child has ADHD, he will demonstrate symptoms of hyperactivity, impulsivity, and inattention all the time and in a variety of settings, such as at home, at school, and with friends. Children with BPD, in contrast, tend to go back and forth between feeling sad and depressed to a state in which they feel manic and wired and are unable to sleep, relax, slow down, or even eat for hours or days on end. They also are prone to drastic mood swings accompanied by explosive temper tantrums that may repeat themselves up to twenty times daily.

Is It ADHD or Oppositional Defiant Disorder?

Marked by aggression, bad temper tantrums, frequent outbursts, and a desire to irritate and oppose others, oppositional defiant disorder occurs in about 40 percent of children with ADHD.

Children with oppositional defiant disorder are usually most comfortable when they are in the midst of an argument, fight, or conflict. They may blast the TV at top volume to drown out their parents' requests, shout "no" to every request from their parents, scream or cry uncontrollably, throw their toys on the floor or break them, jump on furniture, or pick fights with friends.

Discipline Nightmare

Children with this disorder usually wreak havoc on their families and parents, in part because other parents may blame the condition on lax parenting. While a lack of discipline may sometimes be the cause, unfortunately, what works for other children often boomerangs for those with oppositional defiant disorder. Fortunately, behavior therapy can usually help rein in the disorder, and stimulant medication may help.

Fortunately about half of all preschoolers diagnosed with the disorder outgrow the problem by the time they're eight years old. Older children with oppositional defiant disorder are less likely to outgrow it.

If the disorder isn't treated, it can evolve into conduct disorder, a more serious condition that is characterized by physical violence, crime, stealing, running away from home, setting fires, and other destructive and illegal behaviors.

Is It Anxiety and Depression or ADHD?

Studies show that about a third of children with ADHD also suffer from anxiety disorders. Symptoms include unwarranted worrying, fear, and panic, which can manifest as a racing heart, profuse sweating, stomach aches, and intestinal distress. Other types of anxiety that often go along with ADHD include obsessive-compulsive disorder. If your child is suffering from anxiety, he may also have sleep problems.

About 18 percent of children with ADHD, and especially those with the inattentive subtype of ADHD, suffer from some sort of depression. Usually, children with ADHD and depression have family members who suffer from depression as well. Children who are depressed may feel unloved or unwanted, feel inadequate, lack self-esteem and confidence, and feel overly frustrated by failures in school and with friends.

Is It ADHD or a Learning Disability?

Being disorganized, inattentive, distracted, and forgetful can be caused by ADHD as well as by a number of brain disorders that are characterized as learning disorders and language disorders. About 50 percent of children with ADHD suffer from a specific learning disability, especially with reading (dyslexia) and handwriting.

 Essential

Childhood ADHD is not considered a learning disability per se, although symptoms of the disorder are likely to interfere with concentrating, paying attention, being able to focus and sit still, organizing, and getting things done on time.

Auditory Disorders versus ADHD

Children with ADHD as well as a learning disability may also demonstrate problems with listening and retention, but the problems are caused by different mechanisms. A child with ADHD can hear and process information she is interested in receiving, and also tunes out information she finds boring, repetitive, or irrelevant, even if the person talking to her has a very loud voice.

By way of contrast, a child with an auditory processing disorder (suffered by 50 percent of children with ADHD) may not be able to tune out extraneous noise at all, while a child with a learning disability may not be able to understand the material presented, or remember it from one day to the next. Compounding the problem is that all of these problems could coexist with ADHD. If your child appears to have ADHD, these other comorbid conditions must be ruled out first.

 Question

Will stimulant medications help my child regardless of whether she has a learning disability or has ADHD?
Unfortunately, it won't. Giving stimulant medications to a child who does not have ADHD but who does have learning disabilities will not result in an improvement in learning. However, giving stimulant medication to a child who has both ADHD and learning disabilities will result in learning improvements.

Autism

ADHD is present in about a quarter of children with autism, or above five times above the average. People with autism, a neurobiological disorder, suffer from an abnormal absorption with themselves that is characterized by an inability to communicate and interact with others, and a short attention span.

Developmental Coordination Disorder

Children with ADHD are also more likely to suffer from developmental coordination disorder and be extremely clumsy and uncoordinated. This condition is particularly devastating for young boys with ADHD because they often are so clumsy they either can't participate in team sports or they cause so many problems they are teased by classmates and kicked off teams.

The Controversy Regarding TV and ADHD

Research has also shown a connection between attention deficit problems and watching excessive amounts of television. According to the

American Academy of Pediatrics (AAP) guidelines, children younger than two years old should not watch TV, DVDs, computers, video-games, videotapes, or other types of entertainment on screens. Children two years and older should be limited to about two hours daily of "quality" TV programs, such as educational television programs.

A Little TV Is a Good Thing for Children with ADHD

However, many ADHD experts disagree that television is a menace for children with ADHD, and are not overly concerned if young children watch a limited amount of educational television, innocent cartoon shows, and innocent videos like *Winnie the Pooh* or *Thomas the Tank Engine*. Children with ADHD as well as those without it enjoy watching favorite videos over and over again, and often pick up new words and concepts from them that they wouldn't otherwise learn until much later.

Pro-television ADHD experts argue that children who don't watch any television at all are likely to be out of the cultural mainstream, and appear "out of it" to classmates and teachers because they can't share in the excitement of television shows and sports events.

 Alert

Because many children with ADHD already have problems relating to other children, and often come across as odd, secretive, antisocial, and "out of it," not watching television could serve to further alienate them from their classmates and peers, according to ADHD experts.

Survival Tips for Parents

If your infant or preschooler is exhibiting symptoms that you think may signal ADHD, don't panic or jump to conclusions. Your child may be acting normally for his age.

If your child demonstrates extreme behavior that is much different from other children his age, or if he has difficulty making friends, you may want to take him to a pediatrician or child psychologist for a comprehensive medical and developmental history that includes feedback from teachers and health professionals who have worked with your child.

Neuropsychological testing may also be required to rule out conditions that mimic or overlap with ADHD, including anxiety disorder, language-processing disorders, oppositional-defiant disorder, and sensory integration problems.

Behavior Treatment for Preschool Children

Behavior treatment for preschool children with ADHD involves adjusting their environment to help them with social interactions. As a parent, you can help your child overcome challenges by creating more structure, encouraging routines, clearly stating expectations, limiting choices to avoid overstimulation, being consistent when it comes to disciplining your child, setting rewards and consequences, and creating routines that help your child get and stay organized. For more on behavior modification, see Chapter 15.

 Essential

An excellent way to bolster the confidence and self-esteem of your child with ADHD is to help him discover his special gifts and talents, then provide him with the instruction, resources, teachers, mentors, and materials he needs to excel in that gift or talent. Many children with ADHD are extremely creative and intuitive, so look for ways to help your child shine.

Parent Training

Because children with ADHD don't come with an owner's manual and require special care and discipline, you may also benefit from parent training, which can teach you helpful strategies for disciplining your child and tips for getting and keeping him organized.

You may also want to join a support group of parents of children with ADHD to gain insight on the disorder and how to handle it, as well as information on local resources, such as the best physicians and ADHD practitioners.

The Bottom Line

Remember that children with ADHD have problems controlling their behavior without treatment or medication and may be as baffled by their symptoms as you are. Don't mistake ADHD symptoms for intentional misbehaving.

In preparing your child for preschool or day-care, work with teachers and personnel to create an effective learning environment for your child that has lots of built-in structure and routine that substitutes for the chronic disorganization that typically accompanies childhood ADHD.

Be honest about your child's limitations as well as his special gifts so teachers can make modifications that can help your child with ADHD thrive. And understand that even with the best of treatment, your child may still be more hyperactive and impulsive than normal children and require special classes and accommodations.

CHAPTER 5

ADHD in Grade School Children

Children with ADHD struggle in traditional classrooms and are commonly viewed by their teachers as unintelligent or as underachievers. Many come to think of themselves as not very bright or unmotivated. The real problem is that their minds work differently from most people's. They are more holistic in their thinking and are drawn to abstract ideas rather than details. Because they focus on the "wrong" parts of the lessons, they can easily forget, mix up, or simply overlook information that teachers consider important.

The Best Types of Classrooms for Children with ADHD

ADHD experts agree that the best classroom for grade school children with ADHD is informal—that is, not the type of class where children are expected to sit in the same seat all day long. They are better off in a classroom where they can move around, stand up, or work at their own pace.

Your child's classroom should be sufficiently structured so that it provides your child with a framework and lots of cues and tools that help her get and stay organized, such as calendars, schedules, assignments posted prominently and in the same place; designated work spaces for learning tools such as workbooks, dictionaries, etc.; and well-organized supplies, from libraries to art supplies.

Essential

Students with ADHD also thrive in a classroom setting where the schedule is structured and orderly, with the sequence of classes consistent from one day to the next, and special classes, such as art or music, held on the same days every week.

Ideally, your child's teacher will also implement ways for students to organize their work and various subjects so they can find it quickly; for instance, by color-coded folders.

Organizing the School Year or Semester

Children with ADHD often have challenges getting and staying organized and planning ahead. They also tend to have mid-season slumps after the novelty of the first few months of school wear off and the end of school is still months away.

To help your child maintain her focus (another challenge for many kids with ADHD), work with the child's teacher to create a list of academic goals and milestones your child can work toward, and have her cross each one off as she completes it.

Review the list with your child every week to see how things are progressing, to see if deadlines are being met, and to look at what remains to be completed. Remember that setting up lots of external cues for your child can help compensate for her internal lack of organization.

Structuring Assignments and Homework

Many children with ADHD have difficulty completing large, many-step projects with deadlines. Because they are poor at organizing, prioritizing, and handling details, they often become so overwhelmed they give up in mid-stream and never finish the project.

To help your child stay on track and to finish the project on time, encourage her teacher to break up large projects into doable mini-projects, and to give each mini-project a deadline so your child doesn't get behind.

It will also help if her teacher gives your child one instruction at a time, rather than several lumped together. Instead of telling your child to put away her math paper, get out her English grammar book, and turn in her science homework, have the teacher give her one instruction at a time.

Special Services

If your child has not yet been diagnosed with ADHD, but you think he may have it or a teacher has concerns, ask that the school conduct an evaluation to determine if your child qualifies for special education services.

Special Services

Here are some important steps to take to get your child with ADHD the special classes and accommodations he needs to succeed.

- Start by speaking with your child's teacher, school counselor, or the school's student support team, to begin an evaluation.
- Each state has a Parent Training and Information Center and a Protection and Advocacy Agency that can help you get an evaluation. A team of professionals conducts the evaluation using a variety of tools and measures. It will look at all areas related to the child's disability.
- Once your child has been evaluated, he has several options, depending on his specific needs. If special education services are needed and your child is eligible under the Individuals with Disabilities Education Act, the school district must develop an individualized education program specifically for your child within thirty days.

- If your child is considered not eligible for special education services—and not all children with ADHD are eligible—he still can get "free appropriate public education," available to all public-school children with disabilities under Section 504 of the Rehabilitation Act of 1973, regardless of the nature or severity of the disability.

Performance Problems Associated with ADHD

Many students diagnosed with ADHD do well in school one year and founder the next. That should make it obvious that the classroom environment and teaching method are the cause of the student's problems, not the student herself.

Easily Bored

Many children with ADHD are very independent from the time they are young, and this characteristic is especially common among the intellectually gifted. Individualists often clash with their teachers even though they are not disruptive. Some read books in class instead of doing busy-work assignments. Some draw instead of sitting with their hands folded on their desks. Some create complex stories in their imaginations to fend off boredom. They persist because what they are doing interests them. Parents' and teachers' negative opinions are less compelling to children with ADHD than their desire to stimulate and express themselves.

 Alert

Independent thinkers are often diagnosed with attention deficits because they are so intent on what they are doing, they do not notice what is going on around them. If they do notice, they may not care to join in. Getting them to care may be a losing battle.

Problems with Details

Many children with ADHD also have a holistic thinking style that focuses on the big picture at the expense of details they find boring or mind-numbing. They have problems automatically focusing on elements that define subtle differences, which are required to sort and organize.

Many kids with ADHD are adept at comprehending complex concepts and developing new ones, but they are abysmal at performing simple computations that require rote memorization.

Hyperfocus

At the same time, kids with ADHD often hyperfocus on subjects and ideas they find interesting to the exclusion of everything else. For instance, it's not uncommon for a child with ADHD to spend hours on a subject or idea she enjoys, while ignoring her math or grammar homework that's due the next day.

The ability to concentrate intensely can be an asset—especially when a child with ADHD goes to college, where creativity and thinking outside the box are highly valued. Unfortunately, in grade school, a child's hyperfocus often gets in the way of learning or completing nuts-and-bolts ("boring") ideas and assignments that lay the groundwork for grander ideas.

Behavior Problems Associated with ADHD

Most children with ADHD have short fuses and are easily overwhelmed, frustrated, and discouraged. In addition, they may suffer from oppositional defiant disorder, or behavior characterized by disobedience, hostility, and defiance toward authority figures, including teachers, which makes it more difficult for them to get along with people, take directions, and get things done.

The Problem of Hyperactivity

Most children with ADHD are hyperactive, which can make it difficult for them to pay attention, focus, or even stay in their seat. According to the National Institute of Mental Health, hyperactivity refers to children who:

- Fidget and squirm in their seats
- Talk nonstop
- Dash around, touching or playing with anything and everything in sight
- Have trouble sitting still during dinner, school, and story time
- Are constantly in motion
- Have difficulty doing quiet tasks or activities

Hyperactive children often need a constructive way to combat boredom and release excess energy. If your child is restless or frustrated, do not nag or suggest a sedentary activity, such as television or reading. Recommend somersaults, jump rope, hitting a tennis ball against the side of the house, or going for a walk. At least suggest that your child stand up and stretch for a moment.

The Role of Exercise

Another way to ease your child's hyperactivity is to ensure he gets plenty of exercise. For many students, gym is their only chance to move about, but many schools have cut back so that students only attend a few times a week. Even if they go every day, they average only nine minutes of exercise. The rest of the time is spent watching others or listening to the teacher.

A study by U.S. International University and reported in Thomas Armstrong's *The Myth of the A.D.D. Child* found that exercise has positive effects on behavior. Hyperactive, aggressive students participating in jumping or field exercises forty minutes a day, three times a week were less aggressive on the days they ran than on the days they did not.

Regarded as Odd and Different

Highly creative children are in the minority, and the majority does not understand how they think or why they behave as they do. Peers tend to regard them as strange or odd because of their unusual interests. Especially creative types are often branded as crazy because their heightened sensitivity causes them to have stronger emotional reactions than less sensitive people. Even if creative teens find a social niche in high school, they know that most of their peers regard them as odd.

Others label themselves as crazy and withdraw. Some hold everyone at a distance for fear of having their "insanity" discovered. Some embrace the role and spend years moving through the revolving door of the mental health system. When creative children are not accepted by their peers, affirmation from parents becomes all the more important. Most parents love their children dearly. But too many make creative youngsters feel that something is terribly wrong with them.

Daydreaming

In addition, some children with ADHD are accused of being lazy because they daydream. Often the real "problem" is that they devote a lot of mental energy to pondering the material being presented rather than simply trying to commit it to memory. They consider its relationship to other things they have learned and contemplate its implications.

 Fact

Highly sensitive children react strongly to sounds, temperature changes, smells, and tastes that others barely notice. Such acute sensitivity often goes hand in hand with artistic, musical, and literary genius. Do not assume your child is exaggerating when he complains about discomforts that to you seem minor.

Creative children are also more intuitive, so when asked what they are thinking about, they may be unable to articulate what is on their mind. If they try, they are often ridiculed by teachers and peers who cannot comprehend the connection between their comments and the subject under discussion.

Outspoken and Speaking as Equals

Some children with ADHD also tend to be outspoken. They are prone to address adults as equals rather than deferring to their authority. If they are generally insensitive to other people's feelings, they may alienate peers and earn a reputation among adults for being ill-mannered.

Maintaining good relationships with teachers and classmates can be especially challenging for independent types who love to debate. Some children consider ideas more important than people's feelings.

Help your child understand how his behavior affects others, but let him decide whether he wants to change in order to be liked. It is a mistake to take your youngster's side against teachers, but it is also a mistake to try to change your child into someone he is not. A better approach is to communicate in no uncertain terms that you expect your child to be respectful of others. Discuss ways he can assert himself appropriately. And when he hurts someone's feelings, he of course needs to apologize.

Difficulty Being on Time and Adhering to Schedules

Children with ADHD frequently have problems sticking to schedules, in part because dividing time into slots and assigning activities to each one does not strike them as sensible. If they worry about being late, it may be because they are afraid others will be upset. They do not believe that the passage of time is significant or that the clock should rule people's lives.

Help Build Structure and Organization

Poor organizational skills are one of the hallmark signals of childhood ADHD and include having difficulty organizing everything from items and activities to school tasks. In your grade school child, this may manifest itself as having problems getting homework and assignments done on time or in an organized fashion, being unable to find clothing or toys, and living amidst constant clutter.

The first step toward helping your child get organized is to help her overcome her natural aversion to it. The second step is finding ways to help your child get and stay organized. The third and most important is having the entire family commit to using the strategies to help keep the family member with ADHD on track.

Overcoming Aversion

Until your child understands the benefit of getting and staying organized, she will probably resist it. After all, organizing can be tedious, repetitive, and boring—things that children with ADHD already have a natural aversion to. However, most children with ADHD can be motivated to accomplish something. Incentives, such as a raise in her weekly allowance or a special gift, may help motivate your child.

 **Question**

How can I help my child become more organized and enjoy doing it? She always seems to sulk when I suggest anything.
The best way to help your child succeed at becoming more organized is to make organizing fun by making your child feel like a team member rather than a victim, and by keeping an upright and enthusiastic attitude. Nagging your child will only lead her to avoid the task at hand, not do it.

Ask your child what items or activities she wants better organized, discuss some of the problems she can avoid by getting more organized, and the many benefits she'll enjoy—such as having more time to play video games because she's not spending all her time searching for shoes. Keep track of how your child's disorganization sabotages her school grades and friendships, and discuss them with your child so she better understands the ramifications of being disorganized in her own life.

Clean Your Room!

Few things spark more arguments between children and parents than messy rooms. If your child can't find anything in her room, be realistic about what she can accomplish. Your child may not be able to maintain a room that's neat as a pin, but it shouldn't be total chaos either.

Helping Your Child De-Clutter

To speed things along, try these simple tips:

- Give every item in your child's room a designated "home" so your child knows where it belongs.
- Create a daily five-minute routine in which your child puts things away and returns them to their home locations. Then reward her.
- Every two months, help your child get rid of toys and clothing she no longer uses or wants, or store items she only occasionally uses on shelves or in storage.
- Be persistent and provide lots of friendly reminders and supervision, but let your child do the work herself.
- Find a way to make organizing and tidying up enjoyable and fun. Maintain a supportive, enthusiastic attitude, be realistic about what your child can actually accomplish and maintain, and provide clear, consistent requests. Your child won't do anything if she gets discouraged, overwhelmed, or frustrated.

Develop Routines

All children, and especially children with ADHD, thrive on routine, even if they claim they hate it. According to a review of fifty years of psychological research published in *The Journal of Family Psychology*, even infants and preschoolers enjoy better health and behavior when the family has consistent and predicable routines.

Routines are essential for a child or teen with ADHD if he is to focus on daily tasks and activities without getting frustrated or flustered because of ADHD symptoms of inattention, lack of focus, the tendency to get distracted and restless, and low or zero tolerance for boring, repetitive activities.

Morning Routine

To help your child get to school on time, try these simple strategies.

- Have your child wake up at the same time every morning, and go straight to the bathroom. If he has trouble waking up, set an alarm.
- Put out clothing the night before so your child doesn't have to worry about finding clothing to wear.
- Set out a healthy breakfast while he's getting dressed, and have him eat it without the distraction of TVs or computers. If there is time, let him watch TV or use his computer when he's finished.
- Have his coat and school bag by the door waiting for him.
- Have a set time for your child to walk out the door.

The Homework Routine

Most children with ADHD need a mental breather after school, so give your child about thirty minutes to unwind by playing, watching TV or video games, or having a snack. After that time is over use the following routine:

- Create a regular place and time for your child to do his homework.
- To help your child transition from relaxing to doing homework, give him a ten-minute warning.
- Help your child review his homework assignment, and make sure he has pencils and other supplies handy.
- Build in short breaks so your child can get up and walk around and stretch for a few minutes to decrease restlessness and clear his mind.
- Be generous with praise, applauding your child's efforts as well as his results.
- Sit down with him and go over his completed homework.
- Organize assignments and school supplies needed for the next day, put them in his school bag, and set it by the front door.
- Do something relaxing and enjoyable together after your child completes his homework.

The Supper Routine

If possible, have the family eat dinner together at a regularly scheduled time every night. Establish a few dinnertime routines for your child, such as helping prepare the meal, setting the table, clearing the table, or putting the dishes in the dishwasher. Don't discuss work, school, or family problems or issues around the dinner table. Keep the conversation light and friendly, and don't eat with the TV on.

Bedtime Routine

Establish a regular bedtime routine on school nights so your child gets to sleep on time and gets the sleep he needs.

- Give him a five- or ten-minute warning before it's time to start his bedtime routine.
- Have your child turn off the TV or computer or put away his toys.

- Serve your child a light bedtime snack.
- Help your child select and lay out his clothing for the next day.
- Have your child bathe, brush his teeth, put on his pajamas, and get into bed.
- Read a story together or have a friendly talk to help your child unwind.
- Kiss your child good night, turn off the lights, and wish him pleasant dreams.

Helping Your Child Overcome Frustrations, Setbacks, and Competition

It's important to understand the developmental level of your child before she goes to school. She may be able to perform at grade level academically, but be several years behind her peers in terms of maturity and social skills.

If this is the case, it's important that you keep your expectations realistic, and not expect your child to behave as maturely as other children her age. In fact, it may help to simply consider her two or three years younger than she really is.

Solutions at School

As a parent, you should also work with your child's teacher to help her develop simple strategies that will make things easier for your child in a classroom setting.

- Make sure the teacher understands that it's crucial never to humiliate or embarrass your child when she engages in inappropriate behavior. Many children with ADHD don't learn social skills by osmosis like other children, but must be taught them by teachers and parents.
- Ask your child's teacher to work privately with your child to practice appropriate responses to peers until she feels comfortable.

- Request that the teacher provide lots of chances for your child to work in small groups where she can practice her social skills.
- Ask the teacher to monitor your child's interactions with classmates to help minimize problems.
- Talk to your child's teacher about praising her in front of classmates when she does a good job on something. This will help heighten your child's confidence and self-esteem and is a more constructive way to let other students know about your child's special gifts and aptitudes than having your child showing off or resorting to rude comments to get attention.
- Make sure the teacher understands that your child should not be compared with other children in the class, especially if your child has been mainstreamed. Most children with ADHD are not lazy or unmotivated, but are trying as hard as they can to succeed despite their ADHD shortcomings. Many children with ADHD who are forced to compete against others become so anxious their symptoms flare.

Solutions at Home

When talking to your child and disciplining her, it pays to remember that your child has the brain development of a much younger child. Keep your instructions simple and direct, and don't compare your child to other children and expect her to behave in a way that isn't possible for her.

CHAPTER 6

ADHD in Middle School Adolescents

Middle school is a huge leap forward for any child, but for a preteen with ADHD, the leap is longer, higher, and harder. Instead of staying in the same class all day with one teacher, your tween moves from classroom to classroom, interacting with different teachers and students and carrying everything he needs. Many teens with ADHD lack the organizational skills needed to keep track of schedules, homework, and supplies, while the desire to fit in can make the middle school years challenging for tweens with ADHD lacking confidence and social skills.

A Difficult Transition

The many new social and academic demands of middle school aren't easy for a tween with ADHD. To make it worse, research shows that ADHD symptoms often worsen as a child enters his tween years.

Even if your child excelled in grade school, he may struggle with staying organized as he moves from one classroom to another and works with a variety of new and different teachers who have high expectations. Coping with peer pressure, teasing, bullying, and the pressure cooker of adolescent dating and social life may exacerbate his social awkwardness and tax his fragile social skills to the breaking point, and cause him to feel increasingly insecure, self-conscious, and like a social outcast.

As any parent can attest, any tween going through puberty experiences a variety of growing pains. For a child struggling with ADHD, the transition from childhood to adulthood is likely to be even rockier. What's a parent to do?

Continuing Symptoms

Contrary to popular myth, ADHD is not just a condition that affects children. Nearly 80 percent of children with ADHD go on to have symptoms as adolescents, teenagers, and adults, according to the National Institute of Mental Health. Adolescents and teens with ADHD are likely to view the world as an overwhelming whirlwind of confusing activity that requires a host of skills they struggle with.

 Alert

Tweens with ADHD are easily distracted, which means they often lose track of time. Getting to class on time several times a day, as one must do in middle school, can be particularly difficult for your child. Make sure your child's teachers and principal know he has the disorder.

What might come easily or naturally to other tweens may be an enormous, exhausting task for your tween, including such necessary skills as planning ahead; completing projects; staying on track; prioritizing projects; breaking down large projects into small, doable pieces, organizing schoolwork, homework, and activities; following conversations; making new friends; and adapting to a continual onslaught of new teachers and students.

Dealing with ADHD-Related Academic Challenges

The middle school years are the years when students integrate and build on the three Rs they learned in grade school and develop the cognitive skills needed for more complex thinking and reasoning, such as being able to think in abstract terms, deduce and interpret material, and understand ambiguity.

Unfortunately, many tweens with ADHD are two to three years behind other tweens developmentally, and may lack the brain wiring to develop cognitive skills required for more complex and abstract thinking.

How Your Child's Teacher Can Help

If your child is not eligible for special accommodations and services, consider working with your child's teacher to develop strategies that will help your child better cope with ADHD learning challenges.

- Help your child build better study skills. Many tweens with ADHD have poor recall, including problems storing and retrieving subject matter they recently read. Your teacher can help your child by showing her how to isolate material in her textbooks that's most likely to appear on tests by paying attention to boxes, colored fonts, sidebars, and chapter summaries.
- Use who, what, where, when, and how as cues for learning. If your child is studying history, she can ask: Who are the main characters, what is going on, where is it occurring, when did it happen, and how did it happen to help her remember important facts.
- Find tricks to master math. Succeeding at math requires following a succession of steps to solve a problem. By creating sample problems and math formulas on note cards and keeping them in one place, your child will have a handy and helpful reminder.
- Improve your child's reading awareness. Effective reading requires your child to be able to skim and scan to find important facts, and read critically. Many children with ADHD have problems with all of these skills because they lose focus when scanning, and have trouble understanding

ideas that are presented or restated in a different way. High-lighting important information can help your child keep track of facts. Summarizing and elaborating on the major points in the story can also help increase comprehension.

- Encourage your child's teacher to teach to a variety of learning styles. In middle school, many teachers simply lecture. If your child is a visual learner, she may not absorb material presented in a lecture, or lose focus or concentration during a long class. Your child may learn better if the teacher gives her a printed version of the lecture before class so she can follow along and review the material at will.

- Find ways for your child to overcome ADHD restlessness. Many tweens with ADHD are restless, and may require breaks to maintain focus and concentration. Encourage the teacher to find an unobtrusive way to let your child take physical breaks so she can refocus.

How You as a Parent Can Help

Your middle school child will likely benefit from the same type of structure and guidance you provided when she was younger, even if she is more resistant to it as a middle schooler. Here are eight suggestions to try:

Send your middle school child off to school with a "success pack" for each teacher that includes a letter signed by you and your spouse that introduces your child, describes her medical condition, hobbies and goals, explains that ADHD is not an excuse for poor academic performance or behavior, but makes the teacher aware of your child's condition, and provides details about how to contact you if problems arise.

Develop a contract with your child for school-related performance and behavior that needs improvement, and provide incentives for success, such as an increase in her allowance.

Find the best teachers for your child. Ask the principal to switch your child into classes taught by teachers who have experience with ADHD, or rearrange your child's schedule so the most challenging classes fall at a time of day when she's likely to be most alert and attentive.

Be on the lookout for learning disabilities in your child. Many learning disabilities don't surface until middle school, especially in very bright children. Telltale symptoms might include a reluctance to read or write, an inability to comprehend what she reads, difficulty understanding abstract concepts, and poor writing and handwriting skills. If you suspect your child has a learning disorder, see your physician, and request that your school formally evaluate your child.

Children and tweens with ADHD have notoriously sloppy handwriting because of ADHD-related problems with fine motor skill coordination. Ask your child's teacher if your tween can use a computer to take notes and complete homework assignments, reports, and essay tests, instead of doing them longhand.

Network and visit the school to ensure the teachers and administrators know you. Your child will benefit if you get involved at school, and know who to go to when problems crop up. Go to school board meetings, and volunteer to help in the classroom.

Make sure your child's teachers understand how ADHD affects your child's ability to learn and perform. Give teachers ADHD pamphlets, brochures, and books that explain the condition, and steer them to helpful ADHD websites.

Create iron-clad structures and routines at home. Beginning and completing tasks are difficult for children with ADHD. Routines are a good way to help children learn cognitive skills they need at school for organizing, starting and finishing work, and planning. Whether it's getting to bed on time or catching the school bus, create easy, set routines for your child to follow.

Helping Your Tween Get and Stay Organized

Staying organized can be a nightmare for your child when he reaches middle school and suddenly has multiple classes and teachers. Skills that other students might learn naturally or take for granted, such as filing papers; remembering what books, binders, and implements are needed for each class; completing homework; and creating notebooks for each subject, don't come naturally to kids with ADHD—they must be taught.

 Alert

> Middle school work is inherently more complex and demands a higher level of cognitive functioning—such as classifying information, assembling facts, and following a certain progression of steps. If your child already struggles with focus and memory, it's essential that you and your child's teacher establish structures for your child that help keep him on track.

How Your Child's Teacher Can Help

Schedule a meeting with your child's teacher before the start of school, and ask if she can implement some of the following learning tools when teaching your child:

- Post and hand out personal copies of schedules and checklists.
- Post a master monthly calendar in the classroom showing upcoming activities, projects, and deadlines. Leave it up long enough that students can transfer this information into their personal planners.
- Post checklists for procedures and projects and give each student three-hole punched copies for their notebooks.
- Schedule in-class cleanups. Set aside time each week for students to purge their binders, backpacks, and desks.

Inspect students' desk and notebooks periodically, and give rewards (homework passes or tokens that can be redeemed at the school store) for the student who has shown the biggest improvement.

- Provide lots of advance warning about upcoming projects and reports, and give students with ADHD a head start by helping them select a topic, making sure they have the materials they need, and reviewing outlines and rough drafts.

- Break up big projects into bite-size pieces and establish periodic checkpoints so students with ADHD can monitor their progress and stay on track. Post deadlines prominently, and make sure students with ADHD copy them in their notebooks. Refer to deadlines frequently. Contact parents to ensure they know about projects and when they are due.

- Teach students how to take good notes by using outline forms and index cards.

How Parents Can Help

The teacher is only part of the success equation. As the parent of a child with ADHD, it's up to you to make sure your child does his homework on time.

To ensure your child brings home homework assignments, suggest he have a homework buddy he can contact in the event he forgets. If your child has problems copying homework assignments into his notebook, have him read it into a small cassette recorder.

Teach your child how to make good "to do" lists, dividing tasks into "now" and "later." Review his list every evening for the next day, and remind him about projects and assignments that are due the next day.

Before school starts, help your child set up a notebook that's divided into sections, or get him a notebook for each subject.

And don't forget to give your child lots of feedback and praise for a job well done. Kids with ADHD get so much criticism they become adept at tuning it out. Using praise is far more effective.

Teaching Your Child
Time-Management Skills

Prioritizing is a basic time-management skill. A good time to help your child learn is when helping her decide on the order for doing homework assignments. Some students prefer to do the easiest ones first, because it boosts their confidence. Others prefer to tackle the harder items first because they are fresher, and they can relax once those are finished. Or use "chaining," a behavior therapy technique where your child does the task she likes least first, then rewards herself for doing that task by doing something she enjoys more next. An assignment your child enjoys can be started after she completes one she does not enjoy. This motivates your child to get through the first assignment.

 Fact

Children diagnosed with ADHD tend to be remarkably unaware of the passage of time. As a consequence, they commonly misjudge how much time is required to complete routine tasks. A common pattern is to underestimate how long it will take them to get ready to go somewhere or do a chore, and to exaggerate the amount of time they spend on activities they dislike.

Help your child list the tasks and put them in order before she sets out to do any project that has given her difficulty in the past. Consider making and posting lists in convenient locations to guide her through washing the dishes, straightening her room, and packing her book bag. Children with poor memories for such details should use as many aids as possible. After referring to their lists and checking off each completed task and step over a period of weeks, months, or years, they will undoubtedly memorize the procedure.

Dealing with Deadlines

To learn to cope with deadlines, youngsters need to be able to judge how much time various projects will take and set up schedules matched to their capabilities and, whenever possible, their desires.

The first step is to collect lots of data about how long it takes them to do all kinds of routine tasks: taking a bath, completing a set of math problems, gathering their things together for baseball practice, walking home from a friend's house, and so on. That information will eventually enable them to make realistic estimates about how much time they need to allow themselves for various tasks.

Importance and Challenges of Peer Approval

Middle school children feel more socially vulnerable than practically any other age group. For children with ADHD, who are socially awkward, the challenges are even greater to fit in, handle peer pressure, and feel comfortable in a variety of new social gatherings and settings.

Even for children without ADHD, the rules for being accepted can seem so arbitrary and ever-changing that it keeps them constantly on their toes. For kids with ADHD, who lack social confidence and have trouble reading nonverbal cues and body language, committing a middle school social faux pas is practically inevitable.

Tease-Proofing Your Tween

Typical ADHD behavior, such as interrupting others, lack of eye contacts, hyperactivity, an inability to notice social cues, and lack of confidence can make children with ADHD easy targets for teasing and bullying.

How Parents Can Help

Role-playing at home is crucial. Work with your child on maintaining eye contact, using transitional expressions like "Hi," "Bye," and "See ya" when meeting or leaving friends, and the importance of common courtesy and saying "Please," "Thank you," and "I'm sorry" when necessary.

Encourage your child to count to ten in his head before making any comments or trying to participate in a conversation. This will help him avoid blurting out inappropriate things and help him become a better listener.

 Alert

If your tween doesn't understand why he gets such negative attention, he may conclude that he's basically and hopelessly unlikable and simply withdraw. While kids can be cruel and thoughtless, it's important not to dismiss the situation, especially if you have a child with ADHD.

Work with your child on developing social skills that make him less of a target, praise him when he has a successful encounter with a bully, and encourage him to seek out friends who respect and like him. It may also help to tell him about your own tween struggles with teasers and bullies.

Parental Involvement in Extracurricular Activities

Most parents agree that one of the best ways to improve a child with ADHD's academic and social success is to get involved in some way in her school. Studies indicate that the children of parents who are involved at their school tend to get better grades, have fewer behavior problems, have better relationships with their teachers and classmates, and grow up to become more responsible adults. When you participate in your child's school, you're giving your child a message that her school is important to you.

By participating at your child's school, you'll also get a better idea of who your child's friends are, and your child will be less likely to get bullied or teased. You'll also get to know your child's teachers better.

Easy Ways to Get Involved

Getting involved in your child's school is easier than you may think. Here are some suggestions of ways you can participate:

- Attend parent-teacher conferences.
- Volunteer to drive or chaperone a field trip.
- Ask your child's teacher if you can help with special projects.
- Volunteer to chaperone at a class dance or party, or offer to bring refreshments.
- Join the PTA.
- Offer to head up an after-school hobby or sports group.

Can Your Adolescent "Grow Out" of ADHD?

Until the early 1990s, scientists considered ADHD a "childhood disorder" and believed that most children outgrew the condition. For that reason, physicians usually took children off medication before they reached high school. In many cases, teenagers suffered serious setbacks academically and socially—a clear sign their ADHD symptoms had not abated.

Continued research has shown that ADHD symptoms do not necessarily go away by adolescence. According to the American Academy of Family Physicians, about two-thirds of children with ADHD continue to have symptoms as adults.

Does Your Child Still Need Medication?

If your child's symptoms become less noticeable as he gets older, your physician may recommend taking him off medication to see how he fares. If your child's symptoms of hyperactivity, inattention, and/or impulsivity don't return, it's probably a good sign your child is among the one-third of children who grow out of ADHD. Or your child may only need to take medication a few times a week to keep symptoms in check.

Tweens with ADHD and Learning Disabilities

It is common for tweens diagnosed with ADHD to be diagnosed with one or more learning disabilities. Most involve language (especially speaking and understanding what is being said) or a specific academic subject (usually reading or math). A host of educational tests claim to be able to identify learning disabilities, yet many professionals have challenged the whole concept.

Special Education Services

If regular classroom teachers cannot accommodate your child's educational needs, special education help may be a good option. Special education services may involve going to a special classroom all day, getting extra help in a particular subject for an hour a week, or anything in between. It may mean having a specially trained teacher come to the regular classroom to work with your child.

To qualify for special education, your tween's ADHD symptoms must cause significant learning or behavior problems at school. Section 504 of the Individual Education and Development Act legally obligates public schools to ensure that children with a disability have equal access to education.

To qualify to receive services under Section 504, a student must have a disability that "substantially limits one or more major life functions, including education, learning, and behavior."

What to Do If You Think Your Child Needs Special Help

If you think your child needs special services, you may have to be unusually assertive, depending on your child's school district. The first step is to submit a written request for an evaluation via certified mail to the school. Special education classes are expensive due to the small classroom sizes and advanced degrees of the teachers. Parents may have to be assertive to see that evaluations are handled in a timely manner and that the recommendations are implemented.

 Essential

It is a good idea to request a copy of your school district's policies and procedures for complying with Section 504. It will list your rights and the district's responsibilities. If your complaints are not satisfied, you can call the Office of Civil Rights hotline of the U.S. Department of Education at (800) 421-3481 for information about how to proceed.

With its individualized instruction and self-paced learning, special education can help any student. Most students enjoy special education classes and like their teachers. Many students feel a sense of incredible relief and experience heightened morale when their learning problems are finally acknowledged and they are provided with instruction that allows them to progress at their own speed in an accepting environment.

CHAPTER 7

ADHD in Teenagers

High school means coping with academic challenges on top of raging hormones, peer pressure, and sexuality. Add ADHD to the mix, and the transition from childhood to adulthood can be especially trying. As a parent, you can help your teen with ADHD weather his high school years by helping him build the strong organizational skills he needs for academic success, and the strong social skills he needs to master relationships with friends, teachers, and the opposite sex.

Dealing with Academic/Classroom Challenges

The three major symptoms of ADHD—hyperactivity, impulsiveness, and inattention—may also wreak havoc on a teenager's ability to function at school. Many high school students with ADHD have difficulty sitting still, listening, and staying focused. They also experience problems with executive functions like taking and organizing notes, comprehending reading and homework assignments, and getting to class on time. In addition, they may fail to turn in homework assignments or complete projects by the deadline.

Because of their poor social skills, many high school students with ADHD are ostracized by classmates because of their impulsive or rude behavior. To get attention and fit in, boys may adopt sarcastic or smart aleck behavior, while girls may resort to sexual promiscuity. In their desire to be part of the gang, high school students with ADHD may run with the wrong crowd because that crowd is the only one that will accept them.

 Essential

Research conducted by the National Institute of Mental Health shows the teenage brain is a work in progress. Brain scans showed the structural changes in the brain that occur during late adolescence paralleled a pruning process that occurs early in life. It seems to follow a use-it-or-lose-it principle: Neural connections that get exercised are retained, while those that don't are lost.

Mastering Executive Functions

For many teens with ADHD, the biggest academic challenge is handling and mastering the wide range of executive functions required of them by teachers and professors. This includes organizing, prioritizing, delegating, planning, meeting deadlines, and conceptualizing long-range plans and goals.

Strategies to Improve Executive Functions

Staying focused is probably the biggest executive challenge for teens with ADHD. That's because to get anything accomplished, you have to stay focused, concentrate, and stick with it until it's finished.

Unfortunately, teens with ADHD often find it difficult to pay attention, especially when they find the subject boring, dull, repetitive, or uninteresting. Instead of focusing, their mind wanders.

The end result is that the project or task doesn't get done on time— or at all. High school students with ADHD often have to work late on homework and projects and even devote entire weekends to completing them. Others become so distracted that, despite high IQs, they fail subjects or drop out of school. Studies show high school students with

ADHD are more likely to drop out of school, flunk out of college, and perform below their academic abilities than other teens.

 Fact

Many teens with ADHD struggle to find a healthy balance at school. Some hyper-focus on their work to the exclusion of everything else and become loners and social outcasts, while others can't focus at school at all, and are forced to bring work home. While the second group may appear to be workaholics, they are actually compensating for the hours they spend daydreaming or idle at school.

Does Medication Give Your Teen an Academic Edge?

ADHD medications are powerful drugs that can enhance mental abilities, improve clarity, and enhance awareness in those without as well as children with ADHD. That said, if your child suffers from ADHD, he may well need to take stimulant medication to correct brain malfunctions that can lead to underperformance and social problems. In other words, stimulant medication will not give your child with ADHD academic edges so much as help him perform as he would without the disorder.

Unfortunately, there is wide scale abuse of ADHD drugs by people who don't suffer from ADHD. According to *Wired* magazine, many top performers in academic and technology fields abuse these drugs, either through prescription or from friends, to get an extra competitive edge. Parents and even some professionals are also guilty of giving ADHD drugs to students who don't suffer from the condition to enhance their academic performance at school.

This phenomenon is not limited to the high tech industry. In April, *Science Daily* published a similar article claiming that more than 33 percent of college students, and 10 percent of high school students, use ADHD drugs to get them through difficult periods, regardless of whether they have ADHD or not.

 Alert

According to *Wired* magazine, at least one fourth of its readership uses "drugs like Ritalin, Adderall, and Provigil to help them work harder, longer, and better. What this indicates is that people on the cutting edge of technology and science are using ADHD drugs like 'brain steroids' to give themselves an intellectual advantage."

The New Stigma

Your child may prefer to hide the fact that he takes stimulant medications for his ADHD. Teens and college students who don't have ADHD and take these medications illegally are categorized as drug abusers, and your child may not want to tell others he takes medication for fear he'll suffer the same stigma.

In addition, some high school students with ADHD who take ADHD drugs legally for symptoms feel they must hide the fact they take stimulant medications so their friends and peers won't pressure them to share or sell their drugs to them.

Helping Your Teen Get and Stay Organized

Disorganization is a classic symptom of ADHD, and it can make it difficult for your teen to do many tasks at school, including getting things done on time; prioritizing; breaking up large tasks into small, doable pieces; keeping track of books and materials for different classes; and even remembering what classroom to go to at what time.

Organizing Strategies

Here are some strategies you can encourage your high school student with ADHD to adopt to get and stay organized in school.

- Centralize important information. Use a desk calendar, personal organization system, or computer calendar to keep all her essential dates, appointments, reminders, to-do lists, and deadlines in one central location.
- Buy an easy-to-use filing system with color-coded three-sided folders to organize her important projects into separate tasks. Don't use manila envelopes, as materials may fall out of the sides and get lost in the shuffle.
- Start each day by clearing the decks. Have her de-clutter her desk, file important documents, and clear out and file materials in her in- and outboxes. If something is urgent, have her tackle it immediately before she forgets about it or gets distracted.

Helping Your Child Deal with Anger and Criticism

Teen ADHD symptoms may inhibit your child's ability to appropriately interact with others at school or work, be a good team player, handle criticism, deal with authority figures, and conduct himself appropriately during class or with friends. These factors often play a significant role in how teachers and mentors perceive him, and can be the difference between him getting ahead and falling behind.

Managing Emotions

Many teens with ADHD have fragile egos. If your child's self-esteem is wobbly, he may need to be especially careful about acting defensive, continually putting himself down, or letting other people's perceptions or opinions of him affect his conduct.

Instead of letting a bad temper or inappropriate comments jeopardize his schoolwork or job, have your teen role-play managing his temper and communicating thoughts to colleagues instead of keeping them bottled up.

Managing the Effects of Low Self-Esteem

Many teens with ADHD have low self-esteem, and this can manifest at school in a variety of negative ways that can be detrimental to establishing, maintaining, or advancing their career. For instance, low self-esteem may cause your teen to be overly concerned about or sensitive to what others think or feel about him, and cause him to put more time and energy into worrying than working.

Your teen's low self-esteem may cause him to be very self-critical, defensive when it comes to accepting criticism, or angry because he feels he isn't valued or appreciated. A therapist can help your teen uncover some of the reasons or dysfunctional thinking behind his poor self-esteem and help him look for ways to improve or bolster it.

Dealing with Authority Figures

Many teens with ADHD have trouble dealing with authority figures like teachers, professors, and bosses. Many teens with ADHD simply believe they are right about everything most of the time, despite all evidence to the contrary, and that other people are wrong most of the time. Before your teen lets his stubbornness get the best of him, encourage him to consider the possibility that he could actually be wrong this time (or any time).

If your teen still thinks he's right and his teacher or boss is wrong, encourage him to think carefully about what confronting his teacher or boss would accomplish, taking into consideration his personal track record and his personal relationship with the authority figure. Would the teacher or boss be likely to listen and thank your teen for his input, or be so impressed by your teen's insight that he'd change his mind? Or would he be more likely to be annoyed and insulted that your teen had the nerve to defy him and, in turn, give him a low grade?

Discovering Your Teen's Academic Strengths and Weaknesses

ADHD can hamper your teen's ability to look at himself realistically and gauge his strengths and weaknesses. Not knowing what he's good at (or bad at) can have an impact on his academic and job performance in many ways.

He may struggle with a subject, major, or career path that doesn't match his innate talents, or become bored, disgruntled, or disappointed when his efforts don't yield the results he had expected.

A good therapist can help your teen zone in on his strengths and weaknesses so he can minimize shortcomings and maximize his many gifts. Many teens with ADHD decide to change college majors after working with a therapist and wind up in a different career that better fits their ADHD skills and temperament.

Dating, Networking, and Other Social Challenges

Dating can tax a fragile teen with ADHD's social skills to the breaking point. Consider sitting down with your teen to take inventory of her social strengths and weaknesses so she can avoid dating situations that are likely to become awkward or stressful.

Dating Scenarios to Avoid

Encourage your teen to avoid dating situations that will stress her out because they require maintaining strict focus during lengthy and/or complex conversations. These can include large dinner parties where she's expected to participate in conversation, long lectures that cover complex or unfamiliar material, or foreign movies or operas with subtitles that compel her to follow a plot being spoken or sung in a foreign language.

Safer Bets

Better bets for dates for teens who have ADHD include social activities like movies, concerts, and dramatic productions that do not revolve around passively listening and watching rather than actively participating. Other safe dating bets include:

- **Spectator sports.** If your teen is really hyper, spectator sports events may be even better than movies and concerts because there's more opportunity for her to get up, move around, or go grab a hot dog and soda without disturbing the other spectators. Participating in spectator sports lets her blow off stress and anxiety, but doesn't leave a lot of time or room for small talk.
- **Active dining activities.** Rather than formal sit-down dinners that may revolve around long conversations, encourage your teen to choose more informal dining engagements, such as buffets, outdoor barbecue and pool parties, potluck parties, or casual dinners centered around home or rental movies. These options offer more chances for hyperactive types to get up and move around and for inattentive types to focus on short, informal conversations with people of their choosing.

Handling Social Challenges

Everyone needs friends, especially teenagers with ADHD. If your child's symptoms have made it difficult or challenging for her to make meaningful friendships and maintain them during troubled times, she may be going about it in the wrong way. Here are some strategies to help her make and keep friendships that can sustain her through good times and bad.

Have your teen pick her activities carefully. Your teen is already working hard enough to pay attention, focus, concentrate, and read nonverbal cues without forcing herself to do something she dislikes. Engaging in an activity she doesn't enjoy will only cause her to get bored and tune out or drift away.

Encourage your teen to practice being a pal. Making and keeping friends requires time and effort on your teen's part, so make sure she doesn't expect friendships to flourish in a vacuum. Your teen or tween can make staying in touch with friends easy and fast by creating a master list of names, phone numbers, and e-mail addresses on the computer. Have her set aside some time every week to touch base with close friends and set up lunch dates or activities with those that live nearby.

Encourage your teen to contact more casual friends and acquaintances about once a month to keep the connection going. If she has limited time for staying in touch, tell her that it's better to make a quick phone call or send a short e-mail than to do nothing at all. Her friends are probably as busy as she is, and will likely appreciate that she thought of them.

Encourage your teen to surprise friends on important dates in their lives by sending them a card, e-card, flowers, candy, or special gift. Your child's thoughtfulness in remembering birthdays, anniversaries, and special occasions will go a long way toward cementing relationships.

Encourage your teen to flex her creative muscles. If your teen or tween is artistic, encourage her to make her own greeting cards. These are practically guaranteed to win a place of honor on the recipients' refrigerator or mirror. Or, you may want to encourage your child to use her creativity to make unusual, one-of-a-kind gifts, such as homemade cookies and fudge.

ADHD and Addictions

Research shows that teenagers with undiagnosed ADHD may be walking time bombs on a variety of levels. Compared to teenagers without the disorder, teenagers with ADHD are twice as likely to run away from home, three times as likely to be arrested, ten times as likely to get pregnant or cause a pregnancy, and 400 times as likely to contract a sexually transmitted disease.

Many teenagers with ADHD have a penchant for risky behavior as well as a need for constant stimulation. It's no mystery why some of them turn to alcohol or drugs for kicks. Research shows that teens with undiagnosed ADHD are especially prone to drug use because they may be attempting to self-medicate themselves with illegal drugs that bear a resemblance to ADHD drugs. Other children with ADHD abuse drugs or alcohol to mask symptoms of social discomfort or phobias. Talk to your child about the dangers of alcohol and drug abuse and be on the lookout for warning signs.

Is Your Teen Safe Behind the Wheel?

Most parents worry when their teen reaches driving age, and when that teen has ADHD, fears escalate. Car accidents are the number one cause of death for teenagers. Studies show that about 63 percent of those killed are drivers, and 37 percent are passengers. Drivers with ADHD who are in their teen years face a double whammy when it comes to being safe behind the wheel: They have limited experience dealing with driving challenges, and they also lack the maturity required to make good judgment calls.

 Alert

Teenagers with impulsive ADHD are also a hazard behind the wheel and have a 400 percent greater risk of being in traffic accidents than other teens.

Teenagers with ADHD also have a "no fear" attitude that can translate into reckless behavior behind the wheel. Coupled with ADHD symptoms of inattention, impulsivity, lack of focus, and an inability to stop and think before acting it's no mystery why teenage drivers with ADHD are at the top of the list when it comes to fatal car accidents.

Strategies for Parents

If your teenager wants to drive, sit down with him and discuss the effects his lack of driving ability can have on increasing his risk of accidents. Help him develop strategies that will reduce his chances of having car accidents, and make sure he understands that driving is a privilege that can be revoked at any time.

Go on practice rides with your teen to let him improve his driving skills under your supervision. You'll have a better idea of how well he drives, and what he needs to improve to reduce his risk of causing an accident. Make sure your teen understands the dangers of driving while talking on the cell phone, texting, changing CDs, or listening to music or the radio while driving, and limit nighttime driving until you've taken several test drives with your teen. You may also want to set some ground rules about how many passengers your teen can have in the car at the same time to reduce the risk of distractions.

Teenage ADHD Rebellion

The teenage years are a normal time of rebellion for any teen. But teens with ADHD are far more likely to be rebellious than other teens because of the core symptoms of the disorder. Because of their need for constant stimulation and excitement, many teens with ADHD are drawn to risky behaviors such as truancy, drinking, and drug use.

Deciding Not to Take Medication

Many teens with ADHD refuse to take their medication because they don't like the side effects, and/or because they consider ADHD a social stigma and don't want to be associated with the disorder or medications prescribed for it. If your teen wants to discontinue medication, you may want to put off letting her drive until you see how she fares without medication. If her symptoms worsen or remain severe, you may want to prohibit her from driving until she's back on medication and her ADHD symptoms are under control.

Teens with ADHD and Truancy

Because many teens with ADHD have difficulty in school, they are also more prone to truancy than students without the disorder. Repeatedly skipping school and classes means they often fail to turn in assignments, homework, and projects on time, or at all. With repeated truancy, teens with ADHD often fall so far behind their classmates that they drop out of school altogether in frustration.

Teenage ADHD and Dropping Out

Research shows that teens with ADHD, including those with very high IQs, are much more likely to drop out of high school than students without the disorder and wind up in low-paying jobs they find boring and demeaning and which do not tap their special aptitudes or talents.

Helping Your Teen Get into College or Find a Career Path

Every college or university with federal funding is obligated to provide "reasonable accommodations" for the estimated 2 to 4 percent of college students who have ADHD, but the amount of help varies widely among schools.

Some colleges provide the bare minimum to comply with the federal law. Others offer every imaginable service to accommodate students with adult ADHD, including student disability services, study skills programs, specialized help during registration and freshman orientation, on-campus physicians who specialize in treating ADHD, and access to on-campus ADHD coaches, counseling, psychotherapy, and support groups.

If your child has ADHD, you may want to help him look for a college or university that has a welcoming and supportive attitude toward students with the disorder. The college your child chooses should go out of its way to facilitate his transition from high school to college life. Have your child work with his high school guidance counselor to home in on colleges that have small class sizes, low student-to-professor ratios, and an emphasis on personalized attention.

To Disclose or Not to Disclose

Although there is no law dictating that your child must disclose that he has ADHD, it's often a wise choice. By disclosing his disability, your child will provide the admissions department with the information they need to make an informed decision about how well he's likely to fit in at their school. Your child may also be eligible for valuable assistance through the college's disabilities office.

 Essential

College students diagnosed with ADHD may be eligible for services under Section 504 of the Rehabilitation Act of 1973 and the Americans with Disabilities Act. If your child decides to disclose that he has childhood ADHD, he will be required to submit documentation of his disorder. This may include records of psychological evaluations, the date of diagnosis, high school records that document special assistance he received, and a current IEP/504 plan.

Once your child has decided on a college, he should register for disabilities services right away. To ensure he'll get the services he needs from the start, he should apply for admissions and disabilities services at the same time.

College students with ADHD may qualify for the use of assisted technology to help them cope with their disability. These include voice-activated software, books on tape, personal organizers, and computer outlining programs.

Special Challenges for Students with Childhood ADHD

In college, most of your child's life will revolve around being able to concentrate, focus, retain knowledge, take good notes, schedule time for studying, and manage his time so that he gets things done on time. For this reason, typical ADHD problems with executive functions can present a unique challenge to college students with ADHD.

Many students with ADHD overestimate what they can realistically accomplish in one semester. Others, away from the day-to-day assistance of parents and family for the first time in their lives, become overwhelmed with the number of decisions and choices facing them.

Tips for College Success

To ensure your child's college experience is a positive one, make sure you and your child plan ahead. Have him address his inherent limitations and map out a plan of action to deal with them. Make sure your child has access to learning services and academic support to help reduce stress and frustration.

If your child has significant problems with executive functions, you may want to hire an ADHD coach who can help him organize his time and establish good study habits. Joining an ADHD support group or peer study group on campus may help your child make meaningful friendships, help him feel more hooked into campus life, and give him a safe place to vent his fears and frustrations. If the college has a student health center, encourage your child to introduce himself to the physician on staff.

CHAPTER 8

Creating Harmony at Home

Without professional intervention, childhood ADHD can turn the happiest home into a never-ending battlefront. Core symptoms of disorganization, distraction, inattention, and impulsivity can unravel the fabric of family life and cause emotional, mental, physical, and financial turmoil for everyone involved. In addition, parents and siblings of children with ADHD are often stretched to the breaking point in their attempt to raise children and manage household affairs. The following chapter offers lots of tips and strategies for creating a happy home life when one or more of your children have ADHD.

Why ADHD Is a Family Affair

Being a parent is hard enough without adding in ADHD. Even the most organized and efficient parents can end the day feeling overwhelmed, confused, and exhausted when dealing with a child who has ADHD.

Core symptoms of inattention, hyperactivity, impulsivity, disorganization, and distractibility can add to nonstop duties that can often tax parents to the breaking point.

Add in the very real possibility that parents of children with ADHD are more likely than other parents to have the disorder themselves, as well as more than one child with ADHD, and chaos can reign unless some hardcore organizational, discipline, and intervention strategies and techniques are incorporated.

This chapter explores some of the more common challenges facing parents with a child or children with ADHD, and tips and strategies for calming the waters.

Helping Family Members Manage ADHD

Ask anyone who suffers from it, or anyone who lives with a sufferer, and you'll probably get the same response: At times, it can seem that childhood ADHD is synonymous with conflict and disruption. The disorder often creates nonstop chaos and havoc in practically every area and aspect of the home.

The Star in Her Own Soap Opera

Since ADHD is often accompanied by emotional and behavioral volatility, the condition itself makes the child prone to drama. As most family members can appreciate, including the sufferer herself, it's not usually the sort of drama anyone would buy a ticket to see.

One way parents or siblings can pull the plug on ADHD-inspired soap operas is to sit down with a family therapist and get to the bottom of why the child with ADHD feels compelled to spin out soap operas. Once the sufferer and her family members understand the emotional voids the dramas are intended to fill, they can help boost her self-esteem, increase her confidence, and replace her energy-draining dramas with more productive activities that can strengthen rather than deflate her resources, and improve family morale.

Understanding and Recognizing the Root of Mood Swings

In addition to her constant need for drama, a child with ADHD is also likely to suffer from periodic or chronic mood swings. It's important for family members to understand that these mood swings are often not connected or triggered by a particular event or person, but may be the result of neurobiological imbalances, waxing and waning medication levels, side effects of medications, dietary triggers, and coexisting depression or anxiety.

 Essential

Children with ADHD are often extremely sensitive to criticism and may put up a wall to protect themselves from what may feel like a never-ending barrage. Having disappointed many people over time, and having been told countless times they are unpredictable, unreliable, or unproductive, they may react to similar complaints from family members by withdrawing or lashing back.

Exhaustion from having to cope with a daily never-ending parade of symptoms can also make children with ADHD feel helpless, scared, and hopeless. A family therapist can work with family members and the child to take a closer look at mood swings, help isolate likely triggers, eliminate possible causes, and educate the family about mood triggers that may not always be treatable.

Letting Go of the Past

Many children and teenagers with ADHD live with perpetual feelings of guilt and shame about failures of the past, even if their failures were triggered by undiagnosed ADHD symptoms and not caused by their lack of motivation, laziness, lack of productivity, or disinterest. Like a broken record, the song of "failure" plays itself over and over again and often drowns out present-day successes and accomplishments.

By working with a family therapist, family members can help the child with ADHD understand that until she stops dwelling on past failures and begins to live in the present, she will never begin to replace her gloom-and-doom with feelings of contentment and happiness. Once she realizes it's impossible to undo the past and that the more she feeds it negative thoughts, the longer she keeps it alive, a child or teen with ADHD can bury the past and open her eyes to the many possibilities, opportunities, and avenues for joy that exist in the present. Once you're successfully managing your child's ADHD symptoms, you can begin to incorporate some basic ground rules of parenting that will help keep things running smoothly on the home front.

 Alert

Many children with ADHD suffer from depression and anxiety. Living with a gloom-and-doom pessimist who seems hard-wired for continued failure can gradually wear down and pollute the spirits of the sunniest family members and cause them to resent the "downer" in their midst.

Seven Strategies for Quieting Chaos in the Home

Here are some strategies that will help you and other family members become more consistent and loving parents and siblings:

Keep it consistent. Consistency is probably not one of your child's strong suits if she suffers from inattention and has trouble focusing. As a parent, it's important to keep things consistent so your child doesn't get confused or frustrated. As the parent of a child with ADHD, you need to be consistent about everything from house rules to serving meals, to disciplining your children so they understand that your "no" this time will also be a "no" next time, and not a "maybe" or a "yes."

Keep it organized. Again, this is probably not one of your child's strong suits, but an ADHD coach may be your best resource in helping organize the household schedule, finances, and chores. As explained in the last chapter, one strategy that works for many parents of children with ADHD is posting a family calendar of events and commitments.

Lose the Supermom (or Superdad) cape. As the parent of a child with ADHD, don't set unrealistically high expectations for yourself or your child, or commit to more than you or she can do, or both you and your child will feel frustrated, guilty, disappointed in yourself, and overwhelmed. If you're overbooking your child's schedule, it won't take long before something falls through the cracks and your child either forgets or doesn't have time to do something very important. Don't hesitate to delegate.

Create and stick to simple daily routines. While the thought of creating and following set routines may be enough to give your child hives, without set routines, your home life will resemble chaos in no time. To get the day started on the right foot, create a weekday morning routine for you and your child. Create set routines for after school and evening that include after-school snacks and exercise, eating together as a family, and completing homework assignments.

Remember appointments, deadlines, and to take dinner out of the oven by setting alarms. Your child already has a tendency to get hyper-focused on one thing and forget about everything else. To make it easy for your child to remember important things, set kitchen timers, or alarms on cell phones, wrist watches, BlackBerries, and so on so they beep or buzz to remind her no matter where she is in the house.

Create a Grand Central Station for anything that family members use on a daily basis. This will prevent these items from getting scattered around the house or lost in space. To make it easy to keep things organized, build cubbies for your child's backpacks and galoshes, install a key rack by the door for car and house keys (and keep duplicate sets in a set different location), and designate a special place in the house for eyeglasses and sunglasses.

Accent the positive. Remember that children with ADHD are like litmus paper and will absorb any negative vibes you put out there. If you catch yourself feeling chronically depressed or negative, talk with your physician about adjusting your medication schedule so it lasts until bedtime and you have the enthusiasm and energy to devote to your children. Remember to count your blessings and focus on your gifts, and you'll teach your child with ADHD to do the same thing.

Handling Disruptive Behavior

Regardless of how childhood ADHD has unraveled your family or marriage in the past, it's possible to do damage control and get things in order by having everyone in the family master some basic coping techniques and skills aimed at helping the child with ADHD help himself and prevent inflicting chaos on others.

Try a Little Tenderness

Learning how to put themselves in the child with ADHD's place is a good place for all family members to begin. Until everyone in the family understands that their sibling or child with ADHD isn't intentionally screwing up, forgetting to show up, failing to pay attention, or neglecting to listen, they will assume that he is doing it on purpose to make them angry or upset, because he doesn't care, because he's disinterested in what they are doing, or for a million other imaginary reasons.

 Essential

> Once family members understand that their child or sibling with ADHD is a prisoner of his own symptoms, they can start taking steps to help him minimize his ADHD symptoms and maximize his ADHD strengths.

Family members can learn how to deal with the volatile emotions, moodiness, bluntness, critical nature, and high frustration levels exhibited by children with ADHD by not taking things they say too personally, and to remember that some hurtful things children with ADHD say or do are not intentional, but really just ADHD symptoms.

Acknowledge and Release Pent-Up Feelings

Another strategy families can use to weather the unpredictable symptoms and emotions of children with ADHD is to agree to acknowledge and share how things make them feel rather than bottling them up and letting things fester.

Instead of feeling increasingly frustrated with your child with ADHD's inability to do a simple chore, you can acknowledge his ADHD shortcomings, including his own frustration at not being able to get his chore done on time, and help him devise a strategy that can help him master the task next time.

 Essential

One general strategy that can help alleviate conflicts on the home front is to ensure that all family members recognize their child or sibling with ADHD is operating with some basic mental and emotional deficiencies that make doing simple things very difficult for him. By having compassion for him and adjusting their expectations and demands so he can succeed, everyone wins.

This could involve making sure he writes down his homework assignments, helping him develop a way to "flag" his work so he can easily pick up where he left off the next day, calling him at a friend's house to remind him it's time to leave for a doctor's appointment, and acknowledging your gratitude at the extra effort and coordination required on his part to get things done on time.

Effective Intervention Strategies

Maybe you feel guilty because your child with ADHD forgot to do her homework or insulted her teacher or a classmate. Or perhaps you're embarrassed that your child blurted out something confidential and potentially embarrassing at a family get-together.

Regardless of who feels guilt and shame regarding ADHD symptoms, it's important for the entire family to recognize that the child with ADHD is not doing it on purpose—if it's anyone's fault, its ADHD's fault.

Instead of trying to blame a phantom, family members should help the child or sibling with ADHD mend her ways by helping her get more organized by creating family calendars, schedules, and timetables; stay more focused on conversations; and rein in impulsive behavior and comments by counting to ten before saying something potentially insulting or embarrassing.

Helping Children with ADHD Get Organized

One way to keep a child with ADHD organized is to display prominent schedules and timetables at strategic locations throughout the house. Rather than hiding schedules in computer files that are only obvious when opened, post duplicate schedules in the kitchen, in the bedroom, on bathroom mirrors—wherever family members will see them repeatedly and be likely to remember them.

Family members can also help reduce the clutter and disorganization that seems to afflict children with ADHD by designating special places for key items like hats, gloves, school books and homework, gym gear, etc.

Practicing Thanks and Gratitude

Everyone needs to be appreciated, acknowledged, and thanked for their accomplishments, achievements, and attempts, especially children with ADHD who are so accustomed to being criticized and slammed that they are hard-wired for blame, accusations, and negativity and understandably defensive, withdrawn, and unable to express affection.

It's also amazing what a little humor can do to defuse a potentially embarrassing or difficult situation. Instead of focusing on the negative ("You forgot to pick up the take-out pizza on your way home from school, and now it's probably too soggy and cold to eat!") lighten up and reframe it as a funny episode that will go down in time in the family scrapbook.

Join an ADHD Family Support Group

Miscommunications between family members can have dire consequences. Failing to communicate over where your child with ADHD is going or what time he needs to be picked up could leave your child stranded in a dangerous place or situation without supervision.

A family therapist with experience in dealing with ADHD can help your family work on strategies to prevent communication snafus, make sure that everyone in the family understands the limitations imposed by childhood ADHD, and help everyone find ways to overcome the communication gaps that can lead to anger, frustration, resentment, and hurt feelings, and which can create potentially uncomfortable or even dangerous situations in the home.

Another technique your therapist may have you and family members practice is resisting the temptation to criticize, which tends to reduce or shut down communication by building walls or creating conflicts that disguise the real issue at hand.

Children with ADHD are so weary of being criticized, ridiculed, and blamed for doing things wrong they may shut down if you or family members begin your conversation with criticism or negativity. A family therapist can teach family members to set the stage for open communication by beginning every conversation with something they enjoy and appreciate about their child or sibling with ADHD.

CHAPTER 9

Helping Your Child Succeed at School

Unhappy employees can quit their jobs to seek work better suited to their personality and talents. School is a child's job, but students cannot quit—at least, not until they turn sixteen. Because children with ADHD symptoms have so much trouble in traditional classrooms, many mentally withdraw early on and drop out at the first opportunity. This is unfortunate, because some simple classroom changes, special education help, or a change in schools can make for a happy and successful educational career.

Public or Private School?

When looking for the best school for your child with ADHD, your best bet is to forget about getting too concerned with whether the school is public or private, and focus instead on the merits and drawbacks of each school. Both public and private schools have pluses and minuses when it comes to educating children with ADHD.

The Pros of Public Schools

A public school may be the best resource for you and your child for a variety of reasons. For starters, public schools are free. Some private schools can cost as much or more than college. Your child doesn't have to pass admissions tests and interviews to get in—another factor to consider since many children with ADHD do not test well, despite many having high IQs.

Your child's homework load will probably be lighter if he goes to public school, and he can't be forced out if his grades suffer.

The Pros of Going Private

In general, private schools offer smaller class sizes and a higher student-to-teacher ratio, which ensures your child will get the attention he needs. Your child won't be forced to attend a specific public school, but is free to attend any private school in the country, or even in the world.

If your child has a very high IQ and gets bored easily, he may benefit from a private school with an academically challenging, rigorous, and personalized academic program.

 Essential

Many private schools provide additional services to children with ADHD, such as speech therapy after school, rather than during classroom time. This lessens the chance your child will miss out on important classroom education and also eliminates the stigma of being pulled out of class because he's "different" or needs special attention.

Most private schools also rely less on testing than public schools and more on a variety of factors to determine student achievement, and some do away with grades altogether and use a "pass-fail" system.

How to Help Your Child Get the Support She Needs at School

By becoming your child's most powerful ally and advocate, you can help ensure she gets the help and support she needs at school.

While it's never too late to start, you should begin educating yourself, building bridges with school personnel, and keeping detailed records from the day you learn your child has ADHD.

Learn everything you can about childhood ADHD as well as your child's educational and legal rights so you can more effectively work with school personnel.

There are many excellent resources for parents of children with ADHD, including books, medical studies, and organizations. Talk to your physician about where you can find the most accurate, up-to-date information on the condition.

Be sure you understand everything about your child's condition, symptoms, and method of treatment. Ask your physician to explain behavior that may interfere with your child's ability to learn or function at school, and ways you can effectively control them.

Turning Teachers and Administrators into Allies

As a parent, it's essential to build bridges with teachers and other school personnel to ensure your child is getting the help and attention he needs. While most children with ADHD can succeed in a regular classroom, sometimes children need additional assistance or adjustments.

Make sure your child's teacher has the necessary training and experience to deal with your child. Remember that many teachers are already handicapped with too many students, and not enough assistance and materials. If you feel your child's teacher isn't equipped to deal with ADHD, ask the school principal if your child can be placed in a different classroom.

Tips for Building Bridges with Teachers

Here are some tips and strategies to build a good communication line with your child's teacher(s).

- **Reach out to your child's teacher.** Before the school year starts, schedule a get-to-know-you meeting so you can get a better handle on the teacher's teaching and discipline style and determine her experience level in working with children with ADHD. You may also want to use this meeting to provide the teacher with information about your child's symptoms, behavior, and specific learning and academic strengths and weaknesses.
- **Develop a school plan with the teacher that capitalizes on your child's strengths and helps overcome his weaknesses.** Look at constructive ways to deal with behavior problems that may be related to ADHD. This plan is a work in progress that will change as your child gets older and progresses through the school system.
- **Don't be afraid to ask for special help for your child, whether it's tutoring, or special assistance with homework, study, or organizational skills.** Some school districts have tutors and other local resources that can help your child bridge academic gaps.
- **Maintain an open line of communication with your child's teacher so you can work together to resolve any new or ongoing problems.** Keep the teacher abreast of any changes in symptoms and treatments that may have an impact on school work.
- **Show your interest by visiting the classroom and volunteering for activities and projects.**
- **Ask your child's teacher to give you regular progress reports on your child's classroom performance, homework assignments, discipline issues, etc.**
- **Schedule an end-of-school conference with your child's teacher to review your child's progress and look at ways to improve performance in the year ahead.** You may also want to ask about teachers your child may have in the upcoming year and how you can best help your child succeed in school.
- **Keep your child in the loop.** Make sure he understands that you support his teacher, and outline how you expect him to

behave and perform in the classroom setting. You may also want to tell your child how he will be disciplined in the event he misbehaves.

- **Maintain all treatment regimens provided by your physician,** including medication, behavior modification, and other modalities to help control ADHD symptoms at school and at home.

- **Develop consistency between school and home** by using the same language and signals used by your child's teacher to indicate inappropriate behavior and to reward exceptional performance.

- **Help your child get organized by using lists and calendars to keep track of tests, homework assignments, and projects.** Show older children how to use tape recorders or computers to facilitate learning, teach them how to take good notes, and show them how to highlight information to make essential points stand out. If your child is a visual learner, ask the teacher if he can use workbooks illustrated with pictures and diagrams.

Building Bridges with School Personnel

As well as developing a good line of communication with your child's teachers, you should also get to know other school personnel who will have an impact on your child's learning environment, including the school principal and special education teachers.

 Alert

Be proactive by talking to the school principal about specific policies and rules, including how discipline problems are handled, before the school year begins. You may also want to find out if there are other children with ADHD at the school and what special accommodations are being made for those students.

Ask how you can help educate your child's teacher, whether it's providing information on childhood ADHD or supplying the teacher with details of your child's diagnosis and treatment program.

The Importance of Keeping Good Records

When you have a child with ADHD, keeping good records can make or break your child's academic success. Good records can help you monitor your child's academic and behavior progress and help identify academic patterns that may signal the need for adjustments in medication or treatment.

Make sure you keep and continually update the following forms and records:

- ADHD evaluations used to evaluate what type of ADHD your child has. These can be helpful in determining the best course of treatment.
- Evaluations for coexisting medical conditions with similar symptoms
- History of medication to keep track of all medications your child has taken and is currently taking to treat ADHD
- School progress records, including school plans, progress reports from the teacher, grades, end-of-year reports, and standardized testing results
- Individual education plan (If your child is disabled and has an IEP, keep a copy on file so you have it handy in case other health professionals treating your child need to see it.)

Recognizing Different Learning Styles

Many college-educated adults value book learning and have difficulty comprehending that people can learn in other ways. Although there has been a push in educational circles to present more hands-on lessons, most teachers continue to rely on reading, writing, and listening to lectures.

Visual, Auditory, and Kinesthetic

Visual students learn best through written language. Pictures, charts, and diagrams help them understand and process information. Auditory students prefer lectures, films, tapes, and learning through dialogue. Kinesthetic students learn best through hands-on activities.

 Alert

Trying to teach hands-on learners history through lectures is like trying to teach the piano by explaining what to do. Having them read history books is like assigning articles about piano playing. Giving them a written test is like asking them questions about a song to assess their ability to play it.

Because kinesthetic students learn best by touch and movement, simply clapping while repeating the multiplication tables can make memorizing them easier. These students grasp mathematical concepts and solve arithmetic problems more quickly by working with sets of specially designed educational blocks.

When Your Child with ADHD Has Special Needs

If achievement tests indicate that your child is not progressing as expected based on her IQ test score, she is likely to be diagnosed with a learning disability. Special education can help, but so may a better mainstream classroom environment.

Make sure the teacher of your special education child with ADHD is incorporating principles into her regular instruction:

- Intellectual challenges geared to the student's skill level. Lessons that are too easy are too boring to hold students' attention; lessons that are too hard cause undue frustration and cause students to give up.

- Emphasis on understanding and applying concepts. Most teachers place too much emphasis on acquiring information through rote memorization, which many students perceive as useless and tend to forget soon after they are tested on it.
- Involvement in setting learning objectives. Some students benefit more from the opportunity to learn a little about many subjects; some do better exploring a single subject in depth.
- Opportunities to pursue individual interests. Students are more motivated when they choose the topic they want to learn about. Virtually any topic can be investigated from the standpoint of any school subject.
- Self-paced learning. Some students need more time to learn the material. They just do. That is not a reflection of how intelligent they are.
- Instruction that incorporates the student's preferred learning style. Lessons that engage all of the senses tend to be most effective at reaching the largest number of students.

Taking Advantage of Special Services

If your child has a learning disability or special needs, special education help may be a good option. Special education services may involve going to a special classroom all day, getting extra help in a particular subject for an hour a week, or anything in between. It may mean having a specially trained teacher come to the regular classroom to work with your child.

Does My Child Qualify?

To qualify, a child's ADHD symptoms must cause significant learning or behavior problems at school. Section 504 of the Individual Education and Development Act legally obligates public schools to ensure that children with a disability have equal access to education. That includes children with "a physical or mental impairment that substantially limits one or more major life activities including learning and behavior." ADHD falls into this category. Students must receive "appropriate accommodations and modifications" to the regular classroom that are tailored to their individual needs.

Section 504

To qualify to receive services under Section 504, a student must have a disability that "substantially limits one or more major life functions, including education, learning, and behavior." Only the school can determine if a child qualifies. If you think your child needs special services, the first step is to submit a written request for an evaluation via certified mail to the school.

 Question

Why is it so hard to get my child the special help he needs?
Special education classes are expensive due to the small classroom sizes and advanced degrees of the teachers. Parents may have to be assertive to see that evaluations are handled in a timely manner and that the recommendations are implemented. Be persistent and consider getting support from your child's ADHD specialists.

It is a good idea to request a copy of your school district's policies and procedures for complying with Section 504. It will list your rights and the district's responsibilities. If your complaints are not satisfied, you can call the Office of Civil Rights hotline of the U.S. Department of Education at (800) 421-3481 for information about how to proceed.

Mentoring Children with ADHD

Studies show that strong and supportive mentoring relationships between adults and children who have ADHD help children do better in school, and improve their self-image and school attendance.

For a mentorship to work, a child should be matched with an adult mentor who has similar personal traits. In some schools, children with ADHD are matched with college students with ADHD who are having similar ADHD learning challenges. Other mentor programs may match a child with ADHD who has an interest in a specific career with an adult in that career.

 Essential

Project Eye-To-Eye is a national mentoring and advocacy program for students with ADHD that matches young students with high school or college students who also have ADHD. Tutors help children with learning challenges, help them develop special gifts, and work with teachers to develop customized materials for students with ADHD. For more information, visit *www.projecteyetoeye.org*.

Should Your Child Tell His Friends He Has ADHD?

Many children with ADHD and even parents struggle with whether to tell friends they have the disorder. Some believe it is better that friends understand what they are going through so they can be more understanding and flexible when their ADHD symptoms flare up. Others worry that telling friends they have ADHD will scare them away or cause friends to start treating them with kid gloves.

According to experts, there's really no one answer. In many cases, the right decision may be based on the severity of your child's symptoms, and/or the closeness of the particular relationship.

When Symptoms Are Mild

If your child's symptoms are mild and he's able to manage or disguise most of them with medication and therapy, there may be no reason to tell friends or even teachers he has ADHD unless you and your child feel that telling them would strengthen his friendships and relationships with them.

If your child decides to share his condition with friends, encourage him to help friends better understand ADHD symptoms by suggesting good books and websites for them to read or by explaining how they can assist him or avoid being the target of his emotions when his symptoms flare up.

When Symptoms Are Severe

On the other hand, if your child's symptoms are more severe and/or frequently disrupt her life and the lives of others, telling friends and teachers she has the condition is probably essential. It will help friends be more understanding, forgiving, and flexible when your child's symptoms flare, and it will ensure your child receives the special services and accommodations he requires in the classroom setting.

Should I Get Involved at My Child's School?

Studies show that children with ADHD get better grades and have better relationships with classmates and teachers when parents are involved in their schools. This is particularly true if your child is in elementary school or middle school. However, you may want to take a cautious approach if your teen is in high school, as children in this age group are more interested in carving out their own identities than bonding with parents.

Some productive ways to offer your services include coaching a sports team, chairing a special hobby club, assisting your child's teacher with a special class, chaperoning a school dance or field trip, or attending PTA meetings and activities as well as parent-teacher meetings. If your teenager with ADHD is on a sports team, he may prefer you show your support by cheering him on at football games.

CHAPTER 10

Coping with Social Challenges

As a member of society, your child with ADHD is expected to interact and communicate with others on a regular basis, be capable of understanding what friends and teachers say, and be able to read and interpret nonverbal cues so she can behave appropriately in social settings. Unfortunately, many children with ADHD can't follow conversations, stay focused on lengthy discussions, or read body language. Because they exist in an information vacuum, children with ADHD may respond to conversations or social interactions in ways that are not appropriate, consistent, or relevant.

Why Making Friends Is More Difficult for Children with ADHD

Friends are important for youngsters' mental and physical well-being. Stress born of social isolation and peer conflict suppresses the immune system and increases vulnerability to illness and depression.

For your child to master the art of getting along with others, making friends, and maintaining healthy relationships, you will need to teach a number of essential social skills.

Unfortunately, many children with ADHD symptoms have poor social skills because they do not tune in to the subtleties of social interactions or misread social cues. They benefit from reminders to pay attention, and they can often be more objective when watching how peers interact with one another.

Importance of Maturity Level

For children to get along with one another, maturity level is more important than age. If your youngster's social skills are very poor, she may have fewer conflicts and more in common with younger children.

And since older children tend to make allowances for younger ones, they are often more tolerant of immature behavior. Hence, your child may do better with playmates that are younger or older than with people her own age.

 Essential

To help your child make friends at school, you might have the teacher ask a classmate to mentor your child and provide tips for getting along with others. Research indicates that simply having a well-liked student and an unpopular one do a project together provides an enduring social boost.

ADHD Symptoms that Flare in Social Settings

Social situations can be difficult for children with ADHD. Because they feel less confident and more stressed out in social settings than other children, they often experience a flare of ADHD symptoms.

The Most Common "Flare" Symptoms

Even if your child has become adept at making and keeping friends, a particularly stressful social situation is likely to trigger:

- Feeling like he doesn't fit in
- Having trouble following conversations

- Having trouble zoning out extraneous noises or music
- Feeling overwhelmed at the slightest thing
- Feeling the need to dominate a conversation
- Blurting out confidential, inappropriate, or irrelevant information during conversations
- Being unable to read and translate body language, voice tone, facial expressions, or simple nuances of interaction
- Reacting in an overemotional, defensive, or overly intense way
- Jumping to the wrong conclusions
- Feeling defensive all the time
- Feeling that others are always criticizing and blaming him
- Being reluctant to contribute or participate in a conversation for fear of embarrassing himself
- Being viewed by others as standoffish, disinterested, snobbish, or bored

Helping Your Child Deal with Anger and Criticism

Children with ADHD are criticized, rejected, and teased so often that they often become defensive and angry when others criticize them. Many children with ADHD also have very short tempers and explosive mood swings that may erupt without warning in social settings and cause them social embarrassment.

How to Help Your Child Keep Her Cool

Practice with your child so she learns how to control her temper. Here are some helpful strategies you can role-play together.

- Encourage your child to count to ten before reacting or responding to an unkind comment.
- Encourage your child to stick up for herself and to ask someone to clarify or explain if she thinks their comment was untrue or unfair.

- Teach your child to use exercise to walk off her anger. Taking a quick walk around the block can help your child chill out.
- Practice clever comebacks with your child to things she gets teased about frequently.
- Look for ways to bully-proof your child by eliminating common sources of teasing, such as unusual clothing or hairstyles.

Accepting Constructive Criticism

Children with ADHD are often constantly criticized and rejected and may not be able to distinguish valid, helpful criticism from nasty teasing and bullying. Encourage your child to consider the source when deciding how to respond to criticism. If it comes from a classmate who is usually a bully, your child can probably ignore it. If it comes from a well-meaning teacher or school principal, your child will probably want to listen carefully and heed the advice.

Dealing with Impatience

Whether it's butting into conversations without being invited, becoming frustrated for not getting something right, or refusing to wait their turn, children with ADHD are notoriously impatient with others and themselves, a trait that often rears its ugly head in social situations.

Before your child jumps into a conversation, make sure he listens for several minutes to make sure he fully understands what is being discussed. Before responding, encourage him to collect his thoughts, quiet his mind, and think about what he could say that would add to the conversation.

If your child acts on his impulsivity and simply blabbers on without having listened to and digested what was being discussed, he could make a bad impression and drive people away.

Teaching Your Child How to Share and Compromise

Sharing and compromising can be hard for children with low self-esteem, so lots of children with ADHD symptoms need help in this area. Youngsters who are constantly on the defensive commonly fear that if they give an inch, they will end up having everything taken from them.

The Miracle of Sharing

Explain the miracle of sharing: By giving up something, they stand to keep a friend. At the same time, it is not possible to buy friends. They must be able to give without expecting anything in return. The point of compromising is to create a win/win situation. If your child and a friend cannot agree, she needs to toss out some suggestions that she thinks both of them might feel okay about.

 Essential

Role-play and/or give your child examples: "If you want to play one video game and your friend wants to play a different one, offer to play his game for ten minutes if he will then play yours for ten minutes."

Giving Positive Feedback

Direct your child to give positive feedback to her friends by letting them know something that she likes or appreciates about them. She can tell a classmate that she liked her oral report, compliment her on her new haircut, or say something positive about her expertise at jump rope, long division, or anything else. She of course needs to be sincere and to keep her comments simple.

Very needy children make peers uncomfortable by piling on the praise, so stress the importance of confining herself to one positive comment per day. Model this important social behavior by giving your child positive feedback, but aim for one positive comment per hour when interacting with your youngster.

Helping Your Child Make Friends

Research shows that people who have lots of friends not only live longer, but also get sick less often than people with few or no friends. Unfortunately, children with ADHD may find that making and keeping friends takes more energy and focus than finishing their school work. Fortunately, you can teach them many essential skills to making and keeping friends and role-play at home until appropriate behavior and responses become second nature.

Strategies that Work

To help a young child learn to initiate friendships, you may need to take him by the hand and walk him over to meet another child, introduce them, and suggest they play together.

Here are some other ways to help your child develop and keep friendships:

- Teach a child by giving him a mini-lesson en route to a social gathering. On the way to his first soccer practice, instruct him to say, "Hi, my name is Jim. What's yours?" Give him a conversation opener, too. "This is my first time playing soccer. How about you?"
- If your child thinks your suggestions are "dumb," tell him to watch to see how other people start conversations and report back to you. Afterward, ask him what he noticed. The best way to learn social skills is to watch how other people interact.
- Many children with ADHD symptoms have poor social skills because they do not tune in to the subtleties of social interactions or misread social cues. They benefit from reminders to pay attention, and they can often be more objective when watching how peers interact with one another.

- An adolescent may pretend that your recommendations are too old fashioned to be of use. Nevertheless, your teen may re-fashion your ideas to fit his social group's slang and use them. When he's leaving for a dance, you might suggest, "Go up to someone you recognize, and say, 'Hi. Aren't you in Dr. Bob's third period English class?' or whatever. Whether or not you are right, you can start a conversation about your English teachers by asking how she likes her class.'"

Helping Your Child Tune in to Nonverbal Cues

While your child can't "fix" many symptoms of childhood ADHD caused by the neurobiological imbalance in her brain, there are many tips and strategies she can role-play with you to learn appropriate behavior and rein in out-of-control ADHD behavior.

Role-play so your child learns to listen carefully to conversations and respond to playful comments with playful answers, and to serious questions with serious answers.

Rehearsing Likely Scenarios

One way to make sure your child doesn't blurt out the wrong thing is to have her rehearse appropriate responses to a variety of scenarios likely to occur. Before she goes to a party, she might rehearse responses to questions that typically arise in casual party chat, such as, "How do you like your teachers?" or "How is your baseball team doing this year?" Have your child practice responses with you in various fictional settings until she feels comfortable.

By rehearsing appropriate responses with you, your child will also learn to better distinguish between appropriate and inappropriate responses. This will alleviate her anxiety in social settings as well as give her an arsenal of appropriate rehearsed responses to draw on in real-life settings.

Learning Not to Hog the Conversation

Because they have trouble reading nonverbal cues, many children with ADHD have a tendency to dominate conversations or keep talking long after everyone has lost interest.

Role-play being in a group conversation, and encourage your child to listen far more than she talks, keep her comments short, to be kind and honest without being insincere or overly blunt, to be careful about jumping into conversations before she's invited, and to limit her comments to the topic at hand rather than dominating the conversation with irrelevant or unrelated matters.

The Power of Body Language

Make sure your child understands the power of body language. One effective way to bond with someone she's just met is to model their body language. If they cross their arms, she should cross her arms. If they use hand gestures when talking, she should do the same. The trick is to be subtle. If your child is too obvious about modeling, the other person may mistake it for ridicule or mockery and become insulted.

 Fact

An excellent way for children to learn body language is watch movies with the sound off, guess what the characters are saying and feeling, then turn the sound on and match their guesses to the reality. Watching foreign movies with the subtitles off is another useful strategy.

Benefits of Role-Playing

Role-playing with your child is an excellent way to help him rehearse and practice appropriate social behavior and talk so he feels more confident and relaxed in social settings.

Many children with ADHD become nervous and flabbergasted when they go to parties or other social settings and often embarrass themselves by exhibiting ADHD behavior like butting in, dominating the conversation, yammering on and on when no one is interested, saying rude or overly blunt things to others, or saying inappropriate or "clueless" things in conversations.

 Question

Why is role-playing so important for ADHD kids?
Role-playing gives your child a safe place to practice appropriate social behavior until he gets it right so he doesn't blurt things that cause him to be ostracized, shunned, or ignored by classmates. Role-play with your child before he goes to a party to rehearse small talk and clever responses.

The Art of Small Talk

Role-play with your teen so he feels comfortable with the art of small talk. Tell him he just wants to skim off the basics, and remind him that when it comes to small talk, it's better to know a little about a lot of different things than a lot about just one thing.

Another easy way your teen with ADHD can facilitate small talk is to read up on sports and local and international news before going to a party so he has lots of easy conversation starters at his disposal.

Rehearse Bowing Out Before Blowing Out

If your child finds himself in a small group discussion he can't follow or can't keep up with, tell him not to get so impatient with himself that he goes overboard trying to think up an appropriate response that may not hit the mark. If your child is truly confused and/or bewildered by the train of conversation, or if the topic of conversation is simply over his head, practice helping him find a good excuse to bow out politely before he reaches the point of no return—when his hyperactivity or impulsivity may cause him to butt in or blurt out something that may be inappropriate or irrelevant. "Where's the restroom?" or "I'd better rejoin my friend," or "I think I need a glass of water" are always handy excuses for making a graceful exit.

Limiting Personal Disclosure

Many children with ADHD let hyperactivity and impulsivity get the best of their tongue and divulge too much personal information about themselves or they break confidences. Make sure your child understands that divulging too much personal information about herself or gossiping about others makes strangers feel uncomfortable and pressured to reciprocate with personal details about themselves or others.

 Fact

By sharing too much overly positive information about herself, your child with ADHD could come across as bragging or boasting, and leave some people wondering if she's really telling the truth, or simply exaggerating or lying to try to impress or intimidate them.

Tell your child that sharing too much about himself with casual acquaintances could have the opposite effect of what he was hoping to achieve. Instead of making people feel closer to him, it could send them running in the opposite direction and leave him feeling alone and isolated.

Wiggling Out of Difficult Situations

Teenagers benefit from being given the words they can use in difficult social situations. Before your teen leaves for a party, tell him how to respond to antisocial pressures: "If someone asks if you want a cigarette, you can say, 'No, I don't smoke.' If you need an excuse, you can say, 'I can't, I'm trying out for track,' or 'My parents have noses like beagles and will ground me for life if I come home smelling of smoke.'" Do not bombard your teen with a dozen lectures before he gets together with friends. Tackling one issue per outing is plenty.

Correcting Inappropriate Social Behavior

When you observe your youngster making a social blunder, such as being rude, bossy, selfish, or inconsiderate, be careful about how you intervene. Embarrassing your child in front of her peers almost always does more harm than good. That goes for first graders as well as for teens.

The Importance of Keeping It Private

To teach your child to be considerate and respectful of peers, you need to demonstrate appropriate behavior. Call your youngster aside and speak with her privately if you need to make a correction. That is what your youngster needs to do if she is upset with someone. If she criticizes another child in front of a group, she is likely to find herself being shunned or challenged to fight the person she humiliated.

Teaching Without Preaching

Your child will be more willing to heed your advice about social matters if you have a close relationship and if she believes that you understand the social dilemmas she is facing.

An excellent way to achieve a closer relationship and demonstrate that you understand what your child is up against is to share stories from your past. Sharing how you felt about being teased when you were growing up lets your child know that you empathize and have grappled with similar problems.

Telling what you did to try to win friends and influence enemies can give your youngster ideas about new things to try and mistakes to avoid while helping her to consider her situation more objectively. Recounting personal stories is especially effective with adolescents.

Importance of ADHD Buddies and Support Groups

Instead of trying to weather a social function on his own, suggest that your child ask a close friend to go with him who can translate conversations he may have trouble following, as well as interpret nonverbal cues, and give him a friendly nudge or warning look when he starts to dominate the conversation or stray off course.

Testing the Waters

His buddy can also test the waters of small groups at a party by joining the conversation first. If it seems like a friendly group and a conversation he'll be able to participate in successfully, he can wave your child in and introduce him.

Support Groups

ADHD support groups are another place for your child to practice and model appropriate social behavior in a safe, supportive environment. Since everyone in your child's support group has been in a similar dilemma or situation, they can offer strategies to your child that might not have occurred to you.

Helping Your Child Tap into Social Outlets

Most children with ADHD are unhappy at school and feel unsuccessful a good deal of the time. Finding an activity she enjoys that helps her feel successful can go a long way to improving the quality of her life. For extracurricular activities to be positive social outlets, your youngster needs to be able to handle herself in a group setting. When choosing activities, your child's interests need to be taken into account.

Two Sides of Organized Sports

When trying to find an extracurricular activity for their child, many parents automatically think about soccer, baseball, and other team sports. They hope that playing a sport will improve coordination and provide good exercise, and that being on a team will instill discipline, teach sportsmanship, and provide a positive social outlet. Some youngsters are very physical, and their happiest times are spent in Little League practices, at hockey tournaments, and playing in volleyball matches.

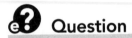 **Question**

Are team sports a good idea for my son with ADHD?
Maybe, but maybe not. Many children diagnosed with ADHD are clumsy and inattentive. They are regarded as liabilities by team members and coaches who are more concerned about bringing home a trophy than about having fun. If your child is clumsy, steer him to solo sports like hiking and cycling.

A teammate who does not follow rules and instructions, stay on task, control his temper, and hold his own athletically is a source of frustration for everyone. The intense stimulation and stress of games can easily undo sensitive, insecure children. Their difficult behavior upsets everyone.

Benefits of Individual Sports

While team sports are not good choices for many youngsters with ADHD, individual sports are another matter altogether. The emphasis on personal development can lessen the pressure to perform while providing healthful exercise and sensory-motor train-ing. Possibilities include swimming, gymnastics, tennis, aikido, Karate, bicycling, skiing, ice skating, and skateboarding.

Dance is not a sport, but the emphasis on rhythm and body awareness can be good physical therapy for physically awkward youngsters who may not be able to participate in team sports or activities because they lack hand-eye coordination and could be a detriment to teams. Other solo activities your child may enjoy include yoga and tai chi.

Tapping into Community Centers and Clubs

From puppet making to pottery, from judo to jewelry making, from basketball to basket weaving, town parks and recreation departments, youth centers, YMCAs, YWCAs, and many health clubs and fitness centers offer a wealth of fun activities for children.

Open courts at local Ys provide children with the chance to shoot baskets without the pressure to show up for scheduled prac-tices, and to practice without risking spectators catcalling from the bleachers.

During the summer, check to see if they offer day camps, nature hikes, trips to swimming pools and museums, and other commu-nity outings. Youngsters can meet new people without having to worry that their negative reputation at school will interfere. Urge your child to take the opportunity to practice new skills

 Alert

If your child is not ready for the intense peer contact of an overnight camp, try a day camp instead. Alternatively, find a camp for children with behavior problems and for at-risk youth at the American Camp-ing Association website at *www.acacamps.org*. There are many sum-mer camps just for children with ADHD.

Making Connections at Churches

Churches and synagogues often have youth groups that are especially kid-friendly. Parents do not have to be members for their children to be welcome. Meetings usually begin and end with a prayer, but the emphasis is on fellowship and fun. Like scouting troops, youth groups sponsored by religious organizations tend to be less structured than school classrooms but more closely supervised than neighborhood free-for-alls. Hence, they can be especially good choices for children with special needs.

If Your Child Is a Loner

Although research shows that loners have more adjustment problems than the social butterflies of the world, that is a group average and is not true for everyone. Some junior technicians would rather build model airplanes, work on the computer, or put together a short-wave radio than trade baseball cards or skateboard with neighbors.

Many youngsters do not want to put time and energy into peers unless they share their interests. Being alone and feeling lonely are very different. It is a mistake to try to cure a child of what does not ail him. If he is happy, that is all that counts. Just be sure that he has not become a loner by default because he has alienated his schoolmates with his inappropriate behavior.

How to Help a Loner

The best solution for a child who is suffering because he lacks friends is to find an activity he likes that he can really get involved in. Like adults, children often bond around shared experiences. Peers with a common interest are more willing to overlook one another's personality quirks. But before searching for ways to fill your child's social calendar, you do need to help your youngster learn some basic social skills.

CHAPTER 11

Parenting Challenges for Parents of Children with ADHD

Parenting children with ADHD can be a real challenge, regard-less of how much you've read up on it or discussed it with other parents. Even when you have the best of intentions, the day-in, day-out grind of dealing with childhood ADHD can exhaust your patience as you try to cope with how the condition affects your child as well as the entire family. Because ADHD is a genetic condi-tion, you or your spouse may also have it, compounding problems and making good parenting skills even more crucial.

Behavior Strategies for Parents

Although trying to raise a child with ADHD can sometimes be overwhelming and confusing, remember that as the parent, you hold the cards when it comes to helping your child coexist with her symptoms and channel her energy in a constructive way.

One of the most important things you can do for your child is to get her a comprehensive assessment with an ADHD expert that explores medical, educational, and psychological evaluations and rules out disorders that mimic or commonly accompany ADHD. Because ADHD is genetic, you may also want to get yourself, your spouse, and other children in the family examined to rule out the presence of ADHD.

Parent Training

Parent training is a type of counseling that teaches parents how to work with children who have ADHD to improve their behavior and also improve the parent's relationship with the child. Ask your child's physicians for information about where you can take parent training classes, talk to people in your support group, or contact local universities or the local chapter of CHADD.

 Essential

Parent training will help you learn to develop limits and boundaries for specific behavior you want to change, be a more effective disciplinarian by using proactive discipline methods that deal with misbehavior by using "time outs" and loss of privileges, and which reward good behavior, and show your child how she can learn and grow from her mistakes.

Parent Survival Strategies

As your child's most important role model and advocate, it's essential that you also stay physically, mentally, and emotionally healthy. If you become overly tired, stressed out, or worn down, you'll have less patience and endurance in dealing with your child's ADHD symptoms. Make sure to follow a healthy diet and exercise program, find ways to minimize stress, and get help for illnesses and injuries immediately. Here are other survival tips to try:

- **Take a break.** Raising a child with ADHD is an exhausting, time-consuming task. Don't feel guilty about giving yourself some down time, especially if you have ADHD yourself. Head to work early so you can relax over coffee at the local coffee shop, hire a baby sitter and go to the movies or out to dinner with your spouse, join a health club and exercise or do yoga at lunch time or right after work, and make time for unwinding with supportive friends.

- **Give yourself a break.** Remember that losing your cool and occasionally yelling at your child or losing your patience with her doesn't make you a bad parent. There are many things you can do to help unwind. Practice a guided visualization, whip up a quick breakfast smoothie, read an inspirational e-book, and so on.
- **Don't blame yourself for your child's condition.** ADHD is caused by a biochemical imbalance in certain areas of the brain. Although the condition is primarily genetic, it is not caused by bad parenting or a hectic home environment, although that can worsen symptoms. ADHD is genetic, but it's not your fault if you passed it on to your child.
- **Join a support group.** Remember that you don't have to do it all alone. Talk to supportive physicians, therapists, teachers, and parents, and consider joining a support group for parents of children with ADHD where you can exchange information and vent your feelings.

Improving Communication

Miscommunication often runs rampant in families with ADHD. Children with the disorder are often so impatient and impulsive that they don't listen well to what family members are saying and misinterpret things. They also are prone to blurting things out without thinking first, violating confidences, and making rude and hurtful comments.

Improving communication issues in the family may require a therapist, although there are also some strategies you can try at home, including:

- **Encourage everyone in the family to become an active listener.** This means repeating what someone else says before adding a comment or response of your own.

- **Encourage family members to ask for clarification if they don't understand something.** Instead of making assumptions or leaping to the wrong conclusions, encourage everyone to ask what something means.
- **Encourage everyone to avoid criticism.** Contrary to the popular phrase, criticism is rarely constructive and usually belittles, angers, or intimidates others. Encourage family members to resist their urge to criticize and remember the age-old maxim, "If you don't have something nice to say, don't say it at all."
- **Tell family members to preface a negative comment with a positive one.** Encourage family members to say something they appreciate about a family member before jumping right into what they don't like.

Remind everyone in the family that the path to effective communication is careful listening and understanding what others are saying. Most arguments occur when one person misinterprets or misunderstands what another family member is saying.

Establishing Structure and Setting Rules

Many children with ADHD have no sense of structure or time. Your child is more likely to succeed if you create a home environment that is organized, consistent, and predictable. Build everyday routines and structures to help your child get and stay organized and on time.

Helping Your Child Stay Focused

Here are some strategies for helping your child stay organized and focused:

- **Create set routines.** Establish a consistent time and place for everything your child does at home, including meals, homework, bedtime, TV time, computer time, play time, etc. Help your child get to school on time by putting out his clothing and school supplies the night before and setting the breakfast table with his favorite cereal and fruit.

- **Put clocks in several locations around the house, including your child's bedroom.** Set timers on clocks and computers to alert your child that it's time to have dinner, finish his homework, or go to bed.
- **Keep things simple.** Many children with ADHD get overwhelmed when they have too many choices. Make sure your child has a few toys or activities to keep him busy, but don't overload him with too much at once or he'll become frustrated.
- **Create a quiet corner.** Your child with ADHD needs a quiet place in the home where he can do his homework or read without being distracted or interrupted by other family members.
- **Be a good role model when it comes to being tidy and organized.** Your child probably won't understand why he has to tidy his room if the rest of the house is a mess.
- **Keep your children busy after school with structured activities without overwhelming him with too many choices.** If your child shows interest, sign him up for music, art, or sports classes after school.
- **Avoid exposing your child to violent TV or video games.** These can aggravate or increase hyperactivity and impulsivity.

Creating Realistic Rules and Expectations

Create clear, concise rules for your child with ADHD, and post them in a prominent place in the house so your child can refer to them often. Create clear-cut expectations for how you expect your child to behave, and provide consistent consequences or rewards he values.

Importance of Praise

Remember that most children with ADHD are used to criticism and rejection, so watch for their good behavior and praise and reward it when you see it to reinforce it, even if it's behavior you'd automatically expect in another child. Rewards can be as simple as a smile and hug, or can take the form of special privileges or gifts.

Improving Organization and Time Management

Many children with ADHD are extremely disorganized, can't prioritize, and lack essential time management skills. These problems create myriad challenges at school and often cause children with high IQs to fail.

Organizational Strategies for Children with ADHD

Disorganization is a classic symptom of ADHD, and it can make it difficult for your child to do many tasks she needs to do to succeed at school, such as getting projects done on time; prioritizing; breaking up large tasks into small, doable pieces; keeping track of books and materials for different classes; and even remembering her class schedule. Here are some strategies you can encourage your child to adopt to get and stay organized in school:

- **Have your child organize projects or tasks on a day calendar and give each task a specific length of time.** Don't underestimate. Have her choose a few of the most essential tasks, prioritize them, and then tackle one at a time. If your child tends to forget appointments, set multiple alarms on your wristwatch, computer, or cell phone to remind her.
- **Develop a methodical system for big projects.** To tackle large or long-term projects, develop a systematic approach. Have your child outline the goal of the project and detail major

considerations like interim deadlines. Then have your child break the project down into smaller steps and determine how much time each will take, making sure her estimates are realistic and in line with those short-term deadlines. Tackle one task at a time, and give your child small rewards when each task is completed. Have your child periodically review her timeline to make sure she has enough time to get the project done on time.

- **Remember that organizational strategies may periodically break down, so don't expect perfection.** The good news is that once your child has established an organizational technique or experienced an organizational success, it becomes easier to reintroduce it and come up with additional strategies for future projects. Expecting perfect solutions can lead to frustration, recrimination, and loss of self-esteem. Sometimes it's better for your child to accept a less-than-ideal solution and pat herself on the back for progress she's made.

- **Tune out distractions.** If your child usually studies in a busy or noisy environment, it may be difficult for her to focus. If she's distracted by noise or people talking, consider getting headsets or a white noise machine. If she tends to gaze out the window, pull the blinds. Use visual reminders to help her stay alert and focused on tasks. Have her shake off tension and stress that may disrupt her focus by taking a breather every hour or so. Have her stretch her arms and legs, shrug her shoulders, scrunch her neck, wiggle her fingers, or take some deep breaths.

Time Management Skills

To help your child with ADHD get things done on time and manage and organize her time so the most important things get done, encourage her to incorporate these strategies:

- Create a daily to-do list. To manage the many details of her studies, write every one down, no matter how small or insignificant, and put the list somewhere she'll be able to see it. Do one at a time.
- Draw a line through each task as it is completed. She will feel some satisfaction each time she crosses off a line, and she will also see that she is making progress. This reinforcement leads to further progress.
- Make sure she consults her to-do list throughout the day so she doesn't get sidetracked.

Breaking the Lateness Habit

Whether it's getting a project done on time or getting to work on time, many kids with ADHD struggle with meeting deadlines. One reason is that children with ADHD tend to underestimate how long it actually takes to accomplish something. In addition, their chronic disorganization and clutter prevents them from acting efficiently.

 Fact

It's not impossible for your child to break the lateness habit, but it will take some effort and practice on her part. Encourage her not to fall into the trap of thinking she can finish just one more thing before she leaves, and encourage her to set multiple alarms to let her know when it's time to leave for school, an important appointment, or a social function.

Until your child breaks the lateness habit, encourage her to double or even triple the amount of time she thinks something will take. To become more realistic about how long certain tasks take, have her write down time estimates in her calendar, and then compare them to actual times after she completes the task, then reset her estimation on the next project to include the extra time. The more she records and corrects how long it takes to do something, the better she'll become at narrowing the gap between how long she thinks it will take to accomplish something and how long it actually takes.

Using Rewards and Consequences

Psychologists have long recognized that the same straightforward principles and simple procedures work well for animals of all kinds, from human beings to fruit flies. Behavior modification programs are effective for helping children and adults alike eliminate troublesome behaviors, break destructive habits, develop better self-control, and respond in healthier ways. It works by incorporating a system of rewards for positive behavior, and consequences or punishments for negative behavior.

How It Works

Effective behavior modification programs help children define goals they are able to reach, and systemically reward each small accomplishment until new habits are formed. Children must be set up to succeed and setbacks result when tasks are either too difficult or children do not consider the rewards valuable. For more information on the system of rewards and consequences used in behavior modification, see Chapter 15.

Financial Interventions for Parents of Children with ADHD

Parents of children with ADHD often have trouble keeping track of household finances, and no wonder. Many parents also have one or more children with the disorder who are seeing a variety of medical experts, and who may be attending special schools or classes, or receiving specialized assistance in college or in the workplace.

Keeping track of the medical expenses and medications incurred by childhood ADHD is an overwhelming challenge for many parents whose children see one or more specialist for their condition and may take one or more different types of medication. Each visit creates a paper trail that needs to be tracked for reimbursement and tax purposes.

 Fact

Many children and teens with ADHD are impulsive spenders who rack up huge debts, but are too inattentive to focus on something as detailed as a household budget or everyday expenses. If your child's spending habits have put your finances in disarray, you can avoid high interest rates, penalties, foreclosure, or bankruptcy by hiring a financial planner or coach.

Establishing Financial Records

The good news is it doesn't take an MBA to set up an easy filing and tracking system for your family. You can do it yourself using these helpful tips:

- Buy an accordion folder for each category of expenses (medical, household, college, summer camp, etc.). The folders are too big for you to lose, and because they are enclosed on three sides (unlike manila folders), they are a safe place to stash papers and invoices of all shapes and sizes without worrying about them slipping out.
- Label each section of the accordion for specific bills, such as doctor's visits, psychologist's visits, prescription medications, medical insurance, specialized classes for children, disability insurance, legal fees, and transportation and mileage. Every time you get a bill, whether it's a physician's

invoice or a credit card slip for a medication, file it in the proper place.

- Remember to keep track of transportation and mileage to and from doctor's visits, as well as receipts for parking, turnpike tolls, gas, and/or mileage, for tax deduction purposes.
- If you'd rather keep track of your expenses via computer, Quicken Medical software is an ideal organizational tool that lets you electronically file insurance information, provider information, exam histories, payments, and disputed claims for each family member in one place. The program also automatically calculates reimbursable mileage, tax deductions, and FSA contributions. Go to *www.QuickenMedical.com* for more information.

By keeping track of medical bills, you'll save money you'd lose on erroneous credit card statements (it happens all the time), higher interest rates and penalties, and lost insurance claims, and avoid the stress and worry of wondering if you've paid a bill on time. In addition, if you feel your child has been denied a legitimate insurance claim for a medical bill, you'll have copies of everything you need to fight your case and win.

Support Groups for Parents of Children with ADHD

You already know how and why ADHD can leave your child feeling lonely, isolated, and often feeling like a social misfit. One of the easiest and fastest ways to make connections with other parents and children struggling with ADHD is to join a support group in your area.

As well as providing an avenue where you can make new friends, share your experiences and problems, and offer moral support, your support group can also keep you informed on the best medical resources in the area as well as special services, disability experts, and colleges and universities that cater to adults with ADHD.

To find a support group near you, check with local colleges, universities, churches and synagogues, community hospitals and clinics, senior citizen centers, or through the local chapter of CHADD, an organization for children and adults with ADHD.

Keeping Up with ADHD Research

To stay up with the latest and greatest research findings as well as acquaint yourself with standard diagnostic and treatment modalities, check out professional magazines that are not only read but also written by experts in the field of psychology and psychiatry. Just a few include *The Journal of Neuropsychiatry and Clinical Neurosciences*, *The American Journal of Psychiatry*, and *Neuropsychology*. You can also find breaking news on the latest studies and research in consumer magazines like *Science and Psychology*, newspapers like *The Wall Street Journal*, and in hundreds of other publications cited in this book. For a list of excellent books on childhood ADHD, see Appendix A.

Online Resources

Medical search databases are another way to find a wealth of information on ADHD research and studies. Some are free while others charge a membership fee. By simply typing in "childhood ADHD," you'll get instant access to articles and abstracts from a variety of magazines and newspapers.

Or try using an Internet search engine like Google. Just remember to be specific about the topic you want to read about, or you'll wind up with thousands of hits to wade through.

Strategies for Parents

The more you know about childhood ADHD, and the more tools and strategies you have at your disposal, the better you'll be able to manage the various mental, emotional, physical, and lifestyle challenges, setbacks, and detours arising from living with the disorder.

Here are ten easy things you can do as a parent to minimize the symptoms of childhood ADHD.

1. Get to the root of things. If your child has been feeling out of sorts or showing signs of depression for two weeks or longer, it's important to get to the bottom of the problem. Children with ADHD can suffer from symptoms of primary or secondary depression, or both. While primary depression is largely inherited and not triggered by life problems like job loss or relationship problems, secondary depression usually results from the accumulated frustrations and disappointments of living with undiagnosed or untreated ADHD. Don't be afraid to ask for help if you feel like your child's life is spiraling out of control because of disruptive thoughts or behavior.

2. Find ways to minimize distractions. If your child has ADHD, he already has trouble maintaining focus, and shifting attention to something else when it's necessary. Help your child reduce distractions throughout the day that are likely to derail him, and which may keep him awake all night. To make sure your child isn't distracted by loud music or television when he's trying to study, turn down the volume, turn it off altogether, or have your child use ear plugs or white noise machines to block or camouflage the noise. Make sure to create a quiet corner where your child can focus on his homework without being interrupted by other family members.

3. Improve your child's quality of life. Don't assume that having ADHD means your child has to put up with depression and anxiety. If your child is on ADHD medication and still suffers from significant to moderate depression, ask your doctor about prescribing an antidepressant. Antidepressants boost levels of the neurotransmitters serotonin and norepinephrine, and will help your child maintain feelings of well-being and happiness. Keep in mind however, that antidepressants require extra caution when used by children and adolescents. This is discussed in Chapter 13.

4. Easy does it on carbohydrates and caffeine. Children with ADHD often resort to high-carbohydrate snacks like candy, chips, or ice cream, or frequent consumption of caffeine, to elevate their mood or increase alertness and energy, The "fix" doesn't last long. Over-doing carbohydrates can lead to weight gain and fatigue, while too much caffeine can make your teen feel nervous and jittery and lead to insomnia. To help your child maintain a healthy low-carbohydrate/high-protein, diet, consider creating meals from cookbooks like *The South Beach Diet* or *The Zone*, both of which have low-carbohydrate meal plans, recipes, and lists of good versus bad carbohydrates. If your teen has trouble sleeping, encourage him to limit caffeine consumption to morning hours. With careful observation, you may detect a relationship between your child's symptoms and his pattern of caffeine and food consumption.

5. Help your child ward off the blues by creating an "anti-boredom" closet. Studies show that many children with ADHD get depressed when they have nothing to do. Children with ADHD sometimes have more nervous energy than others, and this hyper-activity needs to have an outlet of some sort. To prevent idleness or boredom from tanking your child's mood, create an "anti-boredom" closet and stock it with books, games, arts or crafts supplies, sports equipment, and projects that absolutely fascinate him but which he doesn't have time for in his everyday life. The next time your child has an unexpected block of free time, steer him to his "anti-boredom" closet and find something to capture his imagination.

6. Chart your child's sleep. Many children with ADHD have trouble falling asleep, which can in turn worsen symptoms of inat-tention and focus. To get a handle on your child's sleep habits and what needs improving, keep a chart of when he goes to bed every night, how much sleep he gets, how often he gets up at night, and when he wakes up in the morning. Make sure your child goes to bed at the same time every night, gets up at the same time every morn-ing, avoids exercise, TV, and other stimulating activities for at least an hour before going to bed, and limits caffeine consumption to the morning hours. You may also want to avoid giving your child a heavy meal or snack right before bedtime. If your child still has sleep problems, talk to your physician about safe sleep medications for children.

7. Zone in on your child's stress triggers. If your child feels overwhelmed by feelings of stress, encourage him to list the biggest stresses in his day on a piece of paper, then help him start looking for ways to reduce or eliminate them. If your child can't eliminate the source of stress from his life, such as an overly demanding teacher or bully classmate, help your child change the way he reacts to it by role-playing challenging situations with him and rehearsing appropriate responses.

8. Find new ways to calm your child's body and soul. Do some simple meditation techniques with your child. Sit quietly, with your eyes closed, and focus on breathing to meditate. Each time you exhale, silently repeat a one-syllable word—"one" or "peace" or "ohm." Experts suggest meditating for a few minutes or even for a few seconds every time you find yourself in a panic or funk. If your child can't sit still long enough to meditate, try walking meditation, or tai chi, a type of "moving" yoga.

9. Help your child keep a lid on impulsive behavior. If your child has a tendency to say or do things he later regrets, such as interrupting or getting angry at others, encourage him to keep his impulses in check by counting to ten while breathing slowly instead of acting out. Your child will be surprised to find that most of his impulses evaporate as quickly as they appeared.

10. Find constructive outlets for excess energy. Children with ADHD sometimes seem to have more nervous energy than others, and this hyperactivity needs to have an outlet of some sort. A hobby or other pastime can be helpful.

This is just a starter list. Brainstorm for additional ways to keep ADHD symptoms in check with members of your support group, or encourage your child to get an ADHD buddy he can brainstorm strategies with.

CHAPTER 12

Choosing the Right Treatment

While alleviating childhood ADHD symptoms is a top priority of treatment, the overall goal is to help your child function more efficiently, improve her quality of life, and help her cope with the demands of everyday life. Today, experts use many different therapies to treat childhood ADHD, including medication, psychotherapy, neurofeedback, non-drug alternatives, dietary intervention, exercise, relaxation techniques, and strategies to reinforce social skills. Because childhood ADHD is not one disorder but a cluster of syndromes, treatment plans are generally most effective when custom-tailored to meet the needs of individual children.

Evidence-Based Treatment Programs

Most ADHD experts agree that the best way to tackle ADHD is through a multitreatment approach that combines medication, psychotherapy, and social skills.

Although medication is generally regarded as the first line of defense in treating childhood ADHD, and is often so successful at alleviating symptoms that patients do little else to address them, most ADHD experts concur that "pills do not substitute for skills."

While medication can certainly level the neurobiological playing field and allow children with ADHD to learn and develop the skills they need to succeed, it won't always help them improve problems in areas like organization, time management, prioritizing, and using cognitive aids. For this reason, medication should be just one part of a child's treatment plan.

What to Try First

Most experts agree that ADHD medication is the best place to start when contemplating treatments for your child. Medications may offer the most immediate relief from symptoms, tend to have mild side effects that typically decrease over time, and are also more affordable and less time-consuming than treatments that require your child to interact with psychologists or psychiatrists on a weekly basis. For more information on the best medications for treating childhood ADHD, see Chapter 13.

ADHD medications have also undergone years of stringent testing before being approved by the FDA, and are prescribed by licensed MDs or DOs. In some states, properly trained psychologists may also prescribe these medications. In addition, all FDA-approved medications have been subjected to a number of controlled scientific studies that measure their safety and effectiveness.

The same cannot be said for experimental and alternative treatments used to treat ADHD, including dietary regimens, homeopathy, herbal medicine, manipulation therapies, and sensory integration therapies. None of these treatments have been proven to be effective by controlled scientific studies, and often use anecdotal evidence as proof they work. For more information on experimental and alternative treatments for childhood ADHD, see Chapter 18.

Most Reliable Treatments for Your Money

When it comes to containing costs, ADHD medications are usually the least expensive way to treat ADHD, especially if your insurance company has a prescription drug program.

Neurofeedback and behavior modification are more expensive and require that your child work with a therapist on a weekly basis for several weeks, though they may provide good results. For more information on neurofeedback, see Chapter 14. For more information on behavior modification, see Chapter 15.

Experimental and alternative treatments are probably the least effective treatments for your money. They are often quite expensive and time-consuming, and may be administered or monitored by people without medical or scientific training. Most medical experts caution against using these treatments as front line approaches to ADHD.

Overview of Biological Treatments

Biological treatments alter the way the brain functions, either on a temporary or permanent basis. Biological changes can occur as a result of many different factors, including stimulant and non-stimulant medications, and therapies like neurofeedback that may change the way the brain operates over time.

Stimulant Medications to Treat Childhood ADHD

Stimulants continue to be first-line medications for the treatment of ADHD in children. The most commonly used stimulants are regulated as Schedule II drugs by the Drug Enforcement Administration because they have a potential for abuse when not used as prescribed by a medical professional.

Nonstimulant Medications

In the past, nonstimulant medications were generally considered second-line medications, and limited to children who could either not tolerate stimulant medications, did not respond to them, or were not able to use them because of substance abuse issues or coexisting psychiatric conditions. All that changed in 2003, when the nonstimulant drug Strattera arrived on the market.

Fact

Another nonstimulant medication recently approved for ADHD is Intuniv, an extended-release preparation of guanfacine, a blood pressure medication. This medication may be taken in combination with other ADHD medications. It is often effective with the resentment, anger, and defiance often associated with ADHD.

Because nonstimulant medications do not have the abuse potential of stimulants, and because they aren't controlled Schedule II drugs, they can be prescribed with refills and over the phone. However, they may not be as effective as stimulant mediation for some children.

Other Types of Medication

If stimulant drugs or Strattera or Intuniv don't work for your child, or your child can't tolerate the side effects, your physician may prescribe antidepressants. Your ADHD specialist may also decide to go this route if your child is also severely depressed. Research shows that selective serotonin reuptake inhibitors (SSRIs) have a positive effect on the symptoms of ADHD. Tricyclic antidepressants (TCAs) may also help with core symptoms, such as anxiety and depression. However, these medications must be prescribed for children and teenagers with caution. A side effect of suicidal thinking has been reported. Discuss this with your physician.

Types of Psychological Treatments

Psychological treatments for childhood ADHD include treatments that help your child cope with the secondary symptoms of the disorder—in other words, the feelings of anger, frustration, hostility, impatience, low self-esteem, hopelessness, helplessness, guilt, blame, fear, and other feelings that rise from the primary symptoms of childhood ADHD, which include inattention, impulsivity, and hyperactivity. Behavior modification, a form of psychological therapy, may help your child with problem behaviors, for example with completing self-care tasks such as getting dressed for school, and controlling rage.

Some types of psychological treatment help your child see and understand why he is feeling the way he does. Others help him find ways to cope with the effects of living with the symptoms of ADHD, or modify his behavior and thoughts using conditioning and association.

Changing Attitudes Through Counseling and Psychotherapy

Counseling and psychotherapy can involve standard talk therapy, treatment that teaches your child how to change the way he thinks and acts, and therapies that enable him to act out or vent pent-up feelings.

 **Question**

Will counseling help alleviate my child's ADHD symptoms?
While counseling and psychotherapy can't eliminate the symptoms of childhood ADHD, they can help your child develop strategies to better cope with symptoms. Counseling can help your child accept the fact that he has ADHD and help him adjust his personal and school life so things go more smoothly.

Therapy can help remove any guilt or shame that your child may be feeling about ADHD symptoms by helping him better understand their neurobiological origins.

Adjusting Behavior Through Cognitive-Behavior Therapy

Cognitive-behavior therapy may be used with teens to help them adjust their behavior by identifying patterns of thought and behavior, and using techniques to modify them. This short-term therapy has been shown to work as well as antidepressants for treating mild to moderate depression.

In cognitive-behavior therapy, your child's therapist may ask him to write down his thoughts before, during, and after negative behavior, and record how often he engages in negative behavior so he can begin to get a better picture of why, how, when, and how frequently negative thoughts and behavior interrupt his life.

Your child will also learn how to replace self-destructive thoughts with more realistic and constructive thoughts. This practice relieves distress, and helps point and motivate your child toward more positive action.

Behavior Therapy for Behavior Improvement

Behavior therapy, also known as behavior modification therapy, is related to cognitive-behavior therapy, but derives more directly from research on learning in animals. There is less emphasis on thoughts and more emphasis on techniques for rewarding changes of behavior. For a more comprehensive look at this therapy, see Chapter 15.

Monitoring Thoughts with Awareness Training

In awareness training, your child works with a counselor to develop increased awareness of himself and his environment. The goal of awareness training is to help your child become more in tune with how he thinks, feels, and acts.

Unlike cognitive-behavior therapy, in which your child examines thoughts and feelings before he acts, awareness training teaches him to pay attention to his thoughts, feelings, and behavior at every moment. Tapping into this "streaming" information can help him consciously change the way he behaves.

Learning Through Psycho-Educational Counseling

This type of counseling is like taking a course in ADHD, with an emphasis on teaching you and your child about the many aspects of ADHD so you can both better understand the disorder, and find new skills for living with it.

In psycho-educational counseling, your child's counselor acts more as a teacher who enlightens you and your child about ADHD, rather than a therapist. Just a few things your counselor will likely discuss include ADHD symptoms, various treatments and medications, alternative treatments, coexisting conditions, support groups, special assistance at school or work, disability issues, and insurance concerns.

Sharing Experiences Through Group Therapy

In group therapy, a group of people with similar problems meets with a therapist to discuss problems, share experiences, and find solutions. They usually meet for a specific amount of time so group members can become more comfortable with each other, and establish bonds.

 Alert

Children and teens with ADHD often suffer from symptoms such as bluntness, rudeness, lack of patience, and a short temper. Group therapy can give them a safe place to practice more socially acceptable behavior.

In family counseling, the entire family meets with a therapist to better understand family members with ADHD, to find family solutions for creating harmony at home, and to learn ways to support family members with the disorder.

Developing Specific Skills Through Training

Training is a form of counseling that helps kids with ADHD develop or improve on specific skills they may need in a variety of situations, including school, college, and work. It is also a valuable type of therapy for children and teens who aren't comfortable with approaches used in standard talk therapy.

During training, instead of examining their emotions and what motivates them to think and behave in a certain way, your child will focus exclusively on improving or developing concrete skills needed to function in a more efficient way.

 Fact

Training is a type of counseling that focuses on parts of your child's life where he needs to develop specific skills, abilities, and talents. Counselors as well as ADHD coaches use training to help your child develop the organizational, academic, and planning skills he needs to succeed at school, college, and at work.

Although training doesn't alleviate ADHD symptoms, many participants discover that developing new skills helps them think and act in a more positive and life-affirming way. As a result, they find themselves functioning more efficiently and appropriately at school or college and in social settings.

Social Skills Training

As discussed in Chapter 10, social skills training is a type of therapy that helps your child rebuild and correct inappropriate social behavior that may be alienating friends, teachers, and family members and causing her to be a social misfit, outcast, or to feel extremely lonely.

Social skills can also help children rebuild the social niceties they need to get along at school and work, as well as in interpersonal relationships with family and friends. For a comprehensive look at social skills training, see Chapter 10.

Neurofeedback Therapies

Neurofeedback is an exercise program for the brain that aims to help your child change his brain wave patterns at will. As your child repeatedly achieves a more "normal" balance of different types of brain activity, his brain establishes conditions that reinforce those new activities, and makes it more likely that he will function in a different way.

Studies show that children with ADHD experience lower brain activity in specific areas of their brains than people without the disorder.

During neurofeedback, your child is hooked up to an EEG machine, and electrodes are attached to his scalp that (painlessly) deliver a baseline report of his brain activity. Your child's baseline report is then compared against a databank of "normal" baselines to measure differences.

Your child will repeatedly perform learning exercises (usually computer games) aimed at improving areas where his brain function is weak, and computer programs respond to changes he makes to his brain patterns.

Experimental Therapies

Many children and teens with ADHD also use balancing therapies like chiropractic, osteopathy, yoga, transcendental meditation, acupuncture, acupressure, and homeopathy, to reduce stress, slow racing thoughts, and experience feelings of calm and tranquility.

 Alert

Experimental therapies include sensory integration therapies, which allege to help your child process stimuli more effectively; auditory integration training, which claims to assist with the processing of auditory stimuli; and vision therapy, which alleges to help improve visual processing.

Although the results of rebalancing and experimental therapies have not been scientifically documented, some children and teens with ADHD find them extremely helpful in alleviating symptoms. Although these therapies are not usually prescribed in lieu of other biological treatments, they may be useful complements to your child's ADHD treatment program.

Dietary Interventions

Eating a diet low in simple carbohydrates like sugar and starch, and high in dietary protein, as well as engaging in regular aerobic exercise, are two nonmedical ways that may keep childhood ADHD symptoms at bay, although there is no scientific evidence that eating certain foods alleviates or cures childhood ADHD.

The Staying Power of Protein and Whole Grains

A diet high in protein prevents your child's blood sugar levels from spiking, causing hyperactivity and nervousness, or from crashing, which can leave your child feeling tired, lethargic, irritable, and depressed.

Dietary protein also triggers the synthesis of neurotransmitters like dopamine and norepinephrine, which deliver a boost of energy, as well as neurotransmitters like serotonin, which help your child relax and fall asleep.

Eating several servings of whole grains daily also helps prevent wild fluctuations in blood sugar that can either make your child feel wired and hyped-up, or so exhausted and tired that the only thing she wants to do is take a nap.

Although a healthful diet will not eliminate ADHD symptoms, it could help prevent major swings in mood and behavior, ward off hunger (which could cause irritability, grumpiness, and lethargy) and prevent nutritional deficiencies. Eating a balanced diet may also help boost your child's energy, help her relax and sleep, and make it easier for an overweight child to lose weight and keep it off. For a comprehensive look at dietary interventions for ADHD, see Chapter 17.

Exercise as Medicine?

If your child or teen has ADHD and is also a couch potato, your physician may suggest that she embark on a regular program of aerobic exercise such as walking, hiking, swimming, team sports, or cycling.

Although aerobic exercise will firm up flab and tone your child's muscles, it's equally healthy for your child's brain. Just a half hour of exercise four times a week increases your child's brain levels of dopamine, norepinephrine, and serotonin—three neurotransmitters that not only improve focus and attention, but enhance feelings of well-being.

 Essential

Research shows that extremely active teens with ADHD, such as marathon runners or triathletes, may not need to take stimulant drugs to enjoy symptom relief. Studies show that regular intense exercise decreases ADHD symptoms by causing the brain to release the same neurotransmitters that are activated by stimulant drugs.

Exercise is also the ultimate empowerment tool, reducing feelings of helpless and hopelessness and making your child feel like she can conquer, if not the world, then at least her ADHD symptoms.

Feel-Good Endorphins

Because exercise also releases serotonin, the "feel-good" hormone, your child is also likely to feel less stressed, more centered, and more at peace with the world. Your child or teen can time her workout for the benefit she's seeking. She should exercise in the morning to jump-start her day and get herself moving, and work out in late afternoon to unwind and improve the quality of her sleep.

Importance of "Green Time"

Research shows that children with ADHD enjoy a reduction in symptoms when they spend time playing outdoors in nature. If you live in a city, take your child to a park with grass and trees. If you live in the suburbs or the country, encourage your child to play in yards with trees, flowers, and grass, rather than in concrete playgrounds or streets. Or take your child hiking through forests.

Importance of Getting Enough Sleep

Because of their hyperactivity, many children with ADHD need more sleep than other children. Unfortunately, attention deficits can cause overstimulation and make it difficult for them to fall asleep. Here are a few strategies to help your child get the sleep she needs.

- Make sure your child goes to bed at the same time every night.
- Increase your child's activity level, and decrease the time she spends in front of the television or computer.
- Reduce the caffeine level of your child's diet by limiting cola drinks, sports drinks with caffeine, tea, and chocolate.
- Help your child wind down by creating a buffer zone an hour before bedtime where she does quiet activities, such as reading or coloring.
- Use white noise or relaxation tapes to help your child unwind and fall asleep.

Benefits of Multitreatment Approach

Most ADHD experts agree that the best approach for treating child-hood ADHD is using a combination of medication, psychotherapy, and behavior modification.

 Question

Is it better to use one treatment or several for ADHD?
Using a variety of different treatments increases the chances your child will enjoy more continuous relief from symptoms in the event one or more of her treatments are no longer effective, stop working on a temporary basis, or she needs to stop one or more treatments for a variety of reasons.

Perhaps your teen is too busy with schoolwork to exercise, or he's been ill and can't eat a healthy diet. Or maybe your child developed an allergy or adverse reaction to a medication and must stop taking it until your medical experts can figure out what's causing the problem. Using a combination of treatments makes sure your child always has some treatment to fall back on.

Tools for Charting Your Child's Progress

Staying on top of symptoms, medications, and treatments as well as the many other details of your child's life requires a great deal of organization, planning, and attention to detail—some of the very things your child or teen may have trouble with. Here are some easy ways to help you and your child with ADHD stay on top of things.

- **Invest in a day calendar that has a large enough space for each day so you and/or your child can keep track of various and sundry details.** Break it up into home, work, and personal, and put notes, tips, and reminders under each category—from doctor's appointments and important phone numbers, to reactions to medications, stress-busting strategies, and school assignment deadlines.

- **Have your child keep a diary.** Keeping a diary or day journal is a great way for your child or teen with ADHD to relieve stress, rant and rave, and record private thoughts and emotions she may not be comfortable discussing with you or others. Once she writes something down, it's not only off her chest, but it also helps her look at thoughts or actions more objectively. Because remembering things may not be your child's forte, a journal can also help her stay on top of important dates and occasions.

- **Create a medications journal to record when, why, and how your child's symptoms wax and wane, her reaction to new medications, variations in mood based on slight variations in dosages, how various treatments make your child feel, and which treatments work and don't work for her.** Beware that missing a dose or taking two doses at once to catch up on missed doses can have negative consequences. If your child is exhibiting side effects or other problems related to medication, speak to your health care provider as soon as possible.

- **Have your child create a daily "mood" chart with categories for exercise, hours of sunshine, sleep, nutrition, and stress relief.** Have her rate her mood on a scale of one to ten, then engage in activities designed to increase relaxation and happiness, giving herself a check for thirty minutes of daily exercise, thirty minutes of sunshine, seven hours of sleep, a healthy diet low in sugar and carbohydrates, and engaging in stress-reducing activities.

- **Have your child become a list-master.** Have your child create lists of daily tasks she needs to achieve, and then have her strike them off as she completes them to achieve a sense of accomplishment. If your adolescent or teen has problems keeping her class schedule straight, have her list the classes in chronological order, along with a note as to when each class begins and ends. This will help your child correct scheduling conflicts before they occur. Before seeing your doctor, make a list of questions you or your child want to ask him along with a list of medications your child is taking.

CHAPTER 13

Treating with Medication

Medications for childhood ADHD basically work by having an impact on the neurotransmitters in your child's brain that are responsible for attention and motivation. While stimulant drugs have long been considered the first line of defense in treating the disorder and are still widely regarded as the most effective, many nonstimulant drugs, including antidepressants, anticonvulsants, waking agents, and even estrogen, have proven beneficial in treating childhood ADHD symptoms. Many experts believe that Strattera, a nonstimulant drug recently approved for treating ADHD, will eventually replace stimulant drugs and become the standard treatment for the disorder.

Results of NIH Landmark Study on Results of Medication and Therapy

The National Institutes of Health Multimodal Treatment Study of Children with ADHD (MTA), the largest and most comprehensive treatment study of ADHD ever conducted, found that most children with ADHD get significant benefits from stimulant medications, including a reduction in core ADHD symptoms of hyperactivity, inattention, and impulsivity. The study showed that children taking stimulant medications also enjoyed an improvement in academic performance, a decrease in disruptive and aggressive behavior, and an improvement in their relationships with friends, peers, and family members, according to David Rabiner, PhD, senior research scientist with Duke University.

Combined Treatment Benefits

Children in the combined treatment group received both medication and behavior modification. By the end of the study, children in the combined group could take less medication that those receiving just medication.

While children taking medication had fewer ADHD symptoms than children who only received behavior modification, medication did not reduce symptoms of oppositional behavior, enhance relationships with other children, or improve academic performance.

More Research Needed

Experts agree that more research is needed to study the long-term effectiveness of stimulant medication in children. New non-stimulant medications are in many cases proving to be as effective as stimulant medication, although like any medication, they also have side effects. The benefits and side effects of stimulant and nonstimulant medications will be discussed later in this chapter.

Pros and Cons of Medication in Young Children

Stimulant medication is not a universal panacea for childhood ADHD. Although most children will see improvements, academic challenges and behavior problems may persist that require other types of intervention. And studies show that stimulant medications do not work for all children with ADHD.

While most children do not suffer longtime adverse side effects from taking stimulant medication when taken properly, it's important for parents and children to monitor side effects and bring unexpected or adverse side effects to the attention of your physician.

Myths about ADHD Medication

There are many myths concerning stimulant medications. Before letting the myths discourage or frighten you from considering the use of stimulant medications for your child, it's important to get to the truth of the matter.

Here are two of the most popular myths concerning ADHD medication for children, and the truth behind the issues:

Myth 1: Children treated with stimulant medication are likely to become addicted to it and also more likely to abuse other drugs. Truth: There is no data indicating that children with ADHD who take stimulant medications are more likely to abuse drugs than other children. In fact, studies show just the contrary—that they are less inclined to abuse them.

Myth 2: Stimulant medications will turn your child into a zombie. Truth: While some children may become sluggish and withdrawn when going on medication, these symptoms are generally an indication that the dose is too high, or that the child is suffering from a coexisting condition that has not been addressed. In fact, studies show that children treated with stimulant medication show an increase in social behavior, not a decrease.

The Practice of Polypharmacy

Polypharmacy, or prescribing several psychiatric medications at the same time, is often used to treat coexisting conditions in children with ADHD. For instance, if a child has ADHD as well as clinical anxiety, depression, or bipolar disorder, he may need to take medication for both conditions. If done in the right way, polypharmacy can result in a simultaneous reduction of symptoms for both conditions.

But if medications are prescribed without taking into account their side effects, a patient could suffer serious medical consequences, or even experience an increase in ADHD symptoms if one or both medications have side effects like depression, anxiety, brain fog, or insomnia.

Most Commonly Prescribed Drugs for Childhood ADHD

Over the past fifteen years or so, the medication options for treating childhood ADHD have greatly expanded. Today, the most popular medications for treating the disease include many different stimulant drugs, and a wide variety of nonstimulant drugs in various drug categories.

The Popularity of Stimulants

Despite the growing number of medication options, stimulant medications, including methylphenidate (such as Ritalin), and dextroamphetamine compounds (such as Dextrostat, Dexedrine Spansules, and Adderall) remain the most commonly prescribed drugs for childhood ADHD. Many experts also believe they are the most effective.

 Fact

Physicians once needed special permission or a second opinion from the Drug Enforcement Agency (DEA) to prescribe stimulant drugs to children with ADHD. In the past decade, it has become a lot more common and less controversial for physicians to prescribe drugs for the condition, and special permission is no longer needed to prescribe stimulants.

Antidepressants

While stimulant medications like Ritalin and Adderall remain the most frequently prescribed drugs, they are no longer the only line of defense for children with ADHD. Other medications that are sometimes prescribed off-label for ADHD include tricylic antidepressants (TCAs), such as Elavil. Medications that may be prescribed for comorbid conditions include serotonin selective reuptake inhibitors, such as Prozac, Zoloft, and others. Although no antidepressants have been approved by the FDA for treating childhood ADHD, they may be prescribed "off-label" to alleviate its symptoms. Again, they should be used with caution in children and adolescents.

Nonstimulant Drugs

In 2002, the nonstimulant drug Strattera became the first medication approved by the FDA specifically for the treatment of ADHD in adults, and is also used to treat childhood ADHD. Because Strattera is not a Class II stimulant, experts believe that there is also no abuse potential.

The Right Drug at the Right Dose

Drug treatment for childhood ADHD requires that you maintain an open line of communication with your medical experts to ensure your child is taking the right drug at the right dose, and to take corrective measures in the event your child suffers adverse side effects or a drug stops working for her.

It's important to keep in mind that medications are not magic bullets or cures, but part of an overall treatment approach. Because the first medication your child takes may not be the drug that offers her the most benefits, it's important to pay attention to how medications affect your child's symptoms, and what side effects occur.

Remember that you and your doctor may need to experiment with various medications before you find the medication, amount, and dosing schedule that works best for your child, so be patient.

Dosage Concerns

Research funded by National Institute of Mental Health also indicates that medication is most effective when treatment is routinely monitored by your physician. Children may also benefit from a change in dose or scheduling. Long-acting medications that are taken once a day, rather than in multiple doses, seem to work best for most children.

If your child's ADHD symptoms are relatively mild, she may only need to take medication during the school year. If she has a severe form of ADHD, she may need to stay on medication year-round. Consult with your physician to determine the best course of action for your child.

How Long Should Your Child Take Medication?

Physicians advise that most children take medication only as long as it is deemed helpful and necessary. Some children "grow out of" ADHD to the point that they no longer need medication. Others suffer from ADHD symptoms as adolescents and adults. Your physician will probably re-evaluate your child's ADHD and medication plan every year to determine if she still needs to take medication, or if the dose needs to be adjusted as your child grows.

 Fact

According to recent controlled studies, people who took higher doses of stimulant drugs had better results in 70 percent of cases than those who took lower amounts of the same drugs. As blood levels of the stimulant fell, symptoms of ADHD rebounded, and resulted in more intense symptoms as well as increased irritability, according to the studies.

Short- versus Long-Duration Drugs

Short duration stimulants may wear off quickly, and since many children have problems with forgetfulness, taking multiple doses during the day can leave them unprotected if they forget to take the second and third doses.

Taking ADHD stimulants at night to help calm down may leave children feeling so relaxed they can't focus on homework.

In general, medications with gradual onset of effect and long durations of effect in the body before they are excreted are likely to work most smoothly, avoiding emotional ups and downs. These are also the best formulations for children and teens with a history of substance abuse as they avoid the "hit" and "buzz" of recreational stimulants.

Stimulant Medications

The most frequently prescribed, and also among the most effective drugs, stimulants come in a variety of forms and brands. Under medical supervision, stimulant medications are considered safe, and when used as prescribed, they do not make children with ADHD feel "high."

Although the majority of children with ADHD, 60 to 80 percent, enjoy a dramatic decrease in symptoms, some only get some benefits, and others reap none at all. Others suffer from side effects that are so severe that they must go off the drugs.

Fears that stimulants lead to drug abuse or addiction have largely been silenced by controlled studies.

How Stimulants Work in the Brain

Stimulant medications are believed to directly affect the brain neurotransmitters dopamine and norepinephrine, which are responsible for transmitting messages between different parts of the brain.

Dopamine controls the volume or power of the signals coming into your brain as well as areas of the brain that control filtering and screening—or what you pay attention to, while norepinephrine controls your level of alertness, clarity, and wakefulness. Both neurotransmitters have an impact on motivation.

These neurotransmitters are also believed to affect attention and behavior symptoms, although how each neurotransmitter contributes to the alleviation of symptoms remains unknown.

Alert

Although about three-quarters of children with ADHD also have co-existing conditions, there are no controlled studies on the most effective ways to treat children with co-existing or overlapping conditions. To arrive at the best approach, physicians must rely on their previous therapeutic and clinical experience, and continual feedback from patients.

Generic stimulants are usually inexpensive, although many longer-acting stimulants can be quite expensive if your insurance doesn't cover medication costs.

Forms of Stimulant Medication

Stimulant medications come in different forms, such as a pill, capsule, liquid, or skin patch. Some medications also come in short-acting, long-acting, or extended-release varieties. In each of these varieties, the active ingredient is the same, but it is released differently in the body.

Long-acting or extended-release forms ("ER" or "XR") often work best for children who need continuous relief during daytime and evening hours, and who may be too forgetful or distracted to remember to take second and third doses. They are also prescribed to children and teens who have abused other drugs or who are at high risk for substance abuse.

The Half-Life of Medication

The half-life of a drug is the time it takes for one half of the quantity of the drug to be elimintated from the body. It is a measure of the duration of its activity iin the body. Neglecting to take drugs on time that have a short half-life may result in a condition called discontinuation syndrome. Symptoms include irritability, insomnia, dizziness, light-headedness, and flu-like symptoms, and may persist for weeks.

Commonly Prescribed Stimulants

There are many different kinds of stimulant drugs your physician may prescribe for your child. Although they all work in a similar fashion, they differ in how quickly they begin to work, how long they remain in your child's bloodstream, the degree of relief they provide, and in terms of side effects. Through trial and error, you and your physician will be able to determine which medication(s) work best for your child.

- **Methylphenidate.** Marketed as Ritalin, Concerta, Metadate, and Focalin, methylphenidate is one of the most widely prescribed drugs for ADHD and available in a wide range of forms. Different brands use different delivery systems to get the medication to your child's system, and there are also differences among brands in how long the drugs take to reach their half-life and peak, and how long they remain in the bloodstream. Methylphenidate is available in a variety of forms, including short-acting, long-acting, and sustained-release.
- **Dexadrine (d-amphetamine).** One of the oldest drugs used to treat ADHD and still considered one of the best, Dexadrine is marketed in both short-acting and sustained-released forms.
- **Adderall (salts of d- and l-amphetamine).** Similar to Dexadrine, this medication is believed to have more impact on norepinephrine than Dexadrine, and is marketed in short- and long-acting forms.
- **Vyvanse.** A newer medication, it is similar to Adderall in its chemical composition. It is believed to have less potential for substance abuse than most stimulants because snorting it or injecting it will not cause a user to get high. Before it can become effective, it must undergo a conversion in the body from its oral form to a stimulant form. It may result in a smoother onset and result in less restlessness than Adderall.

- **Dexoxyn (methamphetamine).** Biologically identical to the illegal "meth" made in drug labs, Dexoxyn has gotten an undeserved bad reputation. The legal, prescription form of Dexoxyn is not only one of the most beneficial medications for many children with ADHD, but also one of the least expensive medications.

Side Effects of Stimulants

The most common adverse reactions in clinical trails in adult patients were decreased appetite, headache, dry mouth, nausea, insomnia, anxiety, dizziness, weight loss, and irritability, while the most common adverse reactions associated with discontinuation from adult clinical trials were anxiety, irritability, insomnia, and blood pressure increases. However, it should be noted that most side effects are minor and disappear over time, or if the dosage level is lowered.

Dealing with Stimulant-Related Sleep Problems

If your child can't fall asleep, ask your doctor about prescribing a lower dose of the medication or a shorter-acting form for use in the afternoon or early evening. You might also ask about having your child take the medication earlier in the day, or stopping the afternoon or evening dose.

Maintaining good sleep hygiene is also important, and includes going to bed and rising at the same time every day, ending the day with relaxing activities, and establishing a relaxing sleep environment. Using black-out eye shades, ear plugs, and white-noise machines can help eliminate sleep-robbing distractions like bright lights and noise.

Nonstimulant Medications

Although nonstimulants like antidepressants and mood stabilizers have been used for years to alleviate symptoms of ADHD, few have created the excitement and buzz as nonstimulant medications. Strattera is the first no stimulant medication approved by the FDA for ADHD, and also the first medication approved by the FDA for adults, as opposed to children.

 Alert

> Strattera works like an antidepressant to strengthen the chemical signal between nerves that use the neurotransmitter norepinephrine to send messages. Unlike selected serotonin uptake inhibitors (SSRIs), Strattera does not have an impact on serotonin levels in the brain.

Despite its high price, Strattera may be helpful to children who cannot tolerate stimulants, although some patients claim the effects are not as strong as those provided from stimulant drugs. However, there have been indications that Strattera may rarely increase suicidal thinking and that it might also trigger mania. It should be used with care in children, and as with all medications, under the guidance of a qualified physician.

The medication is taken once a day, although those suffering gastrointestinal upset can take a smaller dose twice a day. Full effects are usually felt within four to six weeks, and last all day or even into the next morning. In long-term studies, two-thirds of people taking Strattera enjoyed relief from symptoms for longer than thirty-four weeks.

Common side effects are headache, abdominal pain, nausea, vomiting, weight loss anxiety, sleepiness, and insomnia. Strattera can also interfere with sexual performance in adults.

Antidepressants

With the exception of Strattera, most other nonstimulant medications are generally considered second-line medications for ADHD, and tend to be used in children who either had a poor or bad response to stimulants, couldn't tolerate the side effects, or who have coexisting psychiatric conditions that rule out taking stimulant drugs.

A Warning about Antidepressants

Though the picture is not clear, keep in mind when considering the use of antidepressant medications that suicidal thinking has been found be a relatively rare side effect in children and adolescents in at least some studies. This does not mean that these medications should not be used at all, though in reality they are rarely used for treating ADHD in children and adolescents. A risk-versus-benefit approach based on your child's specific needs and treatment history is highly recommended. Work with your physician to monitor any negative side effects, including any aberrations in thinking and behavior.

Selective Serotonin Reuptake Inhibitors (SSRIs)

Prescribed for depression, anxiety, and obsessive-compulsive disorder as well as for controlling anger and aggression, SSRIs are most useful in alleviating coexisting symptoms of conditions accompanying ADHD. They work primarily by eliminating serotonin from the brain's synapses, though they may affect other neurotransmitters to a lesser degree as well.

Popular SSRIs include Prozac, the oldest SSRI, with a long half-life but many known drug interactions; Luvox, which is similar to Prozac but has a shorter half-life and fewer drug reactions; Paxil, a short-acting SSRI which may pose problems with dosing and discontinuation syndrome; and Zoloft, another short-acting SSRI which may also offer some of the benefits of stimulant drugs.

 Fact

SSRIs have a variety of side effects, many of which are mild or which affect a small percentage of people. The most troublesome side effects may include weight gain, drowsiness, irritability, and thinning hair or hair loss.

Other SSRIs sometimes prescribed to children with ADHD include Celexa and Lexapro. Both have longer half-lives than other SSRIs except Prozac, and fewer drug reactions than most SSRIs as well. Lexapro, which is similar to Celexa, is often preferred by patients and physicians because it is more potent and has fewer side effects.

Serotonin/Norepinephrine Reuptake Inhibitors

These antidepressants have an impact on the levels of both serotonin and norepinephrine, and are useful in treating depressing, anxiety, and ADHD. However, they generally don't offer the symptom relief of stimulant drugs, and are often prescribed when stimulant drugs don't work, or in addition to stimulant drugs.

One widely prescribed drug in this category is Effexor, which seems to stimulate energy as well as lead to a calming feeling.

 Alert

Although there are no controlled studies on the use of Effexor in children with ADHD, several noncontrolled studies indicate that it may be especially helpful in treating ADHD with co-existing depression and/ or anxiety. However, side effects of higher doses may increase blood pressure, and sudden discontinuation of Effexor could lead to nausea and vomiting.

Another popular drug in this category is Remeron, which works on serotonin, norepinephrine, and histamine to promote sleep, increase energy, and increase appetite. However, one major side effect is a dramatic increase in appetite, and a constant craving for carbohydrates. Everything else being equal, Remeron can be a great medication for your child if he is small or has a poor appetite. But if your child is already overweight, Remeron could make it even harder for him to shed unwanted pounds, and, in fact, could lead to him gaining even more.

Tricyclic Antidepressants (TCAs)

Tricyclic antidepressants (TCAs) the first medications developed to treat depression, work by inhibiting serotonin and norepinephrine reuptake significantly.

TCAs have negligible risk of abuse, and are especially beneficial when treating children with ADHD who also have co-existing anxiety and depression. On the down side, it may take several weeks for these drugs to have a full clinical effect, and TCAs generally don't offer the relief of stimulants.

TCAs prescribed for ADHD include Elavil, Sinequan, and Nortriptyline, all of which have sedating qualities (Elavil has the strongest sedation qualities, while Nortriptyline has the least).

Another TCA, Norpramine, has proven beneficial in children with ADHD when given in small doses. Anafranil, another TCA, has an impact on serotonin levels and is often prescribed for children with ADHD who also suffer from compulsive disorders.

Side effects of TCAs range from sleepiness and constipation to light-headedness and dry mouth, although more serious conditions include cardiac problems, and possible death by overdose.

Mood Stabilizers and Antihypertensives

Mood stabilizers, traditionally used to treat bipolar disorder or to reduce or prevent seizure, are also prescribed by psychiatrists to help modulate irritability and rapid mood shifts. The most widely prescribed mood stabilizers include Lithium, Depakote, Tegretol, and Lamictal.

Antihypertensives

Antihypertensives are used to decrease hyperactivity and impulsivity in children with ADHD, and may also help relieve insomnia. Drugs commonly prescribed for ADHD symptoms include Catapres, guanfacine, and various beta blockers, including Atenolol.

Intuniv/Guanfacine/Tenex

A new nonstimulant drug prescribed for childhood ADHD, Intuniv is the extended release form of guanfacine, which is also sold under the brand name Tenex. Intuniv has recently been approved for use in children and adolescents with ADHD.

 Fact

Intuniv shows a lot of promise in controlling symptoms often associated with ADHD, particularly rage, argumentativeness, and irritability, as well as the more common symptoms of ADHD. It can also be safely used with other medications, including stimulant medications.

Some anecdotal reports have been very encouraging. Intuniv provides an alternative or adjunct to stimulant treatment, but is probably not a first-line treatment in most cases.

Tenex and Catapres are also sometimes prescribed to eliminate tics, impulsivity, or aggression. Because of its sedating properties, Catapres is frequently prescribed for children with ADHD and insomnia.

Both mood stabilizers and antihypertensives require closer medical monitoring. Blood tests, and sometimes an EKG, may also be required.

Other Medications for Childhood ADHD

In addition to the above categories of medications, a few others have been used with varying degrees of success to treat symptoms of ADHD.

- **Desyrel (trazodone).** The atypical antidepressant Desyrel (trazodone) is a mild antidepressant that may be prescribed to children with ADHD who have trouble falling asleep.

- **BuSpar.** A serotonin stabilizer usually prescribed to control anxiety and anger, BuSpar is prescribed to control anxiety in children with ADHD.
- **Nicotinic analogues.** These medications act on some of the same brain receptors as nicotine, and may also provide some relief. Although most research on ADHD has revolved around regulating the balance of neurotransmitters, some believe poor regulation of the nicotinic receptors may also be involved.

Short- and Long-Term Benefits

Whether your child has just been diagnosed with ADHD, or is taking a medication for the first time, sometimes it can be hard to figure out what constitutes a positive reaction to a drug. You may wonder if it's the medication or something else that is making your child feel better, or which negative side effects are worth mentioning to your physician.

 Fact

Research shows that taking the right medications in the right dosage can make all the difference in the world when it comes to normalizing behavior in children with ADHD. According to a study conducted by the National Institute of Mental Health, those under a physician's care taking proper medication enjoy normal function 85 percent of the time.

Zoning in on Positive Results

Your child's reaction to medication may be immediate or happen over time, depending on the type of medication and its dosage. In fact, there are many signs that the medication is working. These include:

- Being better able to pay attention
- Feeling less distracted
- Being better able to recall things
- Getting things done on time more often
- Feeling less restless and jittery
- Tending to think before acting instead of blurting things out
- Having more control over emotions and moods
- Suffering fewer and less severe mood swings
- Displaying less erratic behavior
- Having more motivation
- Having an easier time starting things and getting things done
- Getting a better night's sleep
- Finding it easier to make and keep friends
- Feeling less tempted to engage in reckless behavior, such as drinking or taking drugs

Managing Side Effects

Although almost every medication has side effects, not everyone has the same reaction to them. Some people may barely notice side effects while others may be so bothered by them that they have to stop taking the drug or take a lower dosage.

Regardless of how mild or severe your child's ADHD symptoms, or whether or not your child also has coexisting or overlapping conditions, it's important to find medication(s) that not only alleviate her symptoms but facilitate her physical, emotional, and mental health.

When to Call Your Doctor

In some cases, side effects are the body's warning signal that your child and the drug are not compatible. In others, side effects are simply a temporary manifestation. In either case, you'll want to keep your physician abreast of them. If your child suffers from one or more of the following side effects, contact your doctor:

Personality changes. If your child is normally sunny and upbeat, and suddenly becomes doom-and-gloomy, it may be time to switch to another medication.

Trouble falling asleep. While insomnia is a fairly common problem among children with ADHD, if your child's medication makes things even worse, ask your physician to adjust or reduce your dosage, or to time it right before bedtime, prescribe ADHD medications with sedating qualities right before bedtime, or prescribe a sleep aid to help your child fall asleep and stay asleep.

Rebound effects. The majority of children who take stimulants experience "rebound" effects of moodiness, irritability, and restlessness as the level of medication in their bloodstream decreases. Ask your doctor about ways to stabilize the level of medication in your child's body to avoid these annoying fluctuations.

Appetite and weight loss. Many medications for childhood ADHD cause a reduction in appetite and subsequent weight loss. If your child is already overweight, this can be a plus. If not, ask your doctor about timing doses so your child's medication doesn't ruin her appetite for meals. If your child is losing weight despite all your best efforts, consider consulting with a registered dietitian or nutritionist. She can develop a nutrient-dense, high-calorie meal plan that will help your child maintain a healthy weight without overeating sugar, caffeine, and trans fats.

Aches, pains, and tics. In some children, ADHD medications can trigger nausea, indigestion, and headaches. To ward off stomachaches, have your child take her medication with meals. If your child has ADHD as well as a coexisting condition like Tourette's syndrome, and medication worsens her tics and muscle twitches, call your doctor.

Rashes and skin disturbances. Many children are allergic to the dyes and even the cellulose fillers in pills and react by breaking out in a rash. To avoid future rashes, have your physician switch your child to a medication that doesn't have the offending culprit.

Rapid heart beat or increased blood pressure. If your child complains that her heart is racing, she can't catch her breath, she's experience chest pains, or if her usual exercise regime suddenly feels a lot more difficult, it may be a sign that she's taking too much medication.

Side Effects Aren't a Life Sentence

If side effects are seriously interfering with your child's life, make sure she understands that she won't be stuck with them for life. There are many alternatives and "fixes," from changing medication and dosage to taking a drug holiday and giving it a try later.

You may also consider consulting with other medical experts to get a fresh point of view about medications and treatments you haven't yet tried.

The good news is that side effects associated with childhood ADHD medications tend to be mild and temporary. Most of them can be eliminated by simply changing the dosage, dosage schedule, or by switching to a new medication. The even better news is that in many cases, negative side effects simply go away in a few weeks time.

The Fine Print

It's also essential to read and understand the fine print concerning your child's ADHD medication, including information regarding its half-life and peak time, how many doses your child needs to take, if the medication is short-acting or long-acting, and if the medication is available in extended-release forms so your child can take it once and forget about it for the rest of the day.

Tracking Progress

While monitoring the effectiveness of your child's medication will require some effort on your part, the results are well worth it. By keeping track of how well the drug works over time, you and your doctor can make the necessary adjustments in medications and dosages to keep your child functioning at his best.

To maximize the effectiveness of your child's medication and to minimize the side effects and risks, follow these easy guidelines for safe use:

Do your homework. Find out everything you can about the ADHD medication your doctor is prescribing for your child, including potential side effects, how often to take it, special warnings, and other medications and substances that should be avoided or used with caution, including over-the-counter cold and flu remedies containing ephedrine, over-the-counter and prescription weight loss drugs, sleep medications, decongestants, steroids, and asthma medications containing albuterol or theophylline.

Make sure your child takes his medication as directed. He should never take more or less, or take it at a different time than prescribed by your physician.

Don't let a high-fat breakfast sabotage your child's medication. If your child is taking certain stimulant drugs, including Adderall, Metadate, or Ritalin, a high-fat breakfast can compromise its effectiveness by delaying the drug's absorption. Instead of the drug working within the usual twenty to thirty minutes, it could take one to two hours. Rather than serving your child a high-fat breakfast like bacon and eggs, serve him a low-fat option like oatmeal with berries.

Time your child's intake of foods and supplements high in Vitamin C. Fruit juices high in ascorbic acid/vitamin C or citric acid (orange, grapefruit, and other drinks supplemented with vitamin C) may interfere with the absorption of Ritalin because citric acid breaks down the medication before it has a chance to be absorbed by the body. For this reason, your doctor may recommend your child avoid fruit juices as well as high-vitamin cereals and multivitamin supplements an hour before and after taking medication.

Be patient. Finding the right medication and dose is a trial-and-error process. It will take some experimenting, as well as open, honest communication with your child's doctor, before you find the medication(s) that works best in alleviating symptoms in your child.

Don't let your child stop a drug cold-turkey because it is ineffective or has unpleasant side effects. Your child could suffer from discontinuation syndrome, which is characterized by depression, irritability, fatigue, insomnia, and headaches that could linger for weeks or months.

Medication Logs

Keep records of how the medication is affecting your child's emotions, behavior, attention, sleep, appetite, weight, etc. Keep track of any unusual or new side effects that occur, and keep an ongoing record of how effective the medication seems to be at alleviating your child's symptoms.

You may also want to invest in a commercial medication log. For more information about purchasing a medical log, go to *www .information-logs.com.*

Just One Part of Treatment

Remember that medication is just one leg of your child's treatment triangle. By recording your reactions to drugs on a regular basis, it will be easier to isolate unusual emotional, mental, and physical symptoms that appear to be linked to medication, and identify persisting symptoms that may benefit from other types of treatment, such as cognitive or support psychotherapy, coaching, and support groups.

When Your Child's Medication Doesn't Work or Stops Working

Telltale signs that your child's medication isn't working, has stopped working, or the dosage needs to be fine-tuned, include anxiousness, depression, jittery or restless feelings, being unable to sleep, new symptoms your child never experienced before, and experiencing inexplicable mood swings that seem to worsen, no matter what your child does.

Don't Adjust Dosages on Your Own

Don't assume that just because your child is feeling better, she can afford to take less medication, or, conversely, that taking more medication will make your child feel even better.

There's a very small difference between the right dose and too little or too much medication, so avoid the temptation to experiment on your own. Include your doctor in your plans, and discuss your experience with him.

Issues with Substance Abuse

While using stimulants to treat childhood ADHD may seem paradoxical, studies show mild stimulants have a dramatic calming effect on the brains and nerves of children with ADHD, and also reduce the incidence of substance abuse among treated children. Research shows that many children with ADHD experience a dramatic reduction of symptoms after taking stimulant drugs.

However, because some teens with ADHD have a history of substance abuse, some believe there's a chance they may be tempted to use their ADHD medication for recreational purposes.

Case by Case Basis

Whether to use a stimulant medication for teens who have ADHD and a recent history of substance use but no current use needs to be dealt with on a case-by-case basis. Certain extended-release preparations are less likely to be abused. They include Concerta, which can't be crushed and used other than as prescribed orally, and Vyvanse, a new medication for ADHD which the body converts into a stimulant after it's been ingested, a factor that lessens the potential for abuse.

CHAPTER 14

Healing Through Neurofeedback

C hildren with ADHD have lower than normal activity in brain waves that are associated with attention and focus. Neurofeedback, which is also known as EEG biofeedback, is an approach for treating children with ADHD. Children receive real-time feedback on their brainwave activity using computer programs and learn how to alter their typical EEG pattern to one that is consistent with a more focused and attentive state. As your child improves his score, he repeatedly alters his brain waves to achieve a desired balance, teaching his brain how to create conditions that compensate for ADHD.

Overview of Treatment

A global phenomenon that is practiced by specialists all over the world, neurofeedback has managed to enter the American lexicon, yet it remains outside the gates of established medicine. Today, many organizations devoted to ADHD continue to regard neurofeedback as an experimental treatment that can't take the place of more conventional treatments, and which is best approached with skepticism and caution.

That said, many ADHD experts believe neurofeedback is one of the most effective ways to treat childhood ADHD today. A review paper on EEG biofeedback for ADHD published in the *Psychiatric*

Clinics of North America identified multiple published group studies in which the benefits of neurofeedback were either comparable to or exceeded benefits seen in patients treated with stimulant medication.

Expanding Role of Neurofeedback

Since the 1980s, the principles of neurofeedback have expanded from the medical field into the realms of education, professional sports, and even the board room.

Neurofeedback is also used in education settings to help remediate reading and math disabilities, has infiltrated professional sports (where it is used to maximize the "peak performance" of athletes), is used by artists, and used in corporate settings to increase productivity, morale, and profits.

Pros, Cons, and Controversies

Proponents claim that while there are no perfectly designed studies, there is sufficient convincing research to prove that neurofeedback benefits children with ADHD, including studies that show it's even more effective than medication.

Learning a little more about neurofeedback can, at the very least, assist you in making an educated decision as to whether you should incorporate it into your child's treatment program.

 Essential

Research has already proven that a number of neurological disorders, such as epilepsy, can be characterized by distinctive EEG patterns, and that neurofeedback may help clients change those patterns. When children with ADHD undergo the procedure they are better able to pay attention, focus, and concentrate.

Advantages to Neurofeedback

Researchers also cite many other advantages to neurofeedback including:

- Because neurofeedback does not use drugs and is also a noninvasive procedure, it may be used by children and teens who may not be able to tolerate ADHD drugs or who have a history of substance abuse.
- In some cases, neurofeedback may be as effective as stimulants and does not have significant side effects.
- Neurofeedback is ideal for parents who are leery of stimulant medications because they fear they may alter their child's personality, disrupt her natural talent for creativity, or turn her into a pale and boring shadow of herself.
- Most children find neurofeedback to be a fun, exciting, and interesting experience.
- Neurofeedback has a solid track record of treating a variety of conditions, including ADHD. Neurofeedback has reportedly also been a successful intervention in modifying seizures, traumatic brain injury, chronic pain, migraines, depression, anxiety, addictions, and sleep problems.
- Some children enjoy long-lasting positive changes after undergoing neurofeedback, including reduced negative behavior and thinking patterns, and increased self-confidence and self-esteem.
- When the right criteria are used to select candidates for therapy and treatment, the majority of children completing treatment reportedly show marked improvement in brain wave function.

Cons of Neurofeedback

However, it should be noted that critics of neurofeedback argue that to date, there are no entirely satisfactorily controlled studies on it that have been conducted in accordance with the best standards of research. A controlled study relies on rigorous protocol and uncompromising controls, and is usually very expensive to conduct.

In addition, critics point out that neurofeedback may not be appropriate for extremely disturbed children, such as those with bipolar or manic-depressive disorder. Because most families with a child who has special needs have a variety of problems, including unrealistic parental expectations, poor communication, and unsatisfactory relationships, family counseling is usually required, as well as EEG training.

Approach with Caution

Researchers who question the validity of neurofeedback believe parents should approach it with caution for several important reasons:

- Unlike most ADHD medications, neurofeedback is expensive. Because it's still considered an experimental treatment by many insurance companies, you could wind up paying a substantial sum. Sessions average anywhere from $50 to $100.
- Neurofeedback is very time-consuming, requiring that your child commit twice a week for as many as forty sessions. Your child may also need booster sessions from time to time.
- The benefits of neurofeedback may not be long-lasting.
- It may take months for the effects of neurofeedback to kick in.

Latest Findings

According to advocates of neurofeedback, more than twenty studies including more than 700 subjects have been published showing that neurofeedback has a positive impact on ADHD symptoms. Thirteen of those studies were controlled studies involving more than 400 people, three were random-controlled trials, and two were double-blind placebo controlled trials with similar results, which were presented at professional meetings of psychologists and published or are being prepared for publication.

 Alert

> A study of prison inmates demonstrated that EEG biofeedback can significantly reduce aggression. In fact, the drop in recidivism rates among convicts who learned to control their brainwaves was about the best anyone has seen to date: 70 percent for those treated with neurofeedback versus 15 percent for the untreated control group.

Collectively, the studies show that neurofeedback was effective in up to 80 percent of subjects, with improvements equal to those shown from stimulant medication. Improvements were documented by well-validated measures of attention, impulsivity, and hyperactivity, and in changes in brain function as documented by increases in frontal activation shown by EEG and MRI.

How Neurofeedback Works

The brain has five major types of brain wave patterns. Although there are many different patterns in the brain at any given time, these waves can reflect existing mood or mental state.

1. Beta waves. These are the fastest waves in the brain, and the brain waves your child experiences when he's awake. Brain wave frequencies are generally above 12 hertz, which are cycles of activity per second. When your child is feeling alert, attentive, excited, energized, focused, or revved up, his brain is in beta wave mode. He's also in beta wave mode when he's focusing on a project at school, reading a mystery novel, doing a crossword puzzle, or watching an adventure movie.

2. SMR waves. A subgroup of beta waves, these occur when your child is concentrating on how to prepare for a physical challenge, such as climbing a flight of steps, taking a bike ride, working out, or taking a hike or walk.

3. Alpha waves. Slower than beta waves, these are associated with relaxing and winding down. Your child is in alpha wave mode when he's listening to music on his iPod. Alpha waves have frequencies ranging from 8–12 Hz. Some children with ADHD have too many alpha waves, which get in the way of normal communication between different parts of the brain.

4. Theta waves. These are even slower than alpha waves. This is the brain pattern your child is in when he's daydreaming, visualizing, meditating, or about to fall asleep. Theta wave frequencies range from 4–8 Hz. Many children with ADHD have too many theta waves. During neurofeedback, your child does brain exercises to increase the level of beta waves in brain areas bogged down by theta waves.

5. Delta waves. The slowest brain waves of all, this is the mode your child is in when he's asleep. Delta brain wave frequencies range from 0–4 Hz.

A Look Inside the ADHD Brain

When a child without ADHD does something that requires a lot of focus, concentration, and attention, he activates beta waves in certain parts of the brain. But the brains of children with ADHD doing the same task activate theta waves (the daydream brain wave) instead of focused beta waves.

 Fact

Neurofeedback helps strengthen the attentive, or beta wave, muscles of your child's brain that he'd use to do things like concentrate on his homework, pay attention to what his teacher is saying, or focus on a long-term project.

Proponents of neurofeedback believe it helps children with ADHD adjust their brain waves so they more closely resemble the brain waves of people without ADHD.

How Neurofeedback Shifts Your Child's Brain Waves

Before your child undergoes neurofeedback, his therapist will administer a battery of psychological and neuropsychological tests similar or identical to those your child first took when he was diagnosed with ADHD. After test results are analyzed, your child's therapist will input relevant data into a computer program to create a customized program for your child.

 Question

Will neurofeedback cause any pain to my child?
No, neurofeedback is relatively painless and most children enjoy it. New breakthroughs in technology have eliminated the need to attach electrodes to the scalp with messy gels. Your child will wear a cap that contains an amplifier and a wireless transmitter. This has significantly improved the accuracy of EEG readings.

Let's say your child's computer "brain training" is a Pac-Man computer game. Before starting the game, your child's therapist establishes "amplitude thresholds" designed to help your child optimize motivation and learning.

As your child plays the game, a Pac-Man figure advances and sounds a tone whenever your child maintains waves in the 15 to 18 Hz range above a certain amplitude threshold, while keeping waves in the 4 to 7 Hz range below a certain threshold. Your child is rewarded whenever he maintains 15 to 18 Hz above his predetermined threshold 70 percent of the time, while keeping the 4 to 7 Hz frequency above his predetermined threshold 20 percent of the time.

As your child goes through neurofeedback, it will become progressively easier for him to stop daydreaming and fantasizing when he really should be focusing and paying attention. Your child may need up to forty sessions as well as an occasional booster session after several months to maintain his gains.

HEG and Brain Biofeedback

HEG, a new type of brain biofeedback, uses the same concept as EEG biofeedback (neurofeedback), except that instead of learning to control their brain waves, children learn to increase the blood flow to their frontal lobes.

 Alert

HEG is not widely practiced in the United States and there are no studies regarding its effectiveness. You may want to ask your ADHD practitioners about this new treatment before considering it for your child.

During HEG biofeedback, children wear a headband that shines light into and through their skull. Like holding a flashlight against the hand at night, the skin and bones are translucent. Oxygen-rich blood and oxygen-starved blood are different colors, and the sensors in the headband can detect colors. A tone or other signal lets the child know whenever the oxygen level in the frontal lobes increases. Some children can raise it dramatically in a matter of moments simply by imagining that their foreheads feel warm.

Alleged Advantages over Standard Neurofeedback

The training time for HEG in one study was less than ten minutes, as opposed to five to seven hours for EEG biofeedback. HEG biofeedback training reportedly helps many of the youngsters who have not responded to EEG training. In general, the expectation is that children will start with EEG biofeedback and finish up with HEG training.

Short- and Long-Term Benefits of Neurofeedback

Short-term benefits cited by proponents of neurofeedback include improved attention, focus, and concentration; more ability to complete tasks; an increase in organizational skills; and a reduction in impulsivity and hyperactivity.

Long-term benefits can be wide-reaching and affect virtually every aspect of an individual's life. The benefits can include:

- Better behavior at home, at school, and in social settings
- Improved aptitude when learning and mastering new skills
- Higher intelligence test scores
- Increased self-esteem, confidence, and social poise
- Improved school performance
- Better health
- Improved relationships with parents, siblings, peers, and teachers
- A greater realization of his or her innate potential

The Best Candidates and Why

Anyone with a primary diagnosis of ADHD who has low-average, average, or above-average intelligence, can be treated with neurofeedback, according to proponents.

If your child suffers from certain comorbid conditions, however, you're advised to avoid it, at least until those conditions are dealt with. These include severe depression, bipolar disorder, learning disorders, childhood psychosis, significant seizure disorder where medications interfere with learning (i.e., sedating medications), and dysfunctional families who refuse to participate in therapy.

Resource Guide

Several companies are involved in the neurofeedback industry. While most sell equipment to affiliated practitioners, some are more interested in turning a profit and will sell their equipment to virtually anyone. In the wrong hands, neurofeedback programs can be an expensive and frustrating waste of time.

For that reason, it's important to exercise care when choosing a neurofeedback therapist for your child. The practitioner should ideally be licensed in psychology or in a field related to medicine, and her license should allow for independent practice. She should ideally be a state-licensed, PhD-level psychologist with training in brain anatomy and function and be certified by the Behavior Certification Institute of America.

In addition, your practitioner should stay abreast of the latest research, receive ongoing training in neurofeedback, and be knowledgeable in other treatment approaches to childhood ADHD.

Not a Do-It-Yourself Therapy

It is also possible for parents to purchase the equipment and software needed to do neurofeedback biofeedback for less than $2,000. But experts advise against doing this because the potential for misuse and abuse of neurofeedback equipment is very high, and most parents are not trained to do biofeedback properly.

If you or your physician think your child would benefit from neurofeedback, play it safe and make sure your child receives it from an experienced and credentialed practitioner.

CHAPTER 15

The Role of Behavior Modification Therapy

Trying to get children diagnosed with ADHD to behave at home and school is the biggest challenge parents confront. Parents explain, lecture, admonish, nag, criticize, bribe, take away privileges, assign timeouts, and even spank. Too often, their child's behavior does not improve or worsens. Aggressive youngsters become increasingly alienated, defiant, and antisocial with each passing year. Compliant children become more upset, depressed, and self-destructive. Parents simply must end the negativity that creates so much upset and frustration. A behavior modification program may provide the solution your family needs.

Origin of Behavior Modification

Behavior modification is based on a number of different theories and research studies. It was influenced by the conditioning principles set forth by Russian physiologist Ivan Pavlov, theories set forth by American B. F. Skinner, and the work of psychiatrist Joseph Wolpe.

Ivan Pavlov was most famous for training dogs to salivate at the sound of a bell—a case of rewarding and shaping behavior that usually cannot be deliberately controlled. Pavlov demonstrated how such responses can be learned and also can be suppressed. This has implications for treating emotional reactions.

Skinner was a pioneer in the field of operant conditioning, which believes that behavior generally understood as conscious and intentional is modified by its consequences. Consciousness was considered to be relatively unimportant in the control of behavior. Joseph Wolpe, a pioneer in applying these results to therapy, was famous for his pioneering efforts in the areas of desensitization and assertiveness training. By the 1970s, behavior therapy was widely used in treating a variety of mental conditions, including depression, anxiety, phobias, and ADHD.

 Fact

Because behavior modification is often used to treat teens with eating disorders and drug abuse, behavior modification may help your child reduce symptoms of both ADHD as well as one of these coexisting conditions. Behavior modification is most effective when used in combination with ADHD medications and psychotherapy.

What Is Behavior Modification?

By systematically rewarding selected behavior in a consistent, highly organized fashion and ignoring undesirable behavior, trainers teach animals to perform amazing feats. They teach dolphins and lions to jump through hoops. Pigeons learn to carry messages to distant locations. Seeing-eye dogs master the art of guiding the blind about town without becoming distracted by passing cars, animals, and crowds. In short, animals learn to respond in ways most people never would have thought possible.

Psychologists have long recognized that the same straightforward principles and simple procedures work well for animals of all kinds, from human beings to fruit flies. Behavior modification programs are effective for helping children and adults alike eliminate troublesome behavior, break destructive habits, develop better self-control, and respond in healthier ways.

Types of Behavior Modification

While every behavior modification program is different because it is tailored to a specific child, in general there are two basic types:

- Behavior modification (traditional)
- Cognitive-behavior therapy

The secret to a successful behavior modification program is to define small, readily obtainable goals and systematically reward each small accomplishment until new habits are formed. Children must be set up to succeed. Failure results when the tasks are too difficult or the rewards insufficiently motivating or delayed.

Getting Good Results

Impressive results are commonplace when trained professionals conduct modification programs in controlled environments. When scientists methodically follow carefully designed protocols in laboratories and special education teachers work with students in self-contained classrooms, they typically get excellent results.

Why Results Can Be Poor

When ordinary parents and teachers try to carry out behavior programs at home and school, the results often prove very disappointing. Many parents are sure that behavior modification won't work for their child, because their past attempts to solve behavior problems by doling out rewards and imposing punishment followed a predictable pattern: Most everything they tried worked for a time, but nothing worked for long.

Although parents typically conclude that failure means that their youngster is especially difficult, strong-willed, defiant, or resistant, the real problem usually lies elsewhere. The success of a behavior modification program depends on the adult properly applying the techniques involved, not on how the child responds.

 Fact

Some parents wonder if it's wrong to train children as if they were circus animals. Using rewards to control behavior need not feel coercive since both parents and children enjoy increased satisfaction with one another. Behavior modification has been shown to reverse negative communication patterns and strengthen the parent-child relationship.

Creating and maintaining a behavior modification program is often too complex for many parents. Working with a professional trained and experienced in the specific area of behavior therapy will make it easier for you to create and maintain an effective program.

How Behavior Modification Works

While successful behavior modifications differ from child to child, they all incorporate the following ten basic principles:

1. Rewards are given immediately for good behavior.
2. Because immediacy and frequency are essential, a number of small rewards, such as stickers, can be cashed in for bigger, more distant rewards.
3. Rewards need to be things the child desires and does not get in other ways.
4. Rewards are not withheld because a parent is angry with the child.

5. Rewards are never taken away after a child has earned them.
6. Children should be praised for their successes.
7. Children should receive unconditional love from parents regardless of how well they perform in the behavior modification program.
8. Desired behavior should be broken into steps small enough to allow your child to succeed almost every time.
9. Parents should be cautious with punishments. If used, they should be immediate and short-term.
10. If the behavior system is not working, the child should never be blamed. Because behavior modification is a highly sophisticated technique, it should be developed and adapted by a trained professional.

Helping Your Therapist Develop a Customized Program for Your Child

The first step in developing a behavior modification program is to create a list of the behaviors you want to eliminate or to increase. Examples of behaviors to eliminate may be interrupting when someone else is speaking or arguing when told to do homework. Examples of behaviors to increase might include getting dressed in time to go to school, being in bed by 9 P.M., and remaining seated during dinner.

Behaviors that are general, vague, or subject to interpretation such as "don't be rude" must be rewritten so that they reflect specific, concrete, observable actions, such as "do not curse," "do not walk out of the room while I am talking to you," and "do not slam the door."

Similarly, internal states of mind and attitudes such as "don't be so argumentative" must be rewritten as specific behaviors such as "do homework when instructed without arguing."

Importance of Defining Behavior

Defining behavior precisely is a must. Saying that you expect your child to be polite when relatives are visiting really does not tell your youngster what to do. Is she to preface her answers with "yes, sir," "no, ma'am," and "I'm not sure," instead of mumbling, "yeah," "naw," and "I dunno?" Should she say "please" when she wants a piggyback ride, "thank you" when given a present, and "excuse me" before interrupting a conversation? Or would you just be happy if she would refrain from punching her little cousin, using the sofa as a trampoline, or asking the company to go home so she can watch television?

 Alert

Parents often think that their child knows how to behave properly and is simply being stubborn, lazy, or defiant. Time and again it turns out that the youngster truly does not understand that when mother says "do the dishes," she also means "put away the food, wipe the table and counters, and carry out the trash."

Creating Target Behaviors to Modify

After creating a list of target behaviors to modify, try to eliminate the negatives and replace them with positives by changing the "don'ts" to "dos." Saying that your daughter is not to hit her little brother does not explain what she should do when he takes her toys or taunts her. Telling her to ignore a tormentor may not be realistic and doesn't teach her how to set limits and defend herself.

Importance of Rewarding Good Behavior

Children tend to repeat behavior that is consistently followed by positive consequences. Behavior modification programs use rewards to reinforce desirable behavior. There are two types of rewards: material rewards and social rewards.

Material rewards include toys, treats, outings, privileges, and permissions. Social rewards include hugs, smiles, congratulations, compliments, and kudos.

For a behavior modification program to succeed, you must reward your child step by small step for a few simple things he can readily accomplish. Then you must reward him every single time at first, though with care frequency of reward might be reduced later.

 Alert

> It is best to work with no more than one or two simple behaviors at a time. When the desired behavior is inculcated, then another one may be selected until he has thoroughly mastered them before presenting him with more challenging tasks.

Since you will be providing many rewards each day, material rewards must necessarily be inexpensive. Items such as stickers, marbles, or trading cards appeal to some children. Many parents give a piece of candy. This can be very effective, though it may not be wise to give too much candy to children.

It is important to use rewards the child actually wants, and it is generally a good idea to reserve those specific rewards for the behavior modification program so that the child does not become satiated with them by getting them in other ways. If a child loses interest in a reward, a new reward should be used.

Chaining

"Chaining" is a technique for rewarding less pleasurable behavior with more pleasurable behavior. The most aversive behavior comes first. For some children it might be getting dressed in the morning. Using a chaining approach, dressing is the first thing the child would do.

Brushing her teeth might be less of an issue, and might come next. This would then be rewarded with breakfast. Getting herself out the door on time might be rewarded with a special treat to take along to school. Keep in mind though, that any one of these steps might need a specific reward as the program is being developed.

 Essential

Small, immediate rewards should be tallied up for major and more distant rewards. Intermediate rewards might be getting to play a video game for twenty minutes, being allowed to choose the restaurant when the family eats out, or deciding which video the family rents. Outings such as a trip to the mall, city park, or library are popular, distant, and perhaps more expensive rewards.

Role of Social Rewards

Social rewards are interactions that your child enjoys and that are affirming. They can be smiles, hugs, pats on the back, the thumbs up sign, praise, expressions of appreciation, positive acknowledgment, overhearing glowing comments, and spending pleasant time with a parent.

Pleasant time can include wrestling, making brownies, planting a garden, turning off the car radio and singing "Row, Row, Row Your Boat," reading a bedtime story together, etc. When asked, children usually choose material rewards over social rewards, but social rewards are powerful and important. They are more meaningful to most children in the long run. However, a reward is only effective if it is motivating. For this reason, material rewards are often effective, even when they are not considered to be ideal.

Role of Physical Rewards

Make it a habit to administer verbal or physical pats on the back whenever you give your youngster a material reward. Some children are indifferent to praise, smiles, and kudos because every other sentence their parent utters is "good job!" until it sounds like a verbal tic. Youngsters come to regard such glowing comments for what they are: meaningless and empty. At the same time, everyone needs unconditional positive regard. Children should not be deprived of generalized affection.

Importance of Immediate Rewards

Since rewards must be given immediately after a desired behavior occurs, it is usually more efficient to give tokens or other small prizes or treats, for example colorful stickers that can be traded for a bigger prize later.

As anyone who has tried to diet knows, it is hard to remain motivated to work toward a far-off goal. In most cases reward systems only work when children feel rewarded immediately. If you discover that your child is not motivated by certain rewards, change them. If she cannot readily earn rewards, make them easier to reach.

Your Child's Role in a Behavior Modification Program

Children should be involved in all phases of a behavior modification program, and their help determining what rewards they can earn and what they must do to get them is important.

 Essential

Solicit your child's input before deciding how many stickers she needs to accumulate in order to earn a trip to the skating rink or to get a new toy. She must view the rewards as worthwhile and believe she can earn them for a behavior modification program to work.

Explain that you are going to begin rewarding her for good behavior and help her brainstorm a long list of the toys, treats, outings, privileges, and permissions that she would like. Record all of her wishes. You may not be willing to fulfill her heart's desire for a horse by moving Black Beauty into your backyard. But learning that horses mean that much to her may provide clues as to highly motivating rewards. You might consider providing stickers with pictures of horses for her to affix to a chart, renting the *Black Stallion* video, driving to the country so she can pet a horse, letting her take a riding lesson at a stable, going to see a rodeo or horse show, transferring a picture of a horse onto her T-shirt, riding a pony at an amusement park, and helping her arrange to work at a stable.

Increasing the Chances of Success

To increase the chance of success in a behavior modification program, even very small rewards such as tokens and stickers should not be taken away once earned, even if the child does something displeasing or wrong. Remember that children are not at fault when a behavior modification program falters.

Tell your child you love him often, and be affectionate regardless of the progress of the behavior modification program. Children who feel unloved are likely to become depressed, angry, and rebellious.

 Essential

In the context of the behavior modification program, praise specific achievements. And when you do, provide a detailed description of the behavior you like: "I'm impressed that you remembered to ask your brother to pass the salt instead of reaching across the table."

Combining material and social rewards is especially powerful. Trainers provide material rewards such as scraps of meat to puppies at the outset of training. With the combination of praise and pats and the food, dogs soon learn to associate the two. Once they make the association, praise alone serves as a reward and keeps their behavior on track. Similarly, children eventually associate the positive feelings about material rewards with their parent's smiles and expressions of pleasure. In time, approval is enough to keep them going.

Creating Desirable Behaviors

Because a youngster sometimes manages to control his temper or clean his room doesn't mean that he can do either easily. If your child quickly loses interest in earning rewards, you are asking too much of him.

Behavior modification programs work because they set children up to succeed. To do that, you must break each target behavior into a series of small tasks that your child can easily manage and which are rewarded immediately. Each small success builds confidence and creates the can-do attitude that motivates children to tackle new challenges.

Defining Tasks

Perhaps you want your youngster to clean his room without an argument, but his usual response when told to turn off the television and get started is to ignore you. If you turn off the television and firmly tell him to clean his room, he has a fit and promises to clean it later, but later never comes. Or, he goes to his room but does not work.

To solve this problem with a behavior modification program, the first step is to get him to respond when you speak to him, whether he is busy doing something else or is purposely ignoring you. Inform him of this goal, write it on his behavior chart, and specify the reward or the number of tokens he can earn each time he achieves it. Then, when you want to speak with him, go to the room where he is playing, say his name in a normal tone of voice or gently touch his shoulder, and then reward him when he looks up, even if he only glances your way by chance. As you hand him a token, sticker, or another predetermined reward, say, "I appreciate your stopping what you're doing when I need to talk with you. Thanks." After he has been reinforced a number of times in this way, he'll be better at noticing that you are speaking to him.

After your child is consistently responding, compliment him on his accomplishment and announce that he is ready for the next challenge, which might be to accompany you to his bedroom without protest when it is time to clean his room.

Describe the rewards he will earn for each success. Then, if he willingly accompanies you to the bedroom, reward him even if he doesn't clean up his room. Help him pick it up or pick it up for him, and reassure him that he will be able to handle that task in time. Don't advance to the next step until he can consistently walk with you to the bedroom and refrain from arguing. When you are sure he has mastered that challenge, describe the next goal: He will pick up his clothes from the floor and put them in the laundry.

The Role of Punishment

Punishment involves following an undesired behavior with an aversive stimulus that is calculated to suppress that behavior in the future. This could involve taking away an enjoyable activity such as watching television or playing video games.

In a behavior therapy context punishments, if any, are defined in advance in working with your child, just as are rewards. They are never arbitrary or unexpected. A punishment in the behavior therapy context is a brief, predefined event administered in a preplanned manner in response to a specific behavior. It is part of the behavior therapy plan, just as are rewards.

 Question

Should I punish my child with ADHD like my other children?
Punishment is often not very effective in the long run for children with ADHD. Use it with caution, keep punishments brief, and administer them to your child in a private setting to avoid embarrassing your child. Instead of taking away a child's access to television for a week after she's done something wrong, take it away for a half hour each time.

Ask your child's opinion before deciding what the penalty should be for a particular type of misbehavior, and then watch carefully to see if losing privileges really deters misbehavior and motivates your child to behave better.

The Role of Extinction

Extinction involves eliminating something that rewards an undesired behavior so that it will stop occurring. When the reward is eliminated, the frequency of the behavior may increase at first, but it will then drop off to near zero because the consequence that keeps it going has been removed.

Most children find attention to be rewarding. Frequently, if annoying behaviors that are reinforced by attention are ignored, they will at first increase in strength or frequency and then drop off within a few days. This happens because the behaviors are no longer rewarded with attention. Nagging is an example of a behavior that may be reduced in this way.

 Alert

Many youngsters misbehave in order to get a reaction from their parents. Even negative attention is better than no attention, so being scolded can actually be more rewarding than being ignored. Ignoring negative behavior is an example of using extinction.

Many children simply do not know how to get positive attention. Their parents ignore them when they are playing quietly, refuse invitations to play board games, and decline requests to go outside to toss a football. They are chronically stressed and exhausted and only find the wherewithal to respond when a behavior problem compels them to get involved. Behavior modification programs often succeed simply because parents are forced to notice and respond to their child's good behavior.

Overcoming Challenges in Behavior Modification

There are some limits on what can be taught using behavior modification. You must be realistic when targeting behavior to change. It is doubtful that you can turn your shy, artistic bookworm into a football star. At the same time, do not underestimate how much your child can ultimately achieve.

The Challenges of Sustaining New Behavior

Learners usually understand what they are to do and should be able to earn rewards in short order. Being able to sustain their new behavior over time is more challenging, but the positive feelings and consequences the new behavior spurs can help.

Most people can diet or stop smoking for a day or two, but continuing to abstain from fat and cigarettes gets harder rather than easier as time passes. That's because the strain of behaving in unfamiliar ways wears them down. Similarly, although a hyperactive youngster may be capable of sitting still for five minutes at a stretch, doing so requires a tremendous effort.

Until your child finds a way to calm her behavior, she may well feel as if her nerves are on edge, screaming for her to move about. Your child is likely to require changes in rewards to stay motivated. New behavior should come to reinforce itself through improved quality of life and interpersonal relations.

Stress from another problem or difficulty that happens to arise while a behavior modification program is in progress can readily cause a setback. Reverting to old behavior patterns does not mean that no progress has been made. Until new habits develop, lapses are to be expected.

Importance of Continued Rewards

Do not hold back from giving a reward because your child is playing quietly or is busily doing homework for fear your interruption will create a distraction and end your precious moments of peace. Otherwise, you will quickly revert to the same destructive patterns of nagging your youngster when she does something wrong instead of rewarding her for good behavior, and progress will stall. In time, you may be able to reduce the frequency of rewards.

Until rewarding your youngster for virtually every positive behavior as you have planned becomes a habit, remaining consistent is not easy. Be patient with yourself, and reward yourself for your successes at carrying out the program. What you must do to succeed is to modify some of your behavior—perhaps the very same behavior you are trying to get your child to embrace.

You must also plan ahead to be sure you have enough rewards on hand. You must keep your promise so that you reward your child every time she earns one. You must avoid slacking off when you feel stressed, tired, or unmotivated.

Be Patient

If it takes an entire month for your child to pick up her dirty clothes each evening without an argument, don't get discouraged. Many parents of children diagnosed with ADHD have to yell to get their attention for years on end. Many adults are too undisciplined to put their dirty clothes in the laundry each day, and the result is arguments with roommates and marital strife. Do not underestimate the importance of small accomplishments.

Role of Cognitive-Behavior Therapy

Traditional behavior modification uses the consistent use of rewards and consequences to encourage children to behave in a positive way and discourage them from behaving in a negative way. Cognitive-behavior therapy is similar but different. Instead of rewards and consequences, it uses a systematic approach to changing the way your child thinks and acts using conditioning and association.

Fact

> This therapy is called *cognitive* because it attempts to determine what your child's dialogue and thought patterns are and how they relate to his behavior and moods. It's called *behavior* because it uses conditioned responses to your child's internal dialogues to change his behavior.

How Cognitive-Behavior Therapy Works

Your child will work with a therapist to determine his problem behaviors and he and the therapist will determine ways to correct them.

First, the therapist looks at one behavior at a time to try to determine the child's motivations and reasons for acting that way. Next, your child and therapist will look at where and when your child exhibits this behavior, looking at your child's motivations (or feelings and thoughts) for acting that way, and when the behavior typically occurs, or circumstances.

After the therapist and child have a handle on when a behavior occurs and why, they begin to look for ways to change your child's behavior. Once your child is armed with these strategies, he can use them whenever he is tempted to repeat the behavior.

Although children can't usually stop a negative behavior the first time with the first strategy they and their therapist come up with, in time, they can make adjustments until they end up with a strategy or several different approaches that work.

Combining Medication with Behavior Modification

As noted in Chapter 13, a landmark study that researched the most effective treatments for children with ADHD showed that children who used both medication and behavior modification saw a decrease in symptoms and were able to lower their daily doses of medication, while children who just took medication were not able to.

The study also showed that children who received both types of treatment saw a larger decrease in inattention, hyperactivity, and impulsivity than children who received just medication, although children who received just medication enjoyed fewer symptoms than children who just received behavior modification.

The study also noted that while medication was better than behavior modification at reducing hyperactivity, inattention, and impulsivity, it had no effect on the oppositional defiant behavior that sometimes accompanies ADHD, children's relationships with their classmates and peers, and their academic achievement.

CHAPTER 16

The Benefits of Talk Therapy

Although medications for treating childhood ADHD have proven to be very successful in reducing symptoms, they can't teach new skills or improve the organizational and interpersonal challenges that typically accompany the disorder. Talk therapy takes many forms but always involves talking with a trained therapist. Depending on the specific type of talk therapy, your child or teen will learn about the neurobiological natures of the disorder, stop blaming herself, and develop new tools and strategies for coping with everyday symptoms at school, at home, and with friends.

Anatomy of Talk Therapy

Basically, talk therapy is exactly what it sounds like: Your child sits down with a therapist and talks about something she wants to correct, or get over, or forgive.

There are several different types of talk therapy. They include insight-oriented therapy, which aims to help your child understand what she does and why; supportive therapy, where your child gets the support and encouragement she may need to deal with her symptoms; skills training, where she learns specific skills that may be lacking and causing her problems in school; and psycho-educational counseling, where your child learns about the various aspects of ADHD and strategies to cope with them.

Fact

Many children benefit from group counseling, where they work with other children with similar issues; relationships therapy, where they work on skills necessary to make and keep friends; and family therapy, where the entire family gets together to address issues and problems related to ADHD.

Some children also use ADHD coaches to develop and strengthen organizational and time-management skills. For more information on cognitive-behavior therapy, another type of talk therapy where your child learns to change the way she thinks and acts using conditioning and association, see Chapter 15.

Why and When Talk Therapy Works

Everyone in life needs someone to talk to, whether they are going through a major life challenge like childhood ADHD, or just trying to figure out how to cope with a minor setback.

Children with ADHD have myriad issues to contend with, from the symptoms of the disorder to the fact that ADHD is often an isolating syndrome that turns its victims into social outcasts.

From learning about causes and treatments to finding new ways to coexist happily and healthily with the disorder so your child is exercising his innate strengths and playing down his shortcomings, psychotherapy gives your child the coping skills, strategies, and skills he needs to live with ADHD.

Help but Not a Cure

It's important to remember that childhood ADHD has no ultimate cure. While neither medication nor psychotherapy can completely eliminate the symptoms, psychotherapy can help you and your child understand, manage, and minimize symptoms so they are less likely to have a negative impact on your child's life.

Which Talk Therapy Is Right for Your Child?

Just as there are many different regimens for weight loss, there are many different types of therapy. Some focus on helping your child come to a better understanding of why she thinks, acts, and feels differently than "normal" people. Others help your child adjust her behavior, emotions, and thinking so it doesn't sabotage her personal relationships, her ability to perform in school, get into college, or use her unique talent to create startling new concepts.

Learning Through Psycho-Education

If your child has never been in therapy before and has just been diagnosed with ADHD, psycho-education therapy is often a good place to start. In this type of therapy the therapist acts more as an instructor than a therapist to teach you and your child about the disorder.

In psycho-education, you and your child will see that symptoms you might have thought were your child's fault, or which you assumed were caused by your child's innate laziness, lack of motivation, or disinterest, are actually the result of a neurobiological imbalance of neurotransmitters that control attention and impulse.

You'll also learn why it's harder for your child than others to pay attention, focus, remember things, get things done on time, start things, prioritize, and know when to shift gears.

Learning and understanding the biological roots of childhood ADHD can also help you and your child begin to banish years of guilt and blame, and open the floodgates for seeking the help your child needs to overcome symptoms.

Skills Training Therapy

Children with ADHD often feel disordered and as though their lives are spiraling out of control. In order to compensate for their symptoms, they develop idiosyncratic and often ineffective ways of dealing with school and home-related tasks. Another type of therapy, or skills training, helps children with ADHD develop the executive skills they need to function more effectively at school.

 Alert

Disorganization is one of the biggest problems facing children with ADHD. If your child can start projects but can't complete them because she misplaces important documents, a skills training therapist can provide the hands-on help your child needs to get and keep her school work in order.

Skills training helps replace inefficient habits with more effective ones, and also teaches children with ADHD how to enhance their organizational skills through the use of time management skills, audio and visual cues, electronic organizers, date books, calendars, lists, and ways to structure tasks to help your child feel more competent and accomplished.

Insight Therapy

Talk therapy can take many different forms, including insight therapy, support therapy, and group therapy. In insight therapy, your child examines the past for "ah-ha" moments.

The underlying premise of insight therapy is that actions are the result of many conscious and unconscious factors, some of which may stem back to childhood experiences he has completely forgotten on a conscious level, but still reacts to on an emotional level. The goal of insight therapy is to uncover the motivating factors behind what your child does, and find ways to adjust them to result in better outcomes.

 **Essential**

Insight therapy isn't always a walk in the park. Oftentimes, delving into the past to try to figure out present behavior can uncover thoughts, emotions, and memories your child or teen may have suppressed because they were too painful to remember. A trained therapist can help your child deal with painful recollections, and find ways to learn and grown from them.

See Through Excuses

Children with ADHD often have highly creative minds that are adept at brainstorming ideas—not to mention coming up with excuses. Without a trained therapist to help your child cut through the maze, he might never figure out why he routinely "forgets" to do his homework.

Fortunately, an insight therapist is trained to listen closely and carefully to your child's real and fabricated problems and excuses, and help him untangle them so he can come up with a solution to the problem before it has a negative impact on his life.

It could be as easy as making sure all his homework materials are in one place so he can find them and get his homework done promptly, or putting visual cues on his computer to remind him when a project is due.

Your therapist might not always be able to help your child correct or eliminate the problem at hand, but he will probably be able to help your child arrive at a compromise that he can tolerate and live with.

Support Therapy

If an insight therapist serves as a detective to help your child uncover and understand unconscious motives, a support therapist acts more like your child's personal cheerleader. After years of living with the disappointment, rejection, and failure of ADHD, your child may feel like she needs someone to help her pick herself up and dust herself off.

Replacing Negatives with Positives

Many children with ADHD are also mired in negative, gloom-and-doom thinking, primarily because they've spent a large part of their lives internalizing years of criticism hurled their way because of their ADHD symptoms.

If your child is one of them, a support therapist can help your child replace negative thoughts, self-criticism, and low self-esteem with strategies that lead to more positive thinking.

 Alert

Support therapy requires time and patience on the part of your child and her therapist. Your child didn't become negative overnight, and she's not going to emerge from her therapist's office with a positive, radiant glow until she's learned how to stop her negative self-thought in its tracks, and replace it with self-affirming thoughts and feelings.

Time-Honored Strategies

Here are some tried-and-true strategies support therapists use to help children derail negative thoughts and self-image:

Encourage your child to catch herself in the act. The minute she starts thinking something negative about herself, tell her to imagine it's a monster dragging her down to the pits. Becoming more aware of her negative thoughts can help her gain the upper hand on them.

Encourage your child to stop playing that broken record in her head. When your child repeatedly tells herself "basic truths" she believes about herself, such as, "I'm too dumb to pass this test," or "I always screw things up on a date," the limiting self-talk can make her give up before she even tries. Your therapist can help your child practice saying affirmative things to herself that are probably a lot truer than those old, negative songs that have been on autoplay for years now.

Help your child get some perspective. Another problem with children with ADHD is their tendency to magnify their own shortcomings. Maybe your child always thinks she's to blame, no matter what the situation, or she emphasizes the negatives and eliminates the positive when it comes to her past and present accomplishments. As an objective party, your therapist can give your child the reality check she needs to readjust her attitudes about herself.

Encourage your child to learn to reframe. Just like a beautiful picture frame can enhance rather than obscure the beauty of a painting, putting a positive spin on things can turn a mistake into an opportunity for improvement. So your child forgot to turn in her homework? Instead of telling herself she's so stupid she can't remember simple things, teach her to state the obvious in a nonjudgmental way: "I forgot to turn in my homework." Then have her ask herself what she can do to remember to do it tomorrow.

Help your child get rid of the absolutes. If your child is constantly beating herself up for "always" being late, or "never" remembering important dates, have her focus on the many things in life she does right. Replaying that endless (inaccurate) record in her head that says she does "everything" wrong is the sort of negative reinforcement she needs to banish from her life.

Encourage your child to be nice to herself. As a child with ADHD, your child has already had her share of self-criticism and rejection. Have her work with her therapist to find ways to nurture her soul, whether it's listening to inspiring music, reading empowering books, taking a restorative walk through nature, or talking things over with a supportive friend.

Your child will need time and practice to improve her self-image, but once she gets the ball rolling, her positive self-talk may well become a self-fulfilling prophecy. As she gains self-confidence and self-respect, she'll make changes to improve the quality of her life, and feel better about herself in return. Your child will discover that success begets success.

Relationship Therapy

In relationship therapy, or therapy that focuses on friendships and relationships, your child learns how to manage ADHD symptoms that may be affecting his ability to make and keep meaningful relationships, act appropriately during casual dating, feel comfortable in social settings, and work well with people on the job.

Some children with ADHD, especially hyperactive children, manifest their symptoms by jumping into conversations and situations where they're not invited, constantly interrupting others, or behaving in a hostile, arrogant or aggressive fashion—all behaviors that tend to alienate people. Your child's therapist can teach your child effective ways to manage his impulses, such as counting to ten before speaking.

 Alert

Making and keeping friends can be very difficult for children with ADHD. Because of their long history of misunderstanding others, confusing communication cues, and being unable to read and translate nonverbal cues, they are likely to withdraw from social interaction and feel more comfortable alone than with others.

Friends and Children with ADHD

Research shows that children with ADHD get along best with friends who are low-maintenance, don't expect or need regular contact, and who are nonjudgmental. If your child has a friend with ADHD who has "drifted" away, ask your child to make sure he's not overestimating the friend's ability to maintain regular contact.

Because of their forgetfulness, children with ADHD may also forget about friends' needs, and fail to do the many little things required to keep a friendship going and growing. Your child's therapist can teach him the importance of calling friends on the phone, sending a friendly e-mail to check on them, remembering their birthdays, congratulating them, or consoling them for the death of a loved one.

Reining in Impulsive Promising

One problem shared by many children with ADHD is the tendency to make promises and commitments they can't keep, or which they forgot they even made. Unfortunately, the forgetfulness that makes your child's friends feel unloved or unappreciated can also make them wonder if your child is too selfish, self-centered, or narcissistic to care about anyone else's needs but his own.

Your child's therapist can work with your child on strategies that will help him check his impulses before making grandiose promises he can't keep. She can encourage your child to learn how to say "no" when someone's expectations are impossible for him to meet, and to compensate for his inherent tendency toward aloofness and solitude by making a conscious attempt to be more interested and engaged in the lives of others.

Group Counseling

In addition to the individual types of counseling discussed above, children with ADHD often find family or group counseling very helpful. In group counseling, several people with a common issue meet together with a therapist.

Interacting with others and hearing their problems can help reduce your child's feelings of isolation and give her the support and motivation to change troublesome ways of thinking, feeling, and acting.

Many children with ADHD feel awkward in social settings. Because of their impulsivity, they also have a tendency to interrupt others, or to butt into conversations. Group therapy can provide children with ADHD with a safe place to develop and practice appropriate social skills, and to get moral support and feedback in a safe and protected setting.

Family Therapy

In family therapy, the entire family works with a counselor to help family members understand the nature of childhood ADHD and why your child thinks, acts, and feels the way he does; overcome misunderstandings regarding the disorder; change the family's patterns of blame; and help the family make the adjustments needed for family harmony.

Living with a child with ADHD can translate into household chaos. Therapists can help families organize the household so the child with ADHD functions more effectively on a daily basis, and also by removing some burdens from the children who don't have ADHD so they feel more like siblings and less like parents.

Establishing a Family Calendar

Establishing a family calendar where everyone puts crucial dates, doctor appointments, social engagements, social events, birthdays, and anniversaries in one central location relieves the family members without ADHD from having to remember every detail of the family's comings and goings, a chore that can breed exhaustion, frustration, and resentment.

Visual and auditory cues, such as Post-it notes, lists, and alarms that are set as reminders, can also help keep things on track.

Importance of Routines

Your child's therapist can also help you and your child with ADHD create simple routines that help minimize household clutter and chaos. For instance, establishing a central location for house or car keys can help prevent them from getting scattered all over the house.

Essential

Creating orderly routines may also help rein in chaos. While people without ADHD find it easy to establish and automatically follow routines, there is no such thing as an automatic routine for many children with ADHD.

Divide and Conquer

Divide and conquer is another effective way to relieve the burden of household chores in families with a member who has ADHD. Your therapist will help you and your child divvy up the chores so your child with ADHD is responsible for creative tasks like cooking, gardening, and decorating, while your other children tackle chores that require more attention to detail and focus.

How to Find a Therapist

Many parents wonder how they can determine which type of therapy is best for their child. In general, psycho-education and talk therapy can help your child deal with feelings of low self-esteem, inadequacy, anxiety, depression, and feelings of underachievement; while behavior and skills training therapy are useful in helping your child develop new ways to deal with specific issues, rebuild organizational and planning skills, learn time-management skills, and learn more effective communication skills.

Working with a therapist you respect and trust, and who feels like a good match for your child, is usually more important than the type of therapy you choose. You and your child's willingness to be a regular participant in the therapeutic process is also essential to the success of any therapy your child undergoes.

To find a good therapist in your area, talk to members of your support group, or ask your family physician or ADHD practitioners for a referral. Or contact CHADD at *www.chadd.org* for information on therapists in your area.

The Importance of ADHD Support Groups

Many children with ADHD avoid social situations and, as a result, become isolated and out of touch. Support groups can provide kids with ADHD a safe place to develop and practice social skills in a supportive, nonjudgmental, and caring environment.

By sharing their stories with others, and learning that others share the same difficulties, kids with ADHD can help overcome the feelings of isolation that often make them feel like social outcasts, and build the supportive relationships they need to carry them through challenging times. Kids can also practice appropriate behavior.

Learning the Ground Rules

Your child will get the best support from his group if he knows the ground rules going in, and understands that being part of a support group entails listening as well as talking. It's also very important that your child understand the structure of his support group and how it functions. Some groups combine casual socializing with group sharing during the meeting, while others set aside opportunities to socialize and mingle before and/or after the official meeting.

 Essential

Your child should understand that an ADHD support group isn't an excuse to "let it all hang out," but an opportunity to share mutual problems and build on his social skills in a supportive setting. He should check that his impulsivity doesn't cause him to chatter away without thinking and self-censoring, or that his hyperactivity doesn't cause him to jump into conversations before he's invited.

Learning Proper Etiquette

When your child first joins a support group, encourage him to test the waters before taking the plunge. Suggest that he sit quietly and observe for the first few meetings before actively participating. Make sure he understands that sharing too much about himself may make him feel uncomfortable later, while sharing too little may make him seem indifferent or bored to others in the group.

Proper support group etiquette involves taking cues from others to find the right balance between talking and listening. A good rule of thumb for your child to follow is to listen more than he talks, and contribute only when he has something concrete and appropriate to say.

By joining a support group, your child has made an unwritten agreement to listen as well as talk, and to view the support group as a tool for helping himself as well as others gain insight and find solutions to ADHD-related challenges and problems.

CHAPTER 17

Weighing the Effects of Diet

While experts generally agree that bad eating habits do not cause childhood ADHD, and that eating the "right" diet can't eliminate core ADHD problems that are effectively managed by a combination of medication, psychotherapy, and behavior modification therapy, recent studies suggest that what your child eats may exacerbate or worsen existing ADHD symptoms, if not actually cause or trigger them. While it's still not known how specific foods affect symptoms, research suggests that nutrients responsible for brain health may help stabilize mood and alleviate depression, and that reducing sugar intake may decrease hyperactivity.

Pros, Cons, and Controversies

Diet is probably the most controversial issue today in terms of treating and managing childhood ADHD. Consistent research findings have not emerged on how and if specific foods and diets affect children with ADHD.

Two of the most controversial "ADHD diets" are supplementation diets in which your child takes vitamins, minerals, and other nutrients to compensate for deficiencies allegedly caused by the neurobiological and/or lifestyle symptoms of ADHD, and elimination diets in which you remove offending foods or ingredients allegedly contributing to your child's ADHD symptoms. Because neither diet has been sanctioned by the medical community at large, both are considered experimental in nature.

The Pro Side of Dietary Intervention

Brain researchers believe that what's good for the brain is also good for childhood ADHD. They claim that a high-protein, low-carbohydrate diet may help improve concentration and focus, and reduce the time it takes for ADHD medications to work. They advocate a diet high in beans, cheese, eggs, meat, and nuts, with a focus on protein-rich foods in the morning and in the afternoon to bolster concentration and increase the longevity of ADHD drugs.

In addition, they recommend reducing your child's intake of sugar and simple carbohydrates (which break down rapidly into sugar) to avoid sugar "highs" and "lows" that can lead to rapid mood swings, depression, and erratic behavior as well as hyperactivity, restlessness, and insomnia.

This means limiting your child's consumption of candy; honey; products made with corn syrup; snack foods; white flour products; white rice; fruits with high-sugar content like oranges, apples, and bananas; and starchy vegetables like potatoes and yams.

 Alert

Experts agree that consuming large amounts of caffeine is harmful to children with ADHD, although small amounts may promote alertness. Many children with ADHD suffer from insomnia and nervousness. Self-medicating with large quantities of coffee, tea, and other foods high in caffeine to ward off sleepiness or to enhance focus and attention may exacerbate insomnia, and aggravate existing hyperactivity and impulsivity.

Advocates of dietary intervention for childhood ADHD also recommend eating more omega-3 fatty acids, which are found in tuna, salmon, other cold-water white fish, walnuts, Brazil nuts, olive and canola oil, and in supplement form. Taking daily nutritional supplements to counteract deficiencies caused by ADHD is also advised.

The Con Side of Dietary Intervention

On the other side of the fence are those who believe that restricted and special diets have little or limited effect on children with ADHD. They claim when it comes to managing impulsivity, inattention, and other symptoms of ADHD, nothing substitutes for the "holy trinity" of medication, behavior therapy, and psychotherapy.

Sham Treatments

According to the National Institute of Mental Health, restricted diets, allergy treatments, and megavitamins have not been scientifically proven to be effective in treating the majority of children with ADHD.

Other ADHD treatments that lack scientific backing include medicines to correct problems in the inner ear, chiropractic adjustment, bone re-alignment, treatment for yeast infection, eye training, and special colored glasses.

Latest Finding on Nutrients that May Heal ADHD Brain Cells

Some research suggests that children with ADHD suffer from a neurobiological disorder involving a chemical imbalance of brain neurotransmitters. New research on the neuroplasticity of the brain suggests that children can actually grow new nerve brain cells throughout their lives and enhance existing brain cells by eating the right diet. This research also speculates that most children, but especially those with ADHD, lack a sufficient amount of essential fatty acids in the brains.

Because your child's body does not make essential fatty acids, she must consume a sufficient amount every day to nourish her brain. The best source of omega-3 fatty acids is cold water fish such as salmon, herring, tuna, cod, flounder, trout, and shrimp. Other sources of essential fatty acids (omega-3 and omega-6) include nuts, soybean, walnut oil, olive oil, and flaxseed oil.

 Fact

According to research at the University of Oxford in England, a daily fish oil capsule may help ease symptoms of ADHD without medication. That's because a lack of certain polyunsaturated fatty acids may contribute to dyslexia and ADHD. Children in the study who were given fish oil supplements for three months demonstrated significant improvements in behavior, reading, and spelling.

Amino Acids

In addition to omega-3 acids, amino acids may also help nourish brain cells. As the building blocks of protein in the body, amino acids are the fuel that feeds the brain cells and regulate the production of brain neurotransmitters and enzymes responsible for communication between brain cells, cognition, and the transition from thought to action.

Excellent sources of amino acids are complete proteins such as meat, fish, eggs, dairy products, soy, and yogurt. If your child doesn't eat meat, you can "make" a complete protein by combining brown rice with beans, seeds, or nuts.

Preliminary research shows that B vitamins, like amino acids, also help create neurotransmitters that act as chemical messengers in the brain and nervous system.

The Sugar Controversy

When it comes to ADHD, the biggest food war is the one concerning sugar. Although many parents believe that consuming excess sugar exacerbates their child's symptoms and causes fluctuating mood swings, the scientific evidence remains mixed.

Studies published in the *New England Journal of Medicine* saw no correlation between very excessive sugar consumption and adverse behavior, while research conducted at the University of North Carolina showed just the opposite—that the more sugar consumed by hyperactive people, the more destructive their behavior, and the more restless they became. Research conducted at Yale University also suggested that overconsumption of sugar could exacerbate symptoms of inattention.

Because the jury is still out on how sugar affects childhood ADHD, the best barometer may be how your child personally reacts to sugar. If excess sugar makes your child feel and act jumpy, hyper, and restless, it may be a sign that sugar affects him in an adverse way. On the other hand, if your child can eat lots of sugar without feeling hyper, he may be immune to its alleged evil effects.

 Alert

Just because sugar isn't identified as an ingredient in your food or drink doesn't mean the product you're consuming isn't loaded with it. Sugar by any other name includes corn sweetener, corn syrup, corn syrup solids, dehydrated cane juice, dextrin, dextrose, maltodextrin, malt syrup, maltose, molasses, rice syrup, saccharose, sorghum or sorghum syrup, and sucrose—so don't be fooled!

How to Tame Your Child's Sweet Tooth

If your child's ADHD symptoms are aggravated by sugar, reducing the amount he consumes doesn't mean he can never look at a Hershey's Kiss again. By making some simple substitutions and taking advantage of the new wave of sugar substitutes, you can help your child get the upper hand on his out-of-control sweet tooth and enjoy some sugar in moderation. Here are some easy tips to try:

- Switch to sugarless gum. There are many delicious brands from which to choose, and, if nothing else, your children won't subject their teeth to continual sugar-grinding.
- Instead of reaching for a chocolate bar, encourage your children to go for the nuts.
- Substitute veggie sticks and dips for sugary snacks like cookies and crackers. Or look for cookies and crackers made with little or no sugar.
- Instead of giving your children sugary fruit juices, switch to diet sodas or flavored waters. Or if your children are hungry for fruit, give them a whole piece of fruit instead.
- Avoid fluctuations in your child's blood sugar levels by pairing something sweet with protein. For instance, for a healthful snack, pair an apple or a pear with a chunk of Cheddar cheese.

Power of Protein

Studies show that children with ADHD also have imbalances in their brain's neurotransmitters, or the chemical messengers responsible for transmitting messages from one part of the brain to another. Neurotransmitters are responsible for regulating levels of alertness or sleepiness. Some, like dopamine and norepinephrine, are responsible for keeping your child awake, while others, like serotonin, have a calming effect that helps children fall asleep.

 Fact

Research indicates that protein helps regulate the neurotransmitters responsible for feeling alert. For this reason, eating meals that are high in protein can help your child stay energized and focused. In addition, eating a protein-rich breakfast can prevent your child's ADHD medication from being absorbed too quickly, which can make her feel hyper and grumpy.

Protein Buffering

Consuming enough protein isn't difficult—your child doesn't have to eat a pound of bacon and eggs for breakfast, or sit down to a gigantic porterhouse steak for dinner. The average child requires about 45 grams a day. An ounce of cheese provides seven grams of protein, so you can see that meeting your child's daily quota for protein isn't difficult.

Many children with ADHD get off to a bad start every morning by skipping breakfast, which is a crucial link in the daily protein chain. Instead of eating something healthy, they may grab a pop-up pastry, which provides zero grams of protein and lots of sugar and fat.

If you're too busy to make breakfast for your kids, consider jump-starting their day with a fruit-protein shake. You can buy protein shake mixes at the local health food store or Whole Foods–type groceries. Simply toss the mix into the blender with some fruit and ice, push "pulse," and you've got an instant protein shake your kids will think is a milkshake.

ADHD Dietary Guidelines

While it's debatable whether diet alone can treat childhood ADHD, many ADHD experts believe that most children with ADHD function best on a diet that is high in protein and low in carbohydrates and simple sugars. Studies of preschool children showed that children who didn't consume a sufficient amount of essential nutrients suffered reduced attention spans as well as intellectual abilities and thinking capacities.

Some Simple Suggestions

By following some general nutrition guidelines, you can feed your child's brain and body the nutrients she needs, and maybe even alleviate ADHD symptoms in the process. Here are some easy things to incorporate into your child's daily diet:

- Instead of serving three big meals a day, break it up into five or six mini-meals. This will keep your child's blood sugar levels on an even keel and prevent dramatic fluctuations that can lead to mood swings and irritability.
- Make sure your child avoids eating right before bedtime, especially if she has trouble falling asleep.
- Have your child enjoy a serving of protein at every meal, including breakfast. Good sources of protein include eggs, fish, meat, cheese, yogurt, and soybeans.
- Instead of sugary snacks like cookies, crackers, and chips, serve protein-rich snacks like cheese or low-fat yogurt.
- Make sure your child goes easy on empty-calorie snacks that are high in sugar and fat. This includes practically anything you'd buy in a vending machine, including candy bars, cookies, pies, snack cakes, chips, and crackers.
- Encourage your child to eat rather than drink her fruit. It's easy for your teen to drink a large glass of orange juice, which is high in sugar, but she'd have trouble consuming an equivalent amount of raw oranges, or four to five oranges.
- Citric acid can interfere with some kinds of ADHD medications, so ask your doctor about your child's medication. If citric acid is a problem, be sure she doesn't wash down her medication with a glass of orange juice or grapefruit juice. Tangerines and oranges are also high in citric acid.
- Don't feed your children lots of simple "white" carbohydrates. White bread and white rice break down quickly into simple sugars in the body and give your child the same effect as eating cookies and candy. Replace them with complex carbohydrates like whole grains, brown rice, and beans. Because they take much longer to break down in the body, they help regulate appetite and maintain steady energy levels.
- Don't skimp on healthy fats. Your child needs omega-3 essential acids and fish oils found in salmon and tuna to

maintain brain function, so make sure she eats three servings a week to keep brain cells well nourished.

- Avoid unhealthy saturated fats found in butter, margarine, and red meat, and focus on healthy amounts of polyunsaturated fats and monounsaturated fats found in fish, olive and canola oil, and nuts.
- Watch caffeine levels. Caffeine decreases blood flow to your child's brain and may increase ADHD symptoms in some kids and interfere with healthy sleep. Coffee isn't the only caffeine culprit. Tea and hot chocolate also have caffeine, as do many sodas and sports drinks. But some children and adolescents with ADHD do benefit from consuming modest amounts of caffeine, which helps keep them alert. If you're not sure how caffeine affects your child, consult your physician.
- Don't mix alcohol with ADHD medication. The combination can make teens with ADHD woozy, sleepy, and a hazard behind the wheel.

The Bottom Line

Whether you've decided to try a high-protein diet, adding supplements, or eliminating certain foods from your child's diet, you'll also get the best results if you start small and make one change at a time so you can better monitor the results.

It may also help to keep a food diary to record how dietary changes affect your child physically, mentally, and emotionally, and to note what effect they seem to have on your child's ADHD symptoms so you can discuss results with your physician.

Through trial and error, you can determine which foods, additives, preservatives, and supplements increase or diminish your child's ADHD symptoms, and develop a diet that keeps her healthy while avoiding existing problems.

Nutritional Deficiencies that May Aggravate ADHD

Some preliminary studies also suggest that deficiencies of certain nutrients, including vitamin B_6, zinc, and phosphatidyl, are associated with ADHD-like symptoms—and that, in these instances, correcting the deficiency might help curb symptoms.

- **Too little zinc.** Some research also suggests a connection between childhood ADHD and zinc deficiencies in children. One study found a link between zinc deficiency and children and adults who take stimulant medications like Ritalin.
- **Low levels of PS.** Clinical trials have shown that PS, a natural extract of lecithin, can improve cognition in children with ADHD suffering from memory loss, mood, cognitive performance and learning ability.
- **Low levels of B_6.** Studies also suggest that hyperactivity in children with ADHD may be caused by low levels of serotonin in the brain. Children who were given B_6 supplements showed a dramatic increase in serotonin levels. Pyridoxal phosphate, a B_6 member, is essential for the synthesis of the brain neurotransmitters serotonin, dopamine, and gamma-amino butyric acid (GABA).

Combining Diet and Medication

If your child is taking or about to start taking stimulant drugs, you might be wondering if there are certain foods he should avoid, if he is going to lose a lot of weight, or if you should time his meals or medication to ensure optimal effectiveness of stimulant drugs.

Foods that Interfere with Stimulant Drugs

To date, the only food your child should avoid if he's taking stimulant drugs is grapefruit juice, which interferes with the way the body absorbs and breaks down amphetamines. If your child takes his medication in the morning with breakfast and drinks grapefruit juice or eats a piece of grapefruit, he won't get the full benefit of the medication.

Stimulants and Weight Loss

While amphetamines increase metabolism and may cause a temporary loss of weight when your child first begins taking them, most children with ADHD who take stimulant drugs under a doctor's supervision do not lose a significant amount of weight.

 Question

Is it true that some people abuse ADHD drugs to lose weight?
One of the documented side effects of stimulant drugs is weight loss. Unfortunately, some overweight teens without ADHD abuse illegal stimulants to lose weight, including ADHD stimulant drugs. Sadly, some questionable weight-loss doctors have also been known to prescribe ADHD stimulants to overweight patients.

If your child is already underweight and you're concerned about him losing more weight by taking stimulants, ask your physician to prescribe a medication that has less of an effect on weight. In general, methylphenidates cause less weight loss than amphetamines. The weight picture is less clear for Strattera and Intuniv. Intuniv may actually cause weight gain in some children.

Taking excessive amounts of stimulants could result in dramatic weight loss in your child, as well as serious consequences like depression, anxiety, insomnia, and hair loss.

Timing Your Child's Meals

One easy way to ensure your child gets the most from his medications is to time his meals according to medication instructions. Long-acting stimulants, including Adderall XR, Focalin XR, and

Ritalin LA, are best taken on an empty stomach, as high-fat foods could interfere with their absorption and prolong the time they take to kick in. However, Concerta and Daytrana, which are two long-acting methylphenidate preparations, do not appear to have dietary-related absorption problems.

The Battle Over Food Sensitivities and Allergies

The relationship between childhood ADHD and allergic reactions to foods or substances in foods is another hotly contested arena among ADHD experts. Some experts, including the NIMH, claim there is simply no scientific evidence to indicate that an allergic reaction to foods, additives, or preservatives can cause or exacerbate ADHD symptoms. However, other research suggests that such things as artificial food colorings, preservatives, and additives may, in fact, aggravate hyperactivity, irritability, and insomnia in children with ADHD.

The Case for Elimination Diets

Elimination diets work on the premise that by identifying a particular food or ingredient you suspect is causing symptoms and refraining from eating that substance, you can enjoy relief from symptoms.

Elimination diets were brought to the forefront in 1975 by Benjamin Feingold, a well-respected San Francisco pediatrician and allergist at Kaiser Permanente Medical Center, who believed that food additives and preservatives were exacerbating ADHD symptoms in children. Although some parents of children with ADHD claim it helps alleviate symptoms, the diet has not been proven to be effective by scientific studies.

The Feingold Diet bans artificial food colors, flavorings, sweeteners, and preservatives, and salicylates, which are naturally occurring compounds found in some fruits and vegetables. But recent studies suggest that the Feingold Diet appears to reduce symptoms in just 5 percent of children with ADHD.

Exploring the Gluten-Free/Casein-Free Diet

Another treatment used for children with ADHD and autism, the GFCF (gluten-free/casein-free) diet revolves around the unproven theory idea that children with ADHD are sensitive to certain foods containing gluten and casein, and that removing these foods will help alleviate ADHD symptoms.

Advocates of the GFCF diet claim that because children with ADHD process peptides and proteins in foods containing gluten and casein differently than others, their brain treats these proteins like false opiate-type chemicals, causing a certain reaction. They claim that the GFCF diet reduces symptoms and improves social and cognitive behaviors and speech in children with ADHD.

While researchers have found abnormal levels of peptides in bodily fluids of some children with ADHD symptoms, the GFCF diet has not been scientifically proven to be effective for children with ADHD. In fact, because eliminating all gluten and casein from a child's diet could lead to severe nutritional deficiencies, doing randomized studies has proven difficult.

Additives and Preservatives

A number of food additives have been found to cause adverse reactions in many children, although it should be noted that evidence is anecdotal, not scientific. According to anecdotal findings, small quantities of monosodium glutamate (MSG) can cause dramatic behavior changes. Most people associate MSG with Chinese food, but this flavor enhancer is added to a range of foods during processing.

Some people also claim that aspartame, a popular artificial sweetener that is in everything from diet sodas to flavored yogurt, has been linked to brain tumors, movement disorders, and seizures. They allege that it apparently affects the neurotransmitters, especially dopamine, and can trigger depression in susceptible individuals. They also claim that some children are extremely sensitive to small doses and display dramatic behavior reactions. However, this is based on anecdotal findings and none of this is backed up by scientific research. If your child has an adverse reaction to aspartame, eliminate it from her diet. Otherwise, it should be safe for your child with ADHD to consume in limited amounts.

Children Who Use Food to Self-Medicate

Research does show, however, that children with ADHD may be more likely than other children to use food to decrease emotional, physical, and spiritual pain. Unfortunately, as with alcohol, drugs, and habits like gambling, the "fix" is usually very temporary, although the damaging physical and psychological side effects can take years to heal.

Most "binge" foods preferred by children with ADHD are packed with sugar and carbohydrates—and it's no surprise. PET scans showed that ADHD brains were slower to absorb glucose, and had a cerebral glucose metabolism that was eight times slower than other adults. Research indicates that children with ADHD could be binging on cookies, candy, chips, and ice cream in an attempt to alter their brain chemistry.

The Serotonin Connection

Serotonin helps regulate depression, sleep, sexual energy, mood, impulses, and appetite. Some studies show that children with ADHD have low levels of serotonin, which may contribute to their feelings of anxiousness, depression, and irritability.

Because foods high in sugar and carbohydrates temporarily raise serotonin levels and relieve those feelings, children with ADHD may binge on junk food to temporarily raise their serotonin level. Stimulant medications used to treat ADHD are far more effective at elevating serotonin levels than are sugar and carbohydrates.

Eating Disorders and ADHD

If your child has ADHD, he may also have an increased risk of developing eating disorders, including compulsive overeating, binging, bulimia, and anorexia.

Compulsive overeaters can't control how much they eat. Instead of using food to satisfy their hunger, they overeat foods high in sugar, carbohydrates, and salt to alter their feelings.

Binge eaters are compulsive eaters that not only overeat to feed their feelings, but binge because it gives their lives a sense of excitement and risk. Buying the food and figuring out where and when to quickly consume large amounts of food high in sugars and carbohydrates so others won't discover them becomes an all-consuming obsession, even though the binge itself may only last for fifteen minutes.

 Essential

Binge eating followed by purging is called bulimia. In addition to the stimulation, excitement, and rush provided by compulsive eating and binging, bulimics report feelings of release, calmness, and euphoria after vomiting. Unfortunately, this alleged cleansing is short-lived, and many bulimics repeat the process over and over again to get relief, only to quickly regain any weight they hoped to lose through purging.

Anorexia nervosa, or self-starvation, is also characterized by loss of control, in this case, the ability to think about food in a normal way, and to eat in a healthy way. Obsessed with thoughts of food, body image, and diet, anorexics can also use laxatives, diuretics, enemas, and compulsive exercise to maintain their distorted image of thinness. They may also abuse stimulant medications used to treat ADHD, which tend to suppress appetite and often result in weight loss. In fact, studies show that overweight girls and female teenagers who suffer from ADHD as well as eating disorders are at a higher than normal risk of abusing stimulant medications to lose weight.

ADHD Backlash

Unfortunately, many children discover that ADHD traits worsen after they stop self-medicating with food or organizing their lives around food and exercise, forcing them to find new ways of coping and dealing with anxiety and stress.

However, eating disorders can rob the ADHD brain of the nutrients it needs to function, and result in even higher levels of distraction, lack of focus, and spacey-ness. If your child has ADHD and eating disorders, make sure both conditions are diagnosed and treated.

Weight-Loss Tips for Overweight Children with ADHD

Many children with ADHD struggle with their weight for a variety of reasons. If your child is feeling depressed, left out, or sleepy, it can be difficult to muster up the energy or enthusiasm to exercise regularly. If your child binges on carbohydrates and sweets in an attempt to self-medicate and alleviate depression, she may also gain weight. Impulsivity associated with ADHD can also lead to overeating, or trigger eating disorders such as bulimia.

If your child is having trouble following or maintaining a regular exercise program, he may be making some classic "ADHD exercise mistakes." Here are some strategies to give your child to encourage him to exercise safely and effectively:

- **Keep exercise goals realistic.** Is he just starting out? He shouldn't expect to be able to run five miles a week from now. Encourage him to start small and work his way up to his goal. If your child only has the time, energy, and stamina to exercise for ten minutes a day, he should start there instead of trying to force himself into an unrealistic exercise regime he's likely to abandon.
- **Get an exercise buddy.** It's too easy or your child to shirk exercise sessions when the only one "watching" is him. By

teaming up with an exercise buddy or personal trainer, your child will have someone else to be accountable to and a pal to cheer him on and motivate him on those days he doesn't feel like working out.

- **Have him chart his progress.** Put an exercise calendar on the wall and check off the days your child worked out, with comments if desired. Having a visual record of his accomplishments will empower him and motivate him to stay on track. He can also periodically review his exercise chart to see if modifications are needed.

- **Have him reward himself periodically for achieving exercise goals.** You should use behavior modification strategies to give your child constructive and relevant rewards for sticking to his exercise schedule. Incorporating a rewards system can help your child stay on track on days he feels lethargic and unmotivated.

- **Decide on easy-to-earn rewards, then raise the bar as your child improves.** Rewards are more effective if they are immediate and if they are not so difficult to get that they are rare. Keep a written record of your child's changes so he can see the progression, which can further motivate him to stay on track. Once he reaches a goal, he can reward himself with a small luxury. Remember that reaching goals is meant to be an incremental and enjoyable process, so keep the goals easy and realistic.

- **Keep the workout schedule flexible and creative.** If, like many kids with ADHD, your child hates all-or-nothing structures that box him in and give him no way out, have him schedule several possible workout slots every day.

- **Don't let him make excuses.** Don't let your child's creativity let him come up with reasonable-sounding excuses that let him off the hook. Instead of dreaming up excuses, he should use his creativity to envision how great he'll look and feel if he sticks to his exercise program.

CHAPTER 18

Exploring Alternative and Experimental Treatments

Some parents turn to experimental or alternative treatments when their children fail to respond to standard treatment or have adverse reactions. Some of these treatments claim to stimulate and balance the nervous system while others promise to change the way your child processes visual or auditory information. Because experimental and alternative treatments such as homeopathy and herbal medicine are not approved by the National Institutes of Health or the National Institute of Mental Health for treating childhood ADHD, discuss them with your physician before incorporating them into your child's treatment program.

The Controversy Continues

Whether or not alternative treatments without the NIH stamp of approval can be deemed effective is still a matter of debate. Some ADHD experts argue that without large-scale controlled studies, it's difficult to determine the effectiveness or safety of any given treatment for the general public, much less for children with ADHD who have a galaxy of interconnected physical, emotional, and mental issues.

Others claim that experimental treatments may be worth pursuing in the event conventional treatments fail, if only because they seem to have worked for so many others throughout the years, or, in some cases, throughout the ages.

Fact

Many so-called experimental treatments were created by respected ADHD experts who lacked the considerable finances required to conduct large-scale controlled studies, and thus remain experimental treatments. Other alternative treatments are based on age-old theories and principles that have been around since Hippocrates.

Taking a Guarded Approach

As a parent, you want to be careful about where you place your hope and your money when it comes to treatment for your child. Most people do not have the background or the information to know whether medical and psychological treatments are likely to be effective.

Many claims for treatment are made by many intensely sincere proponents. The best approach is to start with therapy that well-conducted scientific research has already shown to be likely to benefit childhood ADHD. In psychology and medicine, there is a sense that every therapy seems to work for someone. Every approach has its very opinionated proponents, especially on the Internet.

However, claims by practitioners and even patient's dramatic personal stories are not sufficient evidence for efficacy. This is a very important point. There are always practitioners and patients who claim that their experience with a certain approach proves that it is effective. They are usually sincere, but sincerity is not enough.

Pros and Cons

Unlike ADHD medication, which may have adverse effects, many alternative and experimental treatments do not have adverse side effects if used correctly. Your child may even enjoy certain benefits she doesn't get from medication.

Fact

Even if so-called alternative treatments for childhood ADHD such as exercise, nutrition, and acupuncture don't directly or indirectly improve your child's ADHD symptoms, many experts believe you have nothing to lose by having your child incorporate them into her life, and perhaps a lot to gain in terms of improving your child's physical, emotional, and mental health.

Likewise, alternative therapies like yoga, tai chi, and medication may help relieve restlessness and hyperactivity caused by childhood ADHD. Studies or no studies, millions of people around the world can attest to the fact that slowing their breathing and staying in the "now" via yoga has helped them more than anything else they've ever tried to feel calmer, clearer, saner, more empowered, more confident, and far more centered.

Cons of Experimental Treatments

A lack of substantial scientific validation isn't the only downside to experimental and alternative treatments. Because many experimental and alternative treatments are not medical treatments, they are not held to the same rigorous testing and regulation standards as medications and psychotherapy. Other potential problems with experimental treatments include:

- Practitioners may also not be required to receive specialized education, licenses, or degrees, and are often not regulated by governing bodies.
- Some experimental treatments are very time-consuming and/or expensive, and may not be covered by insurance plans.
- You may not be able to locate an experimental or alternative physician for your child unless you live in a major metropolitan area.

Herbal Medication

Herbal medicine consists of using plant-based ingredients in high doses to alleviate the symptoms of ADHD. Many people assume that because herbs are natural, they must be safe, but this is not always the case.

Dangers of Herbal Medication

Herbs, like drugs, have the ability to change the chemistry of the body. But herbs are not regulated by the FDA as are pharmaceuticals, which means their potency and ingredients are also not regulated.

Another problem with herbal medications is that they interact with some medications in adverse or even dangerous ways. Because many serious and lethal side effects have been reported in connection with herbal medications, it's important to ask your doctor before giving them to your child.

 **Question**

Why aren't herbal treatments approved for ADHD by the FDA?
Because ingredients vary widely in herbal preparations, these preparations are not regulated by the FDA, and there's always some risk your child may have an adverse reaction. Also, herbs vary in terms of strength and purity. Because there are no regulations for dosage, you never know much is in any product.

Finally, very little research has been conducted on how herbal remedies and homeopathy affect childhood ADHD symptoms. Experts on both sides of the fence agree that more studies are needed to determine their effectiveness and adverse side effects on children with the disorder.

While a growing number of medical doctors are being educated in alternative therapies, and hospitals are opening centers for complementary and integrative medicine at a rapid rate, unless you live in or near a major city, you may find it difficult to find a physician or licensed professional familiar with herbal treatments for childhood ADHD.

Talk with your physician first before starting any herbal remedies for your child. If your child is getting blood tests done, be sure to let your practitioner know ahead of time, as some herbs can skew the results of blood tests.

Caffeine and Childhood ADHD

Caffeine, as found in coffee and other herbal stimulants, is also used as an alternative to stimulant drugs in the treatment of childhood ADHD. Some studies show that caffeine has demonstrated significant benefits in children with ADHD. In other studies, however, caffeine failed to show significant benefits when compared to conventional stimulant drugs.

Some researchers believe that one reason some children with ADHD go into remission when they enter adulthood is because once they start drinking coffee as young adults, they discover it alleviates their ADHD symptoms and start using it to self-medicate. Eliminating caffeine from the diets of children in ADHD remission could possibly unmask their ADHD symptoms, researchers theorize.

Eye on Homeopathy

Homeopathy was founded 200 years ago on the principle that "like cures like," and is still widely practiced today in Europe, India, and South America. The underlying principle behind homeopathy is that a diluted form of a drug will stimulate the body to eliminate symptoms that would be caused if the same drug were administered in its undiluted form.

The Premise Behind Homeopathy

Unlike other types of medication or treatment that treat a single symptom, homeopathy treats your entire body. There are more than 3,000 different homeopathic medicines, and it's up to your homeopath to choose the one that best matches your child's symptoms. Before determining what type of treatment will alleviate your child's symptoms, your homeopathy provider will conduct an extensive interview to find out about his symptoms, lifestyle, and personal and medical history.

Weighing the Benefits

Although some people claim homeopathy helps alleviate symptoms in their children, so far there isn't any scientific research to prove it benefits childhood ADHD. Because homeopathy may also be costly and time-consuming, and administered by practitioners without medical training, it cannot be recommended as a viable treatment for childhood ADHD.

Anti-Yeast Regimens

According to the National Institute of Mental Health, methods to control or destroy fungi, such as certain diet restrictions, removal of fungi in the environment, and medicines to kill fungi (antifungals) do not improve the symptoms of ADHD and should not be considered valid treatments.

While yeast imbalances may share some symptoms with childhood ADHD, there is no research to indicate that yeast imbalances cause or exacerbate ADHD—although your teen may certainly feel worse if she has a yeast imbalance as well as ADHD.

Manipulation Therapies

Manipulation therapies have been around since the time of the ancient Greeks, who used spinal manipulation to adjust dysfunctions in the nervous system. However, only in recent times have manipulation therapies been addressed in terms of their ability to relieve childhood ADHD symptoms.

There are many types of manipulation therapies. Three of the most common ones used today to treat childhood ADHD are chiropractic, osteopathy, and craniosacral therapy. All three purport to improve symptoms by improving the flow of cerebrospinal fluid in the nervous system, and by realigning the spine.

Although manipulation therapies have not been approved by the National Institute of Mental Health as valid treatments for ADHD, some experts believe they are helpful in reducing symptoms caused by neurological dysfunction and imbalance.

Chiropractic Therapy

Chiropractic therapy focuses on realigning bones, although some chiropractors may also be knowledgeable about nutrition and preventive medicine. Chiropractic was invented about 5,000 years ago by the Greeks, who believed that manipulating the spine yielded dramatic health benefits.

While chiropractic therapy is more commonly associated today with sports medicine and back pain than ADHD, a branch of chiropractics called chiropractic neurologists are now working with children and adults with ADHD.

Craniosacral Therapy

Craniosacral therapy was developed by an osteopathic physician in the mid-1990s. During craniosacral therapy, a therapist applies gentle pressure on the scalp to enhance the functioning of the craniosacral system, which is comprised of membranes and fluids that protect the brain and spinal cord.

Although chiropractors generally charge less than physicians, many insurance plans don't cover their services, so the cost may be significant if your treatment entails multiple visits over a period of time. Craniosacral therapy may also be difficult to find unless you live in a major city, and there is no scientific proof it works.

Osteopathy

Founded in the late 1800s on some of the basic tenets of chiropractic therapy, osteopathy is a branch of medical science that focuses on the concept of wellness and preventive medicine.

Osteopaths are similar to medical doctors in that they go to medical school and are trained physicians who can prescribe medication. However, unlike chiropractors (who don't go to medical school and can't prescribe medication), osteopaths also study what impact your skeletal system has on overall health, and are trained in osteopathic manipulative treatment.

Applied Kinesiology

Developed by a chiropractor, this alternative medicine diagnostic tool and treatment revolves around the unproven premise that you can use strength resistance to test the alleged link between muscles, glands, and organs.

Therapists allegedly correct muscular imbalances and problems in associated glands and organs by applying manual pressure to muscles. The therapy is used to "treat" structural imbalances, problems with the muscles and joints, and ADHD.

Applied Kinesiology also purportedly detects food allergies and sensitivities in children with ADHD by tracing them to alleged reversible muscle weakness. There are no controlled studies showing that applied kinesiology works. As with most alternative treatments discussed in this chapter, the "proof" is based on anecdotal evidence.

Sensory Integration

Sensory integration is the relationship between behavior and brain functioning. It refers to the zillions of bits of sensory information that the brain receives at every moment from the five senses (touch, taste, smell, hearing, and vision) and how your brain organizes and integrates these sensations so you can move about and learn normally.

Although many children with ADHD have coexisting problems with sensory integration, it isn't a symptom of ADHD per se, but a separate disorder that is diagnosed, evaluated, and treated separately.

 Essential

Symptoms that may indicate your child has problems with sensory integration include hypersensitivity to touch, sights, sounds, or movement; being overly klutzy, clumsy, or uncoordinated; difficulty with motor skills; being unusually active or inactive; demonstrating behavior or learning problems; and having trouble with mind-eye coordination.

If your child has just been diagnosed with ADHD, your physician may want to rule out the existence of sensory integration dysfunction by administering standardized tests that evaluate his balance, coordination, and posture; how he responds to stimuli; and other things.

If your therapist determines your child has coexisting sensory integration dysfunction, there are several different types of exercises and stimulation techniques that can help your child improve his ability to process the sensory information that gets scrambled up in your brain. Two techniques commonly used with children who have ADHD are auditory and vision integration training.

AIT Therapy

There are several types of auditory integration therapies. Two popular therapies include the Tomatis Method, which was developed in the 1950s by a French ear, nose, and throat physician, and auditory integration training (AIT), which was developed in the early 1990s by another French physician and based on the Tomatis

Method. The basic theory behind both therapies is that an inability to hear specific frequencies results in an inability to process certain sounds. This leads to problems in communication that can trigger behavior problems.

Both types of auditory training require getting hearing tests called audiograms to determine how well the patient hears at various frequencies, followed by twenty sessions over ten days for AIT, and up to seventy-five sessions for the Tomatis Method.

Because the testing and therapies may not be covered by insurance, these treatments can be far more expensive and time-consuming than standard childhood ADHD therapy.

 Alert

A word of warning: Although AIT and the Tomatis Method don't have negative side effects other than the substantial time and cost involved, one significant downside is that once your child undergoes these therapies, he must agree to never again wear headsets when listening to music—so tell your child to be prepared to part with his earbuds.

Today, AIT is far more popular than the Tomatis Method, and has also undergone more research studies. While auditory integration therapy does not have the National Institute of Mental Health stamp of approval as a treatment for childhood ADHD, some experts believe it is very beneficial to children who have hypersensitivity issues as well as ADHD.

REI Therapy

REI therapy, or rhythmic entrainment intervention, was founded in the early 1990s. This type of auditory therapy uses auditory rhythm to stimulate the nervous system, and is based on the premise that certain types of sound can influence brain wave activity.

During REI therapy, your child is directed into a more desired state of consciousness by listening to customized tapes based on his particular symptoms. Because the therapy can be done at home, it isn't as expensive or time-consuming as other auditory integration therapies.

REI experts claim that benefits may begin as early as a few weeks after beginning treatment. They include an increased attention span, a better ability to regulate mood, an increase in language and social abilities, and a reduction in impulsivity, distraction, hyperactivity, and restlessness.

Visual Therapy

Many children with learning disabilities have problems with visual integration. Some experts believe that problems with visual stimuli may exacerbate ADHD symptoms like inattention and distraction.

Although visual integration, like auditory integration, is not considered standard therapy for ADHD, because anything that stimulates vision is also going to stimulate the brain some experts think it may help alleviate specific symptoms.

 Fact

Recent studies showed that children with ADHD are three times more likely to suffer from convergence insufficiency, a condition in which both eyes can't focus on the same things, as people who don't have ADHD. Convergence insufficiency is one of several problems with visual stimuli that are addressed by vision integration therapies.

Like auditory therapy, visual therapy uses stimulation techniques, computer games, vision exercises, and specially colored lenses that reduce eye strain or correct vision imbalances, to "retrain" your child's brain to process visual stimuli in a normal way.

Symptoms of visual integration dysfunction include being unable to follow words along on a page as your child reads, stay focused on something he's looking at in the foreground, and focus both eyes on the same thing at once. Children with this disorder also suffer from a condition called scotopic sensitivity syndrome, in which words or objects seem to jump around on the page, and their eyes tire more easily than normal.

Holistic Treatments

Many parents of children with ADHD are complementing their child's standard therapy with acupuncture and other types of Eastern medicine. Proponents of acupuncture claim it can be a calming influence on children with ADHD and can help alleviate some of the unpleasant side effects of ADHD medications, facilitate healing, reduce pain, strengthen the immune system, and foster health in many other ways.

Acupuncture

A type of traditional Chinese medicine, acupuncture has been used for centuries to calm myriad conditions and diseases. During the procedure, your therapist will gently place extremely fine needles at strategic points in your child's body called "acupuncture points."

The goal of acupuncture treatment is to rebalance your "qi," or the essential energy that flows through the body and every living thing, and is responsible for life. The underlying premise of acupuncture is that illness and pain occur when the qi is out of balance. Placing needles into acupuncture points that correspond to the location of the imbalance restores the balance of the qi so it can flow freely through the problem area and eliminate symptoms.

Most children with ADHD find acupuncture to be a relaxing and completely painless experience. The only sensation of pain your child is likely to feel is a small twinge, or a feeling like a bug bite, if a needle is placed in an area with a high concentration of qi. The pain goes away as the flow of qi is restored. Side effects are usually minimal and may range from bruising, a slight swelling, or soreness, around needle sites, to a feeling of relaxation and sedation.

Acupuncture Pros and Cons

Relatively few complications from acupuncture have been reported to the FDA, which regulates acupuncture needles and requires that they be sterile, nontoxic, and labeled for single use by qualified practitioners only. However, when not delivered properly, acupuncture can cause serious adverse effects, including infections and punctured organs.

While individual acupuncture sessions are usually affordable and may be covered by some insurance policies, since most children require several sessions, acupuncture can be expensive if not covered by your insurance plan.

Acupressure

In acupressure, your child's therapist uses firm pressure with her fingers to press on the same acupressure points that are targeted in acupuncture. The therapy is believed to have the same benefits as acupuncture. Because no needles are used, your child may prefer it over acupuncture.

CHAPTER 19

Is There a Connection Between ADHD and Environmental Toxins?

While controlled studies have not proven that childhood ADHD is caused by exposure to household chemicals and cleaners, environmental pollution, springtime allergens, or heavy metals, preliminary studies suggest that early exposure to lead and other heavy metals in infancy and childhood may contribute to ADHD-like symptoms, such as impaired cognition, hyperactivity—even disciplinary problems and trouble with the law. The good news is that toxic levels of lead have dramatically declined in the United States now that lead has been removed from paint, fuel for motor vehicles, and many other materials.

Controversy Surrounding Environmental Toxins and ADHD

Research is ongoing concerning the association between lead and other environmental toxins and impaired learning, hyperactivity, and other symptoms associated with ADHD. Here are a few leading studies exploring the connection between lead and impaired learning, hyperactivity, and discipline problems—all symptoms that are prevalent in childhood ADHD. Note that none of these studies claim lead or other environmental toxins actually cause or trigger the onset of childhood ADHD.

Connection Between Lead Levels and Cognitive Skills

Research conducted at Children's Hospital Medical Center of Cincinnati showed that blood levels of lead that were below the level currently defined as toxic were associated with poor cognitive skills in children. The team looked at data for nearly 5,000 children between the ages of six and sixteen and found that as blood lead levels get higher, cognitive levels fall. Researchers believe that higher levels of lead may also cause behavior problems in children. While poor cognitive skills are a hallmark symptom of ADHD, this study did not link blood levels of lead to childhood ADHD.

Connection Between Lead and Juvenile Delinquency

Studies conducted at the University of Pittsburgh showed a strong correlation between juvenile delinquency and higher lead levels. Youths arrested in a local juvenile court had bone lead levels that were nearly seven times higher than other teens their age.

While a disproportionately high percentage of children with ADHD get into trouble with the law, this study did not link high lead levels with ADHD.

Connection Between Lead and Impaired Brain Development

Animal studies conducted at Johns Hopkins University showed that low levels of heavy metals may stunt brain development in children by interfering with the development of the brain's neocortex and causing structural changes in the brain. The low levels of lead used in the study were the same as exposure levels suffered by many poor inner city children. While many children with ADHD have impaired brain development, this study did not link heavy metals with ADHD.

Lead and Hyperactivity

Research conducted at the University of Pittsburgh Medical School concluded that hyperactivity may be caused by toxic accumulations of heavy metals in the body, including lead. "Because their bodies are smaller, and because their nervous systems are still in early stages of development, children are particularly vulnerable to the effects of element imbalances," the researchers concluded. "Lead is a potent toxin very commonly associated with a host of neurobehavior problems in children, including hyperactivity, attention deficit, and other learning disorders." Follow-up studies indicate that these effects often last into adulthood.

 Fact

According to the American Academy of Child and Adolescent Psychiatry, about one of every six children in the United States has blood lead levels in the toxic range. Researchers now believe that the level of lead necessary to cause central nervous system effects is far lower than previously estimated.

Lead Poisoning from Paint

Lead paint was used in most homes and apartments built prior to 1978. Covering it with several layers of nonleaded paint is no guarantee of safety. Family members inhale it when breathing the dust that is in the air and crawling babies ingest minute flakes while sucking on their hands and toys.

Antique toys and furniture painted with lead paint are other sources of poisoning. The lead content of paint manufactured before 1960 is especially toxic, with concentrations as high as 50 percent.

Toddlers standing by rocking chairs, at windows, or in cribs ingest lead as they mouth wooden arms, sills, and railings. Even if a youngster's home is free of lead, his daycare center, and the homes of babysitters, relatives, and friends, may be contaminated.

Lead Poisoning from Food

Some 13 to 22 percent of the lead children absorb from food comes from canned goods. U.S. canners agreed to stop using lead solder to seal food cans in 1995. Nevertheless, the Food and Drug Administration estimates that 10 percent of the canned goods coming in from other countries are sealed with lead solder.

Avoiding Risks

The Center for Disease Control recommends that after opening a can containing lead solder, the food should be removed and placed in a different container and should never be stored in the can. It would seem that a safer solution is not to buy food packaged in cans sealed with lead.

Leaded crystal contains lead, so food should not be stored in it. Glazed pottery and ceramic ware may contain lead. The glaze eventually cracks and the lead can seep into food. If there appears to be a dusty or chalky gray residue on the glaze after washing, do not use the pottery for food.

Pottery manufactured in the United States with lead glaze must bear a label that says "Not for Food Use," but small crafters working from home do not always provide consumer warnings.

Lead from Imported Herbal Products

Beware of imported herbal products that come from countries where lead is an even more serious problem than in the United States. A popular Mexican remedy that is used to treat children for symptoms resembling colic is 90 percent lead. It is known by various names: Azarcon, Luisa, Liga, Greta, Coral, and Rueda. Similarly, a popular fever remedy from Indochina called Pay-loo-ah has been found to contain up to 90 percent lead.

The Case for Contaminated Water, Air, and Soil

Scientists have known since 1925, when some products containing lead were briefly banned, that lead from pipes was leaching into the water of homes and businesses across the country. Further installations of lead pipes were banned, but that did not have an impact on existing pipes, most of which are still in place.

Additionally, plumbers continued to use lead solder in other types of water pipes until the 1980s. Lead faucets and fittings were not outlawed until 1998, so only the newest homes and ice makers are certain to have lead-free pipes.

Dangers of Potable Water

Water faucets do not have to meet modern lead standards unless they lead to a fixture specifically designed to dispense drinking water. Otherwise, it is legal for them to contain 8 percent lead. Children must be taught never to drink the water from the bath, shower, garden hose, utility sink, and laundry tub.

Water that has been sitting in water heaters contains the highest concentration of lead, so the EPA says not to drink water from the hot water tap. Turn on the cold water tap and let the water run until the temperature changes before drinking it. That way, water that was sitting in leaded pipes or solder is cleared away.

Dangers of Municipal Water

However, letting the water run for a while will not help if the entire municipal water supply is contaminated, which is often the case. This is an especially big problem on the East Coast, where some water systems have been in place since the Civil War.

Well water in rural areas is not necessarily safe to drink, either. Depending on the type of fertilizer that has been used in nearby fields and pastures, run-off that ends up in wells can contain heavy concentrations of lead and aluminum.

Ensuring Water Safety

To learn about the quality of your local water supply, contact your water department and request a copy of its annual report. The report will list the EPA standards and indicate whether they are being met. Your local department or the EPA's Safe Drinking Water Hotline (800-426-4791) can provide information about testing and safety.

Water filters that remove lead and other heavy metals can be purchased from any department store. Be sure to get one that meets ANSI/NSF standards for health effects.

Some filters are designed to improve "aesthetics," which means taste and odor are improved but harmful chemicals are not removed. The filters must be changed regularly to be effective, so follow the instructions carefully.

Lead Poisoning from Contaminated Air and Soil

Lead from automobile emissions ends up in the air and settles in the soil, so children living near congested traffic and heavily traveled roads run an especially high risk of lead poisoning.

Playing in areas where leaded gasoline, leaded paint, or ceramics were once manufactured, sold, or used in quantity is very dangerous. Long after the gas station has been demolished or the building containing lead has been razed, heavy lead concentrations remain.

Also, dust blowing in from contaminated areas causes youngsters living at a distance to be poisoned. The bottom line is that soil in densely populated urban areas and the air near high traffic areas are major offenders.

Symptoms of Lead Poisoning

Because the liver and kidneys are especially affected, common physical problems include mild anemia, loss of appetite, constipation, and diarrhea. Visual and motor disturbances affect children's fine and gross motor skills.

According to experts, intellectual problems from lead poisoning range from learning difficulties and reduced scores on IQ tests to serious developmental delays and severe mental retardation. In mild cases, the results are clumsiness, poor handwriting, and various learning difficulties; tremor, paralysis, and seizures result from more serious poisoning.

Effects of Prenatal Exposure

Damage from prenatal exposure to lead does not seem to be reversible. The severity of the symptoms from postnatal exposure and the extent to which they can be reversed depends on how much lead was absorbed and the duration of the exposure. Ingesting large quantities can cause permanent brain damage and can be fatal.

Some experts believe that even a slightly elevated level of lead in the body may produce ADHD-like symptoms ranging from mild to severe. Because brain development is so rapid before birth and during the baby years, the effects of lead on unborn children, infants, toddlers, and preschoolers may be especially great as their livers are less efficient at ridding the body of toxins, causing stronger reactions to very low levels of lead.

Behavior Problems that May Result from Lead Poisoning

Some experts also believe that lead poisoning can cause attention deficits, distractibility, hyperactivity, restlessness, aggression, hostility, violence, anti-social behavior, anxiety, irritability, and lethargy.

Acute cases of lead poisoning do occur, but chronic, low-level exposure to lead is by far the most common. Symptoms usually disappear once lead has been cleared from a child's system. Some experts claim that IQ test scores then increase an average of nine points, although this has not been proven by controlled studies.

The Need for Testing

Every child with ADHD symptoms should be tested for lead poisoning. Some of the inexpensive do-it-yourself lead poisoning test kits may not register the low levels of lead that the government has now determined are harmful.

Your child may be eligible for free testing through your local Child Health and Disability Program (CHDP). To find out, contact your local public health department. Phone the National Lead Information Center at (800) 424-LEAD for information about how to have your home tested.

How to Treat Lead Poisoning

The good news is that ADHD-like symptoms often disappear once lead is out of a youngster's system. The alleged treatment for lead poisoning is chelation therapy, which involves speeding the excretion of the lead through urination.

However, chelation therapy is controversial for children with problems stemming from chronic, low-level lead exposure. The medications that are used can be dangerous, and chelation therapy can actually increase lead absorption. Previously chelation was only used for extremely severe cases of lead poisoning since blood lead levels fall quickly once the environment is cleaned up.

Many traditional physicians remain leery of chelation and claim that cleaning up the child's environment and letting time work its wonders is usually the best solution, unless the situation is very serious.

Do Heavy Metals Cause ADHD?

Some experts believe that other heavy metals may cause ADHD symptoms. Artists are familiar with paint colors "cadmium blue" and "cadmium red" (often called "cad blue" and "cad red" for short). They may not realize that cadmium is a highly toxic heavy metal. Young artists should handle these paints carefully and avoid getting them in their mouths.

Eyeing Heavy Metals

Certain heavy metals are essential for the human body to function properly, but in excess they cause problems with brain functioning. Heavy metals can disrupt thyroid gland functioning, which helps to regulate activity level.

Copper is a brain stimulant and can cause racing thoughts and thinking disturbances. Copper also destroys histamine; low-histamine children are hyperactive. An excess of aluminum has been implicated in learning disabilities and behavior problems.

New Research on Mercury Fillings

Although mercury in fillings was once believed to be so dangerous that people were advised to get older fillings removed, a new study indicates that older mercury fillings are less toxic than formerly believed. The study showed that the chemical forms of mercury in fillings changed over time. While new fillings contained metallic mercury that could be toxic, older filling usually contain a type of mercury that was not likely to be toxic to the body.

Dangers at Home

Medical experts agree that it is highly unlikely your child would ever be exposed to enough lead in such household items as utensils, cups, bowls, or bathtubs to suffer ADHD-like symptoms. Children who are most at risk for lead exposure are those who live in older buildings in inner cities where lead paint remains on the walls.

That said, if your child suffers from unexplained mild anemia, stomachaches, constipation, forgetfulness, attention problems, aggressiveness, and mood swings, you may want to double check him for lead poisoning, although it's more likely he has a cold or the flu. While it is highly unlikely that lead poisoning is the culprit, it's better to be safe than sorry.

CHAPTER 20

Finding the Silver Lining

The three major symptoms of childhood ADHD—hyperactivity, impulsivity, and inattention—create many challenges for children who suffer from the disorder. These include problems performing at school, difficulty making and keeping relationships, and an inability to function comfortably or appropriately in social settings. But these symptoms may also have a silver lining. Hyperactivity can give your child the energy she needs to work longer and harder, impulsivity can provide the courage and drive your child needs to take great leaps of faith, and inattention can make it easier for your child to move between projects.

Counting Your Blessings

As discussed in previous chapters, childhood ADHD doesn't have to be a curse for life. Many famous inventors, scientists, writers, movie stars, filmmakers, artists, musicians, rocket scientists, and politicians and others have used their unique ADHD strengths to carve out a permanent place in history.

In fact, as researchers discover more and more about the disorder, they are redefining what it means to be a child with ADHD as not just a group of negative attributes, but a group of positive traits as well.

Scientists believe that one reason children with ADHD may excel at creative tasks is that their brains are wired in a way that limits inhibition. Children with ADHD may find it easier to follow the beat of their own drummer than children without ADHD, who feel compelled to conform to societal norms.

The Hidden Gifts of ADHD

Motor-driven and built to invent, create, think outside the box, find similarities between disparate things, and to hyperfocus, the child with ADHD is wired for peak performance and success in the complicated and ever-changing twenty-first century.

When it comes to excelling at school or later in his career, match a child with ADHD with something that interests him and you'll likely wind up with a child that happily devotes hours to schoolwork without running out of steam or focus.

True, a child with ADHD may have problems focusing on things that are mundane and boring, such as where he put his pencils. But because his thinking process is different from that of other children, he has the sort of creative mindset that leads to great works of art, science, invention, a surplus of ideas, great enthusiasm and excitement, prolonged interest, and an ability to see the big picture, or see things in a holistic way.

Right-Brain Masters

Children with ADHD also have the skills and right-brain power required to succeed in the twenty-first century. Because they thrive on visual imagery and stimulation, they are naturally attracted to computers, which are accelerating the rate at which new information and knowledge can be disseminated and interrelated.

Because they tend to be less inhibited in their thinking, and more easily distracted by linear or logical thought, many children with ADHD are able to see connections and associations between seemingly disparate things, which accounts for their ability to think outside the box, come up with new solutions to old problems, and piece together unrelated ideas or concepts and create entirely new genres of art, music, writing, mathematics, etc.

 Fact

> While chronic disorganization and clutter are problems that are shared by most children with ADHD, many of them are highly adept at functioning in chaotic environments. In fact, they may actually require chaos to create, invent, or function at their peak.

Natural Entrepreneurs

Because children with ADHD are usually very eager to try something new, are highly intuitive and imaginative and get the gist of things very quickly, they also grow up to make excellent entrepreneurs.

Studies show that children with ADHD turn into adults who are most effective and productive when they are their own bosses, or when they are allowed to work independently, at their own pace, and on their own time clock. Mavericks by nature, children and adults with ADHD may not always be good followers, but they often excel as leaders.

If your child's school or teachers are stifling her creativity and motivation, consider looking for one that is flexible and open to dialogue, where your child will have some freedom to arrange her environment, schedule, and study habits.

Tapping into Special Talents

The brain chemistry of children with ADHD differs from "normal" brains in its relationship to dopamine. As a result, children with ADHD crave stimulation just to feel alive.

Because of this craving, they are also more likely to seek thrills, take risks, discover new ways of doing things, act and think more boldly, stand out from the pack, and have a higher degree of personal charisma because they are bold, brave, and adventurous.

Your child may already have the raw material it takes to gain great fame and wealth. But why does the ADHD gene help a few people achieve outrageous success, while leaving many others struggling just to get by? While luck and chance always play some role, the real secret may lie in your child understanding how to harness her innate strengths and minimize her ADHD weaknesses.

Harnessing ADHD Strengths

One of the most important things you can do to ensure your child's strengths have a chance to shine is to manage her ADHD symptoms consistently and effectively.

 Fact

Make sure your child takes her medication regularly. While medication alone can't fix poor grades in school, it can help your child manage mood swings and alleviate the restlessness, impulsivity, and inattention that may contribute to poor study habits.

The best treatment approach for most children with ADHD is a combination of medication, therapy, behavior modification, a healthy diet, regular exercise, support groups, relaxation techniques, and other lifestyle changes that enhance their lives.

How Your Child Can Make ADHD Work

In addition to following her treatment program, encourage your child to turn many of her ADHD symptoms into assets by using the following tips and strategies:

- **Encourage your child not to repress her ADHD gifts.** Instead, have her look for ways to express her creativity, inventiveness, imagination, enthusiasm, and energy, at work, at home, and in social settings.

- **Encourage your child to let her inattention be her guide.** If she finds her mind constantly drifting and wandering, she shouldn't ignore the danger signs. Inattention can be a red flag that she's bored, disinterested, or unchallenged. ADHD can be the radar she needs to switch to a new line of study in school or college.

- **Have your child make a list of her strengths and weaknesses, then match up her strengths and weaknesses to find out what sorts of jobs and careers are a good match.**

- **If your child doesn't know how to best use her ADHD skills, or if she's not even sure what they are, have her work with a career coach or therapist.** Aptitude tests can help her home in on jobs and careers that would set her brain cells firing.

- **Make sure your child understands that ambition alone is not enough to propel her to success.** Many students with ADHD find it easy to get enthused about a new major in college, but aren't realistic about the time and effort required to get there. Help your child create a road map to get her from point A to point B, then encourage her to use her tremendous energy and drive to propel her down the road to success step-by-manageable-step.

- **Encourage your child to use rather than abuse her innate ability to take risks.** Harnessed properly, her ability to take a calculated leap of faith that would leave others teetering on the brink can be a tremendous asset. But taking careless or needless risks can set her back light years, and even endanger her physical or financial health. Make sure your child understands that before taking a leap, to consider if it's worth the risk, and that she has a good chance of landing on solid ground.

- **Have your child take inventory of her personal likes and dislikes to figure out what she wants to be.** Does she like working on her feet in front of people (like a teacher) or by herself in front of a computer (like a writer)? If she's hyperactive, she might fare best in a job that lets her move around, or which requires physical exertion, such as a sales job that gets her out and about, or a career that requires physical exertion, such as a personal trainer.

- **Tell your child not to stick with a line of study that doesn't match her personal profile just because she's worked extra hard to master it, or worked against some of her natural gifts or characteristics to be successful.** Your child will be happier, less stressed, and more effective at a job that uses her natural gifts.

- **Encourage your child to test-drive another line of study if she doesn't like the one she's in.** If her current major in college isn't using her imagination or creativity to the fullest, tell her to make arrangements to sit in some classes she thinks she might enjoy more.

- **Encourage your child to be patient with herself, and not to expect instant success if she decides to change course.** Tell her she should prepare to spend some time examining her talents and skills, and talking with professionals to find a better match.

The Importance of Owning Up

Many children with ADHD have become adept at masking their symptoms or covering them up with learned behavior. While masking negative symptoms can certainly help life go more smoothly, if your child masks positive ADHD traits such as creativity, spontaneity, or thinking outside the box, for fear of being "discovered," she could be sabotaging herself and limiting her ability to live life to the fullest.

If you and your child with ADHD are in denial about her symptoms, and/or you and she have been telling the world she's "normal" out of fear of social stigma, it may be time to let your child's ADHD genie out of the box. Your child's therapist can help you and your child "own" her positive ADHD traits and help her explore ways to use them to her best advantage.

Harnessing the Power of Friendship

Deciding whether or not to tell his friends he has ADHD may not have legal implications, but it could have a major effect on the way friends interact with and support your child, and it may also have an impact on feelings of trust.

If your child's symptoms are so mild that they don't interfere with his ability to make and keep friends, or if his symptoms are controlled by medication so that he is able to behave as a reliable and trustworthy friend, telling his friends he has ADHD is probably a decision he'll make on a case-by-case, or need-to-know basis.

If his symptoms result in periodic moodiness, irritability, withdrawing, socially awkward behavior (like putting his foot in his mouth), a tendency toward reckless behavior, impatience, restlessness, and so on, he may want to inform close friends of his disorder so they are more understanding of his symptoms, better able to put his ADHD-inspired idiosyncrasies into perspective, and more forgiving when he says or does something inappropriate.

Bonding with Fellow ADHD Sufferers

In fact, close friends in the know can help your child avoid embarrassing faux pas and help him function more effectively in social settings by acting as his personal interpreter when he can't follow a conversation, loses track of his thoughts, or is unable to read nonverbal cues or body language.

Friends who also have ADHD can help your child deal with the many challenges posed by the condition. Whether it's providing a safe place for him to rant about his symptoms, or providing him with ADHD information on ADHD resources, your child's ADHD friends can give him the sympathy, support, and empathy he needs to cope.

The Latest and Greatest ADHD Research

Although scientists have yet to find a cure for ADHD, sophisticated, high-tech research and equipment are shedding new light on what may cause or contribute to the disorder, and what types of treatments are most effective.

 Alert

Many researchers now believe that ADHD is not one condition, but a cluster of conditions or disorders, each of which may be able to be treated. By discovering treatments for the individual conditions that make up ADHD, scientists one day hope to find an overall cure for the disorder.

The rapidly evolving technology of brain-imaging techniques is letting scientists observe how the brain functions when it has ADHD. By comparing such brains to brains without ADHD, they are finding distinctive differences in brain chemistry and makeup that categorize ADHD.

Scientists are hopeful that brain-imaging techniques can one day be used in the diagnosis and subsequent management of ADHD.

Eye on Maternal Contributors

Studies have also been conducted that have isolated how specific maternal factors cause or contribute to childhood ADHD. For instance, research indicates that mothers who smoke and drink alcohol during pregnancy are more likely to give birth to a child who develops ADHD.

In addition, new studies show that excessive maternal stress during pregnancy can contribute to a severe type of ADHD in children.

Better Criteria for Better Diagnoses

The current criteria for the diagnosis of childhood ADHD are taken from the *Diagnostic and Statistical Manual of Mental Health Disorders, 4th ed. (DSM-IV)*, which was published in 1994 and revised in 2000. The next edition will be published in 2013 and will reflect the latest research findings. Researchers are pushing for modifications in the 2013 edition that would establish different diagnostic criteria for childhood, adolescent, and adult ADHD.

New Directions in Research

Researchers are studying the long-term effects of established ADHD treatments, such as medication, psychotherapy, and behavior modification, and are also looking at the long-term outcome of children with ADHD who are not diagnosed or treated.

In addition, scientists are looking for safer and more effective medications to treat patients with ADHD alone, and with ADHD and co-existing conditions such as chronic anxiety, depression, and bipolar disorder.

Resources for Parents of Children with ADHD

Organizations and Support Groups

Children and Adults with Attention-Deficit/Hyperactivity Disorder (CHADD)

A nonprofit organization and support group for children and adults with ADHD.
www.chadd.org

National ADDA

A national organization for adults with ADHD with conferences and teleclasses.
www.add.org

National ADHD Service

A national organization with a provider directory and free resources on ADHD.
www.addresources.org

National Center for Gender Issues and ADHD

An advocacy group that promotes research and awareness on ADHD in women and girls.
www.ncgiadd.org

ADDvance

An online resource network for women and girls with ADHD.
www.addvance.com

Books

Adem, Daniel. *Healing the Hardware of the Soul* (New York: Free Press, 2002).

Adler, Leonard, *Scattered Minds* (New York: G.P. Putnam, 2006).

Breggin, Peter R. *Talking Back to Ritalin: What Doctors Aren't Telling You About Stimulants for Children* (Common Courage Press: Monroe, ME, 1998).

Brown, Thomas. *Attention Deficit Disorder: The Unfocused Mind in Children and Adults* (New Haven: Yale University Press, 2005).

The Diagnostic and Statistical Manual of Mental Disorders, Fourth Edition, Text Revision (American Psychiatric Association: Washington D.C., 2000).

Flick, Gary. *ADD/ADHD Behavior-Change Resource Kit* (Jossey-Bass: San Francisco, CA, 1998).

Garber, Stephen, Marianne Garber, and Robyn Freedman Spizman. *Beyond Ritalin: Facts about Medication and Other Strategies for Helping Children, Adolescents, and Adults with Attention Deficit Disorders* (Villard: New York, NY, 1996).

Hallowell, Edward and John Ratey. *Answers to Distraction* (New York: Bantam Books, 1996).

Hallowell, Edward, and John Ratey. *Delivered from Distraction* (New York: Ballantine, 2005).

Hallowell, Edward, and John Ratey. *Driven to Distraction* (New York: Simon and Schuster, 1994).

Keirsey, David, and Marilyn Bates. *Please Understand Me: Character and Temperament Types* (Prometheus Nemesis Book Company: Del Mar, CA, 1978).

Matlin, Terry. *Survival Tips for Women with AD/HD* (Plantation, Fla: Specialty Press, 2005).

Robbins, Jim. *A Symphony in the Brain: The Evolution of the New Brain Wave Biofeedback* (Grove Press: New York, NY, 2000).

Rosenberg, David R., John Holtum, Neal Ryan, and Samuel Gershon. *Pocket Guide for the Textbook of Pharmacotherapy for Child and Adolescent Psychiatric Disorders* (Brunner/Mazel: Washington, D.C., 1998).

Spratto, George R. *PDR Nurse's Drug Handbook* (Delmar Learning: Clifton Park, NY, 2004).

Videos

Don't Pick on Me! (Sunburst Communications: Pleasantville, NY).

Shapiro, Joan M.D., and Jeffrey Freed. *4 Weeks to an Organized Life with AD/HD* (New York: Taylor Trade Publishing, 2007).

Websites

ADD.about.com

This site is a great introduction to ADHD in children and adults.

www.add.about.com

Additude Magazine.com

This is a free website covering most aspects of ADHD in adults and children.

www.additudemag.com

ADD Forums

This website is an online support network for parents, children, and teens.

www.addforums.com

ADHD News.com

This is a support and information website for adults and children with ADHD.

www.adhdnews.com

ADD Consults.com

This online virtual clinic offers free one-on-one advice from ADHD experts.

www.addconsults.com

APPENDIX B

Recipes

While research on ADHD diets remains limited and results are mixed, many experts believe dietary changes may help relieve symptoms when used in combination with "first-line" treatments such as ADHD medication, neurofeedback, and psychotherapy. According to WebMD's ADHD expert Richard Sogn, MD, "Whatever is good for the brain is likely to be good for ADHD." Brain researcher and ADHD expert Daniel Amen, MD, recommends that children with ADHD eat a high-protein diet, cut back on sugary snacks, eat more complex carbohydrates, and consume more omega-3 fatty acids. For more information on ADHD diets, see Chapter 17.

A gluten-free/casein-free diet is not commonly accepted as a valid treatment for ADHD by experts in the field, and the authors don't recommend that this be your primary approach to finding help for your ADHD child. We understand that you, the reader, may have heard about the GFCF diet and may have wondered about its effectiveness. The authors present some recipes here for illustrative purposes only, and so that you, the reader, can better understand alternative treatments for ADHD.

BLUEBERRY APPLE MUFFINS
Makes 12

Calories: 223 | Fat: 7 g | Protein: 3 g | Fiber: 4.4 g

Ingredients:
2 cups gluten-free all-purpose flour
1 teaspoon xanthan gum
1½ teaspoons baking powder, divided
½ teaspoon salt
1 cup chunky applesauce, divided
½ cup flaxseed meal
¼ cup coconut oil
¾ cup packed brown sugar
½ cup soy milk
1 teaspoon gluten-free vanilla extract
1 cup blueberries

- Preheat oven to 350°F.
- Lightly oil a standard muffin pan.
- In a small bowl, combine flour, xanthan gum, 1 teaspoon baking powder, and salt. Stir with a whisk.
- In a medium bowl, combine ½ cup applesauce with ½ teaspoon baking powder.
- Add remaining ½ cup applesauce.
- Mix in flaxseed meal, coconut oil, brown sugar, soy milk, and vanilla.
- Slowly mix dry ingredients into wet.
- Gently mix in blueberries.
- Spoon batter into oiled pan.
- Bake 25–30 minutes or until a toothpick inserted into the center of a muffin comes out clean.

VEGGIE OMELET

Serves 2

Calories: 224 | Fat: 19 g | Protein: 10 g | Fiber: 1 g

Ingredients:
½ cup thinly sliced mushrooms
¼ cup chopped green pepper
¼ cup chopped onion
1 tablespoon diced pimiento
3 eggs at room temperature, separated
2 tablespoons gluten-free, casein-free mayonnaise
¼ teaspoon salt
⅛ teaspoon pepper

• Combine mushrooms, green pepper, onion, and pimiento in a 1-quart casserole; cover loosely with heavy-duty plastic wrap and microwave on high for 3 to 3½ minutes or until vegetables are tender. Drain and set aside.

• Beat egg whites until stiff peaks form. Combine egg yolks, mayonnaise, salt, and pepper; beat well. Gently fold egg whites into egg yolk mixture.

• Coat a 9-inch glass pie plate or quiche pan with ½ teaspoon oil. Pour egg mixture into pie plate, spreading evenly. Microwave at medium (50 percent power) for 8 to 10½ minutes or until center is almost set, giving pie plate a half-turn after 5 minutes.

• Spread vegetable mixture over half of omelet. Loosen omelet with spatula and fold in half. Gently slide the omelet onto a warm serving platter.

CHICKEN NOODLE SOUP

Makes 8 cups

Calories: 141 | Fat: 4 g | Protein: 7 g | Fiber: 5 g

Ingredients:

1 pound boneless chicken breasts cut into ¼-inch pieces

½ red onion, diced

2 celery ribs, sliced

1 medium carrot, sliced

¼ red bell pepper, diced

3 garlic cloves, minced

2 tablespoons gluten-free, casein-free margarine

2 tablespoons olive or canola oil

1 teaspoon dried basil

½ teaspoon dried oregano

⅛ teaspoon pepper

3 (14½-ounce) cans organic chicken broth

1 (14½-ounce) can diced tomatoes, undrained

½ summer squash or zucchini, sliced

4 cups gluten-free rotini, cooked according to package directions

5 ounces fresh spinach, chopped

- In a large saucepan, sauté the chicken, onion, celery, carrots, red pepper, and garlic in margarine and oil for 5 minutes.
- Stir in the basil, oregano, and pepper until blended.
- Slowly add organic chicken broth, tomatoes, and zucchini or squash.
- Bring to a boil. Reduce heat; cover and simmer for 1 hour.
- Return to a boil; stir in the pasta and spinach.
- Reduce heat; simmer, uncovered, for 5–10 minutes or until spinach is tender.

TURKEY CHILI
Yields 12 cups

Calories: 195 | Fat: 6 g | Protein: 11 g | Fiber: 5 g

Ingredients:
2 tablespoons canola oil
1 red onion, chopped
1 clove garlic, minced
1 pound ground turkey breast
1 pound butternut squash, peeled, seeded and cut into 1-inch cubes
½ cup gluten-free, casein-free chicken broth
2 (14½-ounce) cans petite diced tomatoes
1 (15-ounce) can black beans with liquid
1 (15½-ounce) can white hominy, drained
1 (8-ounce) can tomato sauce
2 teaspoons chili powder
1 tablespoon ground cumin
⅛ teaspoon cinnamon
8 ounces gluten-free, casein-free plain soy yogurt

- In a large pot, heat the canola oil over medium heat. Add onion and garlic; cook and stir for 3 minutes until clear, add turkey. Stir until crumbly and no longer pink.
- Add the butternut squash, chicken broth, tomatoes, black beans, hominy, and tomato sauce; season with chili powder, cumin, and cinnamon.
- Bring to a simmer, then reduce heat to medium-low, cover, and simmer until the squash is tender, about 20 minutes.
- Top each bowl with 1–2 tablespoons of yogurt to serve.

TABBOULEH SALAD

Yields 8 cups (6 servings)

Calories: 190 | Fat: 10 g | Protein: 6 g | Fiber: 4 g

Ingredients:

3 cups quinoa, cooked
1 cup cannellini beans
1½ cups parsley, finely chopped
3 large tomatoes
3 green onions, sliced
1 tablespoon mint, finely chopped
¼ cup extra-virgin olive oil
¼ cup lemon juice

- Combine all ingredients.
- Chill for 2–3 hours and then serve.

BROCCOLI QUINOA CASSEROLE

Makes 6 cups

Calories: 218 | Fat: 4 g | Protein: 8 g | Fiber: 6 g

Ingredients:

1 cup vegan creamy corn soup
½ cup gluten-free, casein-free soy Cheddar cheese
1 large bunch of broccoli
3 cups cooked quinoa

- In a small sauce pan, heat soup over medium-high heat.
- Add cheese and stir until melted. Set aside.
- Cut broccoli into small florets and steam until tender.
- Combine quinoa, cheese sauce, and broccoli.

BAJA-STYLE FISH TACOS
Yields 8 tacos

Calories: 258 | Fat: 15 g | Protein: 13 g | Fiber: 4 g

Ingredients:
1 teaspoon canola oil
1 pound cod; cut into 2-ounce portions
1 lime, juiced
¾ teaspoon sea salt; divided
½ cup gluten-free, casein-free sour cream
½ cup gluten-free, casein-free mayonnaise
2 limes, juiced
½ fresh jalapeño pepper, deseeded, halved, and deribbed
½ teaspoon dried oregano
½ teaspoon dried dill weed
¼ teaspoon ground cumin
¼ teaspoon cayenne
8 gluten-free corn tortillas
½ medium head cabbage, finely shredded
½ medium head red cabbage, finely shredded

- Lightly oil a shallow baking dish with 1 teaspoon canola oil. Arrange fish in dish.
- Sprinkle fish with the juice of 1 lime and ½ teaspoon sea salt. Cover with foil and bake at 400°F for 10–15 minutes. Remove from oven when done.
- In a blender, combine ¼ teaspoon sea salt and next 8 ingredients to form sauce for tacos.
- Heat corn tortillas lightly in skillet on stove, top with portion of cooked fish, drizzle with sauce, and place handful of both types of finely shredded cabbage on top. Serve.

SHEPHERD'S PIE

Yields 10 servings

Calories: 275 | Fat: 11 g | Protein: 18 g | Fiber: 4 g

Ingredients:

3 large potatoes, peeled
1 tablespoon olive oil
1 red onion, chopped
½ cup diced carrots
1½ pounds organic ground beef
2 tablespoons flaxseed meal
¾ cup gluten-free, casein-free beef broth
¾ cup green peas
¾ cup corn
1 teaspoon Worcestershire sauce
1 teaspoon ketchup
1 teaspoon Dijon mustard
2 tablespoons gluten-free, casein-free margarine
½ cup gluten-free, casein-free soy milk

- In a large pot bring to a boil enough water to cover potatoes. Cut potatoes and place in boiling water.
- In large skillet, heat 1 tablespoon olive oil. Sauté onions and carrots until tender. Add ground beef and flaxseed meal to pan and brown. Drain ground beef and return to hot skillet.
- Add next 6 ingredients to skillet and allow to heat for about 10 minutes.
- Meanwhile, remove potatoes from boiling water when tender. Mash with margarine and soy milk. Be careful not to make these potatoes too thin.
- In a 9" × 13" pan, first layer and press meat mixture into the bottom of pan evenly. Then for the top layer, spread mashed potatoes on the top of meat mixture. Use a fork to arrange the potatoes into an even but pointy layer. There should be peaks of potatoes sticking up to get brown.
- Bake at 400°F for 30 minutes. Broil for 5 minutes at the end to crisp up the top.

SESAME-CRUSTED CHICKEN BREASTS

Serves 4

Calories: 440 | Fat: 27 g | Protein: 24 g | Fiber: 4 g

Ingredients:

¼ cup pineapple juice

¼ cup orange juice

1 tablespoon lime juice

½ cup gluten-free, casein-free soy sauce

1 inch gingerroot, peeled and minced

2 cloves garlic, or to taste, minced

2 large boneless, skinless chicken breasts, halved

1 egg, beaten

½ cup sesame seeds

- In a glass pan, whisk together the juices, soy sauce, ginger, and garlic. Rinse the chicken breasts and pat dry with paper towels. Add the chicken to the sauce and turn to coat. Cover and refrigerate for 4 hours.
- Drain the chicken; dip in beaten egg and then in sesame seeds. Grill or sauté in oil for 6 minutes per side. Serve hot.

HUMMUS

Yields 2 cups

Calories: 234 | Fat: 12 g | Protein: 6 g | Fiber: 5 g

Ingredients:

2 cups cooked garbanzo beans (canned)

2 teaspoons lemon juice

3 tablespoons olive oil

1 clove garlic

¼ teaspoon cumin

⅛ teaspoon salt

- Drain and rinse beans. Combine all ingredients in a food processor or blender. Process until smooth.

BARBECUE CHICKEN PIZZA
Yields 4 servings

Calories: 267 | Fat: 12 g | Protein: 10 g | Fiber: 2 g

Ingredients:
3 tablespoons barbecue sauce
½ cup marinara sauce
1 prebaked gluten-free pizza crust
8 ounces shredded chicken
⅓ cup red onion, sliced thin
1½ cups vegan mozzarella cheese (optional)
2 tablespoons chopped cilantro (optional)

- Preheat oven to 425°F.
- In small bowl, combine barbecue sauce and marinara sauce. Spread on prebaked pizza crust.
- Top pizza with chicken and red onions and cheese, if using. Bake about 15 minutes.
- Remove from oven, sprinkle with cilantro. Serve.

VEGETABLE BAKED RISOTTO
Makes 4½ cups (Serves 6)

Calories: 200 | Fat: 1 g | Protein: 7 g | Fiber: 5 g

Ingredients:
3 cups gluten-free, casein-free vegetable broth
½ cup green beans
1 cup Arborio rice
1 cup broccoli florets
1 small zucchini
1 garlic clove
1 cup cooked great northern beans
1 teaspoon dried basil
1 teaspoon dried oregano

- Preheat oven to 325°F.
- Bring broth to a boil.
- Drain and rinse green beans and rinse rice.
- Trim ends from green beans, cut into 1-inch pieces.
- Divide broccoli into small florets, and coarsely chop zucchini.
- Mince garlic.
- Drain and rinse great northern beans.
- Combine all ingredients in a covered casserole. Bake 1 hour.

HOMEMADE POTATO CHIPS
Makes about 50 chips (Serving = 10 chips)

Calories: 312 | Fat: 23 g | Protein: 3 g | Fiber: 3 g

Ingredients:
4 large Yukon Gold potatoes
1 cup canola oil
Salt to taste

- Peel and slice the potatoes. The best way to slice these chips is with a mandolin or the slicing blade on your food processor.
- Place 2 inches of oil in the fryer. Heat the oil to 340°F and watch the temperature throughout the cooking time.
- Carefully add potato slices, a few at a time, to hot oil. Remove when golden and drain on brown paper bags or paper towels. Sprinkle with salt. Serve hot or warm.

SWEET POTATO FRIES
Yields 4 cups

Calories: 120 | Fat: 0 g | Protein: 4 g | Fiber: 4 g

Ingredients:
4 sweet potatoes, peeled and cut into matchsticks
Large pot of boiling water
Large bowl of ice water
2 egg whites
⅛ teaspoon garlic powder

- Preheat oven to 450°F.
- Blanch the potatoes: Bring a large pot of water to a boil. Place potatoes in and cook for 5 minutes. Drain and immediately plunge into bowl of ice water.
- Dry the potatoes well. Combine egg whites and garlic powder.
- Toss potatoes with egg white mixture.
- Line baking sheet with parchment paper and bake for 14 minutes.
- Turn once about 7 minutes into cooking.

GRANOLA

Makes 10 servings

Calories: 153 | Fat: 8 g | Protein: 3 g | Fiber: 2 g

Ingredients:
2 cups gluten-free oats
⅓ cup chopped pecans
¼ cup chopped almonds
¼ cup apple juice
¼ cup maple syrup
2 tablespoons canola oil
1 teaspoon cinnamon
½ cup dried apple pieces

- Preheat oven to 350°F.
- Oil a cookie sheet.
- In a large bowl, combine oats, nuts, apple juice, syrup, oil, and cinnamon.
- Spread mixture on cookie sheet.
- Bake 15–20 minutes or until golden brown.
- When cool, combine with dried apples.

PINEAPPLE SALSA

Yields 4 cups (4 servings)

Calories: 70 | Fat: 0 g | Protein: 3 g | Fiber: 4 g

Ingredients:

1 cup diced fresh pineapple
½ cup red pepper, diced
½ cup yellow pepper, diced
½ cup black beans, drained and rinsed
¼ cup red onion, diced
¼ cup cilantro, finely chopped
¼ cup orange-pineapple juice
2 tablespoons lime juice
Salt and pepper to taste

- In large bowl, combine first 6 ingredients and mix well.
- In small bowl, combine orange-pineapple juice and lime juice. Pour into large bowl.
- Mix all ingredients together, season with salt and pepper to taste.

LIMEADE SORBET

Makes 2¼ cups (Serves 4)

Calories: 280 | Fat: 0 g | Protein: 0 g | Fiber: 0 g

Ingredients:

1½ cups prepared limeade from frozen concentrate
¾ cup frozen white grapes

- Combine ingredients in a blender or food processor; blend until smooth.
- Pour into a freezer-safe container.
- Freeze for 2 hours, then fluff with a fork.
- Return to freezer.
- Continue fluffing every 1½ to 2 hours until serving.

CRANBERRY OATMEAL COOKIES
Makes 48 cookies

Calories: 73 | Fat: 3 g | Protein: 1 g | Fiber: 1 g

Ingredients:

1 cup gluten-free all-purpose flour
1 teaspoon xanthan gum
2 cups gluten-free old-fashioned rolled oats
½ teaspoon cinnamon
½ teaspoon baking soda
½ teaspoon salt
¼ cup applesauce
¼ teaspoon baking powder
½ cup packed dark brown sugar
¼ cup pure maple syrup
½ cup canola oil
½ cup dried, sweetened cranberries (gluten-free)
½ cup gluten-free, casein-free chocolate chips (optional)

- Preheat oven to 350°F.
- Combine flour, xanthan gum, oats, cinnamon, baking soda, and salt in a medium bowl. Stir with a whisk to combine.
- In a large bowl, combine applesauce with baking powder.
- Add brown sugar, syrup, and canola oil.
- Mix dry ingredients into wet.
- Stir in cranberries and chocolate chips, if using.
- Drop by tablespoon-full onto ungreased cookie sheets.
- Bake 13–15 minutes or until golden brown. Remove to cooling rack to cool.

CHOCOLATE CHIP COOKIES

Makes 60 cookies (Serving = 3 cookies)

Calories: 246 | Fat: 14 g | Protein: 3 g | Fiber: 3 g

Ingredients:

3 cups gluten-free all-purpose flour

1 teaspoon xanthan gum

1 teaspoon baking soda

½ teaspoon salt

½ cup applesauce

½ teaspoon baking powder

¾ cup coconut oil

1½ cups packed dark brown sugar

1 tablespoon gluten-free vanilla

2 cups gluten-free, casein-free chocolate chips

- Preheat oven to 375°F.
- In a medium bowl, combine flour, xanthan gum, baking soda, and salt.
- In a separate bowl, combine applesauce and baking powder.
- Add coconut oil, brown sugar, and vanilla to applesauce mixture.
- Beat wet ingredients together using an electric mixer for 1–2 minutes, or until well combined.
- Blend dry ingredients into wet.
- Mix in chocolate chips.
- Drop batter by the tablespoon onto ungreased cookie sheets.
- Bake 10–12 minutes or until golden brown.
- Remove cookies from cookie sheets, and cool on cooling racks.

APPLE PEAR CRISP

Makes 4 cups (8 servings)

Calories: 229 | Fat: 6 g | Protein: 2 g | Fiber: 4 g

Ingredients:

3 medium pears

3 large apples

¾ cup packed light brown sugar

1 teaspoon gluten-free vanilla

½ cup gluten-free all-purpose flour

¼ cup gluten-free, casein-free rolled oats

½ teaspoon xanthan gum

¼ cup butter or gluten-free, casein-free margarine, melted

Canola oil spray

- Preheat oven to 400°F.
- Peel and thinly slice pears and apples.
- In a small bowl combine remaining ingredients.
- Spray a 2-quart casserole with canola oil.
- Spread fruit in bottom of casserole.
- Top with sugar mixture.
- Bake 40 minutes.

CHOCOLATE COCONUT BROWNIES

Makes 12 brownies

Calories: 302 | Fat: 19 g | Protein: 4 g | Fiber: 3 g

Ingredients:

¾ teaspoon light brown sugar

½ cup coconut oil

1½ teaspoons gluten-free vanilla

1 (12-ounce) package gluten-free, casein-free chocolate chips

1¼ cups gluten-free all-purpose flour

1 tablespoon xanthan gum

½ teaspoon baking soda

½ teaspoon salt

½ cup applesauce

½ teaspoon baking powder

½ cup finely shredded coconut

- Preheat oven to 350°F.
- Combine brown sugar and coconut oil in a large microwave-safe bowl. Heat on high for 1–2 minutes until coconut oil is melted.
- Stir oil and brown sugar, mix in the vanilla and half the chocolate chips. Set aside.
- In a medium bowl, combine flour, xanthan gum, baking soda, and salt.
- In a small bowl, combine applesauce and baking powder.
- Mix applesauce mixture into coconut oil–chocolate mixture.
- Mix dry ingredients into wet.
- Stir remaining chocolate chips and shredded coconut into batter.
- Lightly oil an 8- or 9-inch-square pan with coconut oil.
- Spoon batter into pan.
- Bake 35 minutes or until a toothpick inserted into the center comes out clean.
- Cool completely before cutting.

Index